"Today, when the complaints against Time Square can be summed up in the single word 'Disney,' there is even some lingering affection for the Peep Land, Travis Bickle dystopia of the 1970s. As Mr. Traub writes, 'the layers sit atop one another like geological strata.' *The Devil's Playground* drills through those strata with Mr. Traub's characteristic intelligence and brio."

—*The New York Sun*

"The charm of *The Devil's Playground* . . . rests on the author's determination not to romanticize the most over-dreamed plot of real estate this side of Eden. The narrative combines a wonkish fascination for contemporary deal making with glamorous tales from the days of lobster houses, Runyonesque gangsters, and naked chorines on glass platforms."

—*Time Out New York*

"Well-written . . . mellifluous and reflective."

—*The New York Review of Books*

"In eloquently detailed prose, enlivened by stories of myriad Broadway personalities, Traub's narrative reviews the area's history and poses complex questions. . . . Traub is a fair, careful reporter and an engaging writer."

—*Library Journal*

"Traub has made a career out of writing about New York and its institutions. He has the right: he lives and breathes the city, and his prose tumbles out sparkling and effortless. His history of Times Square—its name was changed from Longacre Square in the spring of 1904 for the newspaper headquartered there—is a vivid and remarkably nonjudgmental tale. . . . A fabulous read that quite nearly captures the 'gorgeous disarray' and 'epic higgledy-piggledy' of the world's gathering place."

—*Kirkus Reviews* (starred review)

PHOTO: ELIZABETH W. EASTON

JAMES TRAUB has been writing about the politics, culture, characters, and institutions of New York City for twenty-five years. Currently a contributing writer for *The New York Times Magazine,* he has also served as a staff writer for *The New Yorker* and has written for the country's leading publications in fields as diverse as foreign affairs, national politics, education, urban policy, sports, and food. He is the author of two books with New York City settings—one on the Wedtech scandal of the mid-1980s and a second on the City College of New York. He lives in Manhattan with his wife and son.

THE DEVIL'S PLAYGROUND

RANDOM HOUSE TRADE PAPERBACKS NEW YORK

A CENTURY OF PLEASURE AND

PROFIT IN TIMES SQUARE

JAMES TRAUB

THE DEVIL'S
PLAYGROUND

2005 Random House Trade Paperback Edition

Originally published in hardcover by Random House,
an imprint of The Random House Publishing Group,
a division of Random House, Inc., in 2004.

Library of Congress Cataloging-in-Publication Data
Traub, James.
      The Devil's playground: a century of pleasure and profit in
Times Square / by James Traub.—1st ed.
          p. cm.
      Includes bibliographical references (p.) and index.
      ISBN-13: 978-0-375-75978-9
      1. Times Square (New York, N.Y.)—History—20th century.
2. New York (N.Y.)—History—20th century.   3. New York (N.Y.)—
Social conditions—20th century.   4. New York (N.Y.)—Biography.
5. Popular culture—New York (State)—New York—History—
20th century.   I. Title.
   F128.65.T5T73 2004
   974.7'1—dc22   2003061629

Random House website address: www.atrandom.com

Book design by Barbara M. Bachman

144782292

TO ALEX,

MY SPARRING PARTNER,

AND BUFFY,

MY PARTNER

CONTENTS

ONE NIGHT IN THE FALL OF 2002 I took my son, Alex, then eleven, to see the play *42nd Street*, which was showing at the Ford Center—on 42nd Street. It was a Saturday night, and the balcony was full of loud, happy out-of-towners. To our right, four girls chattered away in Chinese. The row in front of us was full of sailors—a nostalgia trip all by itself, for sailors and soldiers have been coming to Times Square for a night of fun for a good three-quarters of a century. These boys, the drill team from the Groton sub base in Connecticut, were polite, talkative, and positively button-eyed with excitement; a few of them had never been in New York before. And on their one night out in New York, the submariners had decided to take in not a strip show but a Broadway musical—and what a musical it was! The curtain rose, and then stopped, about eighteen inches up. All we could see were disembodied shoes, in crazy shades of yellow and green and orange and blue, moving at a blur; and the theater echoed with the obbligato of rapid-fire tap dancing. No music; just rhythm. It was a moment of pure Broadway virtuosity. The first time I had gone to the show, a few months earlier, an old gent with a cane sitting down the row from me had loosed a spontaneous shout when the feet came out. Now the boys from Groton, and the Chinese girls, and Alex and I, were all cheering with delight. I was also furtively dabbing at my eyes.

That's Broadway for you—bright lights and gaudy colors, energy and talent, the old-fashioned chorus line and the old-fashioned emotions. *42nd*

Street punches the same buttons they've been punching in Times Square for a hundred years. But *42nd Street* is also *about* those buttons, and about that old Times Square. The play is a musical about the making of a musical, *Pretty Lady,* in the worst years of the Depression. To say that *42nd Street* is about the Depression would make the play into a far more weight-bearing instrument than it aspires to be; insofar as it is about anything, it is *about* the "kids" of the chorus who are the true citizens of Broadway, who under all the wisecracking and makeup believe ardently in the dreams in which shows like *Pretty Lady* traffic. The Depression exists not as a social phenomenon to be examined, but as a giant piece of rotten luck, which makes us root for the show, and admire the kids, all the more. When *Pretty Lady* is threatened with sudden collapse, the kids wonder where their next meal is going to come from; but we know that the indomitable Broadway spirit will rise above misfortune.

The musical *42nd Street* began its life as a 1933 Busby Berkeley movie— actually, it began its life as a novel, now long forgotten, by one Bradford Ropes—so, for the first audience the setting was contemporary, and the show's yearning and escapism reflected the audience's own deepest wish. Now, of course, that's no longer true. The appeal of *42nd Street* is overtly nostalgic. The air of desperation and fear that must have seemed terribly familiar in 1933 gives the play its authenticity today; here is the mythical Times Square of the thirties, the "Runyonesque" Times Square, right up to Nick Murphy's hoods, who threaten to break a leg or two (but don't). Who doesn't know the song: "Naughty, bawdy, gaudy, sporty . . . 42nd Street!" We don't pity the kids; we envy them, for the sheer vitality, the electricity, of their world. When we watch *42nd Street* we look not only backward but outward—to the street of the play, which of course is also the street of the theater, the street right outside the door. We compare their 42nd Street with ours.

Our 42nd Street was a consciously, sometimes even lovingly, reengineered urban space. For, by the 1960s and 1970s, the naughty and bawdy had descended into the squalid and pathological; and in the ensuing decades New York City and State had undertaken a massive project of urban re-creation. And it had worked. The very fact that we were watching a musical on 42nd Street was proof, for the theater we were sitting in had been showing pornographic movies twenty years earlier. The Ford

Center had been built from the wreckage of two splendid old theaters, the Apollo and the Lyric, the latter dating from 1903; the glorious scroll-work and arabesques of the Lyric's 43rd Street façade now constituted the rear entrance of the Ford. Just down the street, toward Broadway, was a children's theater known as the New Victory and reconstituted from the ruins of the Republic, built in 1900; and directly across 42nd was the renovated New Amsterdam, an art nouveau masterpiece that in the early years of the previous century had been considered the most architecturally innovative theater in the United States.

At intermission, Alex and I walked out onto the street. It was nine-thirty on a Saturday night, and the crowd was so dense we could scarcely move. A big circle of people had gathered around Ayhan, the Turkish master of 42nd Street spray painting. Farther west, toward Eighth Avenue, was a Russian guy who sold 3-D pictures, and a few Chinese men who would render your name in calligraphy. The entire street was bathed in acid light, purple and green and orange and yellow, from the giant signs advertising the chain stores and restaurants that lined the street; an immense gilded palm, a glittering gesture from the god of kitsch, perched high above Madame Tussaud's Wax Museum. Gangs of tourists eddied up and down the sidewalk, taking photos of one another and of the signs and of the cops on horseback gazing balefully at the entrance to the Broadway City arcade. I held on to Alex's hand, not because there was anything ominous in the scene—there wasn't—but because I worried he might be swept away by the crowd. The truth is that there's no place in New York more fun for an eleven-year-old boy than Times Square.

This new Times Square of office towers and theme restaurants and global retailers and crowds and light and family fun is so utterly different both from the pathological Times Square of twenty years ago and the naughty, gaudy Times Square of seventy years ago that we almost need a different name for it. Certainly we need a new way of thinking about it. What are we to make of this place? For the city's financial and governmental elite—for the leading forces in real estate and tourism and entertainment and retail, for civic boosters and public officials—Times Square is overwhelming proof of New York's capacity for self-regeneration. Indeed, former mayor Rudolph Giuliani virtually adopted Times Square as the emblem of the safe, clean, and orderly New York he had erected on the ruins of the chaotic and deviant New York he believed he had inherited. Few things pleased Giuliani more than officiating over the New Year's Eve "ball drop" in his new Times Square. The willingness of tourists from all over the country and the world to gather in Times Square, as they had in generations past, was a vivid symbol of New York's rebirth.

But, unlike the mayor, most of us do not consider orderliness the cardinal virtue of urban life; nobody moves to New York—or Paris or Tokyo or Bombay—to revel in the predictable. For that very reason, many people who think about cities, and many people who simply love cities, find the new Times Square profoundly unnerving—in the way that so many modern, reconditioned urban spaces are, whether train stations or waterfronts or warehouses-become-gallerias. Say "Times Square," and the instant association is "Disney." And "Disney," in turn, is shorthand for a deadening depletion of the old teeming energies, a corporate-theme-park version of urban life. To its many critics, Times Square isn't a place, but a simulacrum of a place, an ingenious marketing device fostered by global entertainment firms. Times Square is now home to the world's biggest McDonald's, and to the world's biggest Toys "R" Us; the ground floor of the Times Tower, the center of Times Square and thus the pivot around which the universe rotates, is, as of this writing, scheduled to be given over to a 7-Eleven. And so Times Square, which over the last century has been the symbol of so much, is now understood as the symbol of the hollowing out of urban life, the decay of the particular in the merciless glare of globalization.

I'm one of the people who loves cities. I love crowds and noise and light and hubbub. I love overhearing conversations in the subway. I love the accidental quality of city life, the incongruous and the surreal. And to say that you love cities is to say that you love *old* cities, for only cities built before the advent of the automobile have the density that makes these myriad accidents and incongruities possible. (I do not love thee, Phoenix.) Jane Jacobs, that great champion of cities and dauntless foe of urban renewal, believes in density to the exclusion of almost everything, including open space and grass. And when I think of Times Square during the epoch I am most inclined to sentimentalize—the era of Damon Runyon and A. J. Liebling, the era just before and after *42nd Street*—I think of an infinitely dense and busy asphalt village, or even a series of micro-villages, such as Jacobs loves, in the space of a few blocks.

I am also, if not an urban theorist, then at least an urban journalist. I have spent much of the past twenty years writing about urban schools and crime and politics and policies, mostly in New York City. And I am not inclined to sentimentalize New York's decline, or that of the other old American cities. I did not like Times Square in 1985, when I used to work there. I did not share the view that predatory street people were its authentic citizens, or that the proposed renovation constituted a kind of unholy "gentrification." I cheered Mayor Giuliani as he spoke of the dangers of "defining deviancy down," and as he declared war against New York's pernicious street culture. I believe deeply in civility—perhaps a great deal more deeply than did our famously uncivil mayor. And so as I walked through the Times Square that was a-building, I felt the magnitude of the achievement, and I felt it as a reclaiming of abandoned urban territory— even as, at the very same moment, I felt the pang of loss, the loss of specificity, of locality, of eccentricity, of the micro-villages that were no more and never would be again.

The question "What are we to think of this place?" compels us to think beyond the particulars of this one intensely particular spot. It forces us to consider how, or whether, we can be at home in the global cities we now see evolving all around us. What, if anything, can we attach our feelings to—not just the ironic and resigned acceptance of the inevitable, but the delight that city life has inspired in cosmopolitan folk since merchants plied the narrow lanes of Siena or Tangier a thousand years ago? What exactly are we to do with our nostalgia for what we know very well can never return? Should we wield it as a weapon against the encroachments of the new? Should we, alternatively, discard it as a mere hindrance as we embrace the new?

Last, and perhaps most important, is a practical question: How, as citizens, should we wish to see our cities shaped? The new Times Square— or at least the new 42nd Street—was a product of choices, even if they weren't always very clearly stated. And some of these choices plainly contradicted others, for the renovation of Times Square was designed both to preserve its traditional ambience and to promote the development of office construction. Other choices could have been made. Ought they have been? Is this, in retrospect, the best Times Square we could have had? Perhaps we could have had a more "authentic" place; and yet nothing would be more ludicrous than a Colonial Williamsburg version of Times Square, with Nathan Detroit and Nicely-Nicely stalking up and down Broadway in their chalk-striped suits. How, then, should we negotiate the passage from the old and exhausted to the new and—we fear—soulless?

And so this book began with thoughts about Times Square as it is today. But it quickly became obvious that I could not make sense of Times Square without understanding what it had meant in the past. More than that, I had to understand how this place had come to mean so much—how it had come to be seen as the central spot not only of New York but of the country, and even, not so fancifully, of the world. Surely one answer is geography. William Taylor, perhaps the most distinguished historian of Times Square, has written, "The center of the classical city was the forum and the agora. Times Square, located at a major transportation hub, was neither. Because of its location, it became a new kind of center of amusement, recreation, and vice; the kind of area that in earlier cities was located off-center, its activities discreetly muffled. Times Square's very centrality meant that whatever took place was immediately in the national spotlight." Times Square, that is, became New York's zone of popular culture and entertainment because it was so readily accessible to the millions who lived and worked in the city, or who were visiting from out of town; and because this pleasure district occupied the center of the city that was itself the center of the nation's culture, Times Square came to be seen as the capital of fun, the place that instructed the nation in the fine art of play and furnished the dreams of young people languishing in what the great Broadway columnist Franklin P. Adams always called Dullsboro.

Times Square's meaning evolved along with popular culture itself. The Times Square of the early years of the century was the place where men—and, increasingly, women—began to throw off the moral restraints that had governed public behavior in the Victorian age, to enjoy themselves among strangers as they might have in the privacy of home. In the twenties, with the sudden rush of prosperity, Times Square became a national theater of urbanity and wit, as well as of a giddy revolt against Prohibition. In the late 1930s, when Times Square was already beginning its long slide into decrepitude, Liebling described it as "the heart of the world," the home of the con artists, auto-mythologists, and stoic philosophers whom he loved, and who flourished in the famine culture of the Depression. And then, after the war, came the carny Times Square of sailors and soldiers and shooting galleries and hot dogs and dime museums, and of swing and bebop. Television was sapping the force of Times Square, as it was of all the great urban gathering places. And then—the deluge. Even then, in the seventies, Times Square still stood for something, though what it stood for was the collapse of the urban core. Times Square has always been understood in symbolic terms. Its meanings have changed, but the sense of its centrality has not. It is still the heart of a very different, if not quite so welcome, world.

ON APRIL 8, 1904, Mayor George B. McClellan declared that the area around 42nd and Broadway would no longer be known as Longacre Square, but as Times Square. Times Square will celebrate its hundredth birthday at approximately the time this book is published. And so *The Devil's Playground* will tally a century's worth of accumulated and shifting meanings, from rise to fall to reconstruction to a booming but ambiguous rebirth. It is constructed in such a way that the layers sit atop one another like geological strata, so that the archaeologist-reader can recognize how much incident and meaning has gathered at this one tiny site, and also register the way in which Times Square has changed while remaining true to some underlying destiny. The question at the bottom of this book is, Does Times Square serve us—New Yorkers, Americans, lovers of urban life—as it served us in its various heydays? Or, put otherwise, How should we feel when we step out of *42nd Street* onto 42nd Street?

PART ONE

THE RISE AND FALL OF FUN

THE CHILDREN
OF NECESSITY

THE WORD "SQUARE" DOES NOT have the same meaning in Manhattan as in Paris or London or Rome. Belgrave Square and the Piazza della Repubblica are rectilinear spaces that serve as punctuations or pauses in the street plan. Here the business and the pace of the city slows, cars are forced to the periphery, and pedestrians are invited to wander across broad spaces, often around and amidst a garden. Think of the Place des Vosges, that quintessential seventeenth-century square in the heart of Paris, with its grand brick-faced houses and elegant cafés looking out over a park where schoolchildren in uniform play on swings. This is the Paris of Madeline, and of our dreams.

New York City has, or rather had, several such gracious spots, in the districts developed in the nineteenth century—Washington Square, in Greenwich Village; Gramercy Park, in the East Twenties. But most of the places New Yorkers call squares are, in fact, axial points where Broadway crosses another north–south avenue. Some of those places, including Union Square, at 14th Street, and Madison Square, at 23rd, also featured charmingly landscaped parks, with fine houses gathered around the perimeter; but because they were also traffic hubs, these places eventually became large-scale commercial centers, so that New Yorkers now think of them as places to shop rather than to stroll. And as Broadway continues north it slices straight through the adjacent avenue, putting an end both to parks and to pedestrians. The square immediately to the north of

Madison is Herald Square, which consists of a few rows of benches, a statue of Horace Greeley, and an enormous number of cars. The next square after that is Times Square, which is neither square nor safe to cross by foot, and which is possibly the least serene place in the Western Hemisphere—"a ganglion of streets that fuses into a traffic cop," as the essayist and urban bard Benjamin de Casseres put it in 1925. Is it any wonder that our dreams of Paris are so different from our dreams of New York, when the one has the Place des Vosges, and the other Times Square?

Why does Manhattan have traffic jams where other cities have plazas? A reasonable guess would be that the sheer force of growth wiped the old gathering spots off the map. That would be reasonable; but it would be wrong. The curious truth is that Manhattan looks the way it does because it was designed that way. Possibly the unlikeliest aspect of this fact is that Manhattan was designed at all. Whereas political capitals, whether Washington, D.C., or Rawalpindi, have often developed according to a blueprint, mercantile centers normally expand willy-nilly from some original core, according to the ambitions and appetites of the people who shape them. And this was certainly true at first of Manhattan, which expanded northward from the tip of the island. The narrow, crooked lanes around Wall Street offer a reminder of what the entire city once looked like.

But Manhattan's street plan is, in fact, a monument to political control of private behavior. By the beginning of the nineteenth century, Manhattan was a flourishing port city of perhaps 100,000 souls which extended about as far north as the stream that is now Canal Street. The farmland beyond was controlled by large landlords, who often carved out private streets for their own convenience. It was by no means clear whether the power to map out the rapidly growing city belonged to the municipal governing body, the Common Council, or to private landowners. In 1807, the city appealed to the state to settle the issue, and the state agreed to appoint a commission that would have "exclusive power to lay out streets, roads and public squares," and to "shut up" streets already built by private parties.

Whatever the original intention, the commissioners chose to interpret their charge as a mandate to utterly transform the map of the city. In 1811, they published one of the most audacious documents in the history of urban planning. It was a work that bore the stamp of the new republic—though it was Benjamin Franklin's rationalism and unsentimental materialism, rather than Thomas Jefferson's sense of romance and grandeur, that infused this extraordinary design. In remarks accompanying the plan, the commissioners noted that they had wondered "whether they should confine themselves to rectilinear and rectangular streets, or whether they should adopt some of those supposed improvements, by circles, ovals and stars, which certainly embellish a plan, whatever may be their effects as to convenience and utility." Note the stacked deck—on the one hand, "embellishments" of "supposed" value; on the other, "convenience and utility." "In considering that subject," the commissioners continued, "they could not but bear in mind that a city is to be composed principally of the habitations of men, and that strait-sided, right-angled homes are the most cheap to build, and the most convenient to live in. The effect of these plain and simple reflections was decisive."

So the commissioners straightened out Manhattan's twisty street plan into a relentless, unvarying grid—twelve avenues, placed at unequal intervals and running on a roughly north–south axis, and 155 streets crossing the avenues from the settled northern border of the city far up into the wilds of Harlem. As there were to be no ovals or stars, so there were to be no plazas, no public gathering spots. The commissioners went on to observe, "It may be, to many, a matter of surprise that so few vacant spaces have been left, and these so small, for the benefit of fresh air, and consequent preservation of health. Certainly, if the city of New York were destined to stand on the side of a small stream, such as the Seine or the Thames, a great number of ample places might be needful." Pity Paris or London, languishing beside "a small stream," while in Manhattan the health-giving sea dispelled the vapors attendant upon urban life. And then the commissioners returned to their commercial preoccupations: the very fact that Manhattan was an island, they noted, ensured that the price of land was "uncommonly great"; so "principles of economy" would have to be given more weight than might otherwise have been prudent. Thus, no plazas.

Generations of urban thinkers, from Frederick Law Olmsted to Lewis Mumford, have reeled in horror at a master plan that obliterated topography in favor of the endless multiplication of identical units, and could find no larger rationale for doing so than cost. And yet everything about the plan bears the stamp of this new democratic republic: its simplicity and horror of adornment; its blunt practicality; its faith in the marketplace as a democratic instrument, equally open to all. The grid was a blow against the large landholder with his private streets; even the decision to identify the avenues and streets by number rather than name was an act of "lexicographical leveling," removing from the great families the privilege of memorializing themselves in the city's street plan. The grid was an abstraction, but an abstraction placed at the service of the citizen—intended not to thwart the city's appetites and ambitions, but to facilitate their satisfaction.

The commissioners did permit several interruptions in the pattern. There would be "places," such as Union Place, formed at the conjunction of various streets and thus "the children of necessity," and "squares," large areas to be set aside for parade grounds or marketplaces, though not for strolling or the taking of fresh air. Besides these, only one exception to the relentless principle of the grid would be permitted: Broadway. This boulevard was already the city's main street, crossing over the canal and running all the way to Grace Church at 10th Street (where it formed the southern boundary of Union Place). The path continued as the Bloomingdale Road; as it slanted northward, this roadway cut at a sharp angle through the avenues, forming triangles which, though children of necessity as well, apparently seemed to the commissioners too unimportant for further comment.

THE "SQUARES" NEVER had a chance before the city's growth, and before the simple principle—which the commissioners seem to have anticipated—that land would be converted to its most valuable use. Neither the parade ground nor the marketplace was ever built. And as New York became, first, the great port city of the eastern seaboard, and then the nation's chief source of capital, the city's boundary pressed out into the numbered streets of the new grid. The grid did not, of course, lend itself to the idea of a "city center"; instead, the center moved steadily north, from the area around City Hall, to what is now SoHo, to Washington Square. In 1832, a developer gained control over the waste area the commissioners had laid out as Union Place, and renamed it, in the great tradition of real estate marketing, Union Square. By the late 1840s, Union Square was lined with fine houses and shops. The opening up of Madison Avenue in 1847, with its headwaters at Madison Square at 26th Street, made possible a new elite neighborhood; and soon the rich were moving northward along Madison and Fifth.

New York City underwent a radical transformation in the middle decades of the nineteenth century. An economic boom turned lower Manhattan into one of the world's great commercial centers, with buildings that, for the first time, towered above the highest church steeples. Eight- and ten-story office buildings went up at the tip of the island; the offices of the city's great newspapers clustered around City Hall; wholesalers and small-scale manufacturers moved into cast-iron buildings in the area around Houston Street, and printers and publishers gathered around Astor Place, just below Grace Church. The tremendous growth of downtown propelled everything else northward. As recently as 1840, virtually the entire population of the city was jammed below 14th Street; by 1870, more than half the city lived to the north, mostly in the rapidly developing East Side.

The city's theaters and amusements, which in the late eighteenth century centered around City Hall Park, headed north along with the population generally. This happened both because the fine stores and office buildings and government offices that occupied lower Manhattan could afford to pay more in rent than theaters and restaurants could, and also because culture followed its consumers. (The poor remained downtown, in what is now called the Lower East Side, or lived along the wharves on either side of the island, where much of the city's manual labor was employed.) Nevertheless, in mid-century the city had no real entertainment district. New York was a city of pedestrians, and people lived where they worked; most neighborhoods, save the most exclusive, necessarily had a mixed character, with factories, taverns, shops, and private homes all on the same street, and often in the same building.

But the rise of mass transportation changed the face of New York. The first elevated railroad, immensely noisy and dirty and inefficient but still positively miraculous at the time, was completed in 1870; it carried passengers up the West Side from Dey Street, far downtown, to 29th Street. A Sixth Avenue line followed in 1878, and then Third Avenue, and then

Second. Public transportation meant that New Yorkers could live in one neighborhood, work in another, and enjoy themselves in a third. Basil March, the hero of William Dean Howells's 1890 novel, *A Hazard of New Fortunes,* lives with his wife in the dignified precincts of Washington Square, but commutes by "el" to his office at the raffish magazine he edits in the East Forties. Though he also explores the city on foot and by coach, March always seems to take the el when he wants to go "uptown," where yet newer worlds await him. By Howells's time, the East Side had been developed up to 125th Street, though the West Side remained largely pastoral.

An incidental effect of this new capacity to take large numbers of people from one place and deliver them to another was that those peculiar junctures created by the periodic intersections of Broadway with an avenue suddenly presented themselves as nodal points in the city—not squares, but traffic convergences. Broadway itself never had an el, but it was flanked by els, and the avenue itself was served by horse-drawn "omnibuses" and by "horsecars," which were horse-drawn trolleys whose wheels ran along tracks in order to make for a smoother and swifter ride. And so the entertainment district consolidated around juncture points along Broadway. Theaters were still scattered around the city—along Second Avenue, and 125th Street in Harlem, and in Brooklyn—but by the 1870s, the city's first true entertainment district had emerged, at Union Square.

What was new about Union Square was that it supported not just the theater but an entire industry brought into being by the theater, as well as all the other forms of pleasure associated with theatergoing. In and around the square were legitimate theaters, such as Wallack's, as well as "variety houses"—featuring what would later be called vaudeville—such as the Union Square Theater and Tony Pastor's New Fourteenth Street Theatre; Steinway's piano shop; theatrical agencies; theatrical printers; show publications like *Leslie's Sporting and Dramatic News*; Sam French's play publication store; the costume house of Roemer and Kohler; and the studio of Napoleon Sarony, photographer to the stars. Union Square's southern boundary, 14th Street, was known as the Rialto, because it was so heavily frequented by theater people; among the show folk themselves, the area immediately in front of the Union Square Theater, at the south-eastern corner of the square, was known as the Slave Market, because it served as an open-air hiring hall. Indeed, the society novelist Richard Harding Davis wrote that "it is said that it is possible to cast, in one morning, any one of Shakespeare's plays, to equip any number of farce companies, and to 'organize' three Uncle Tom's Cabin combinations" from the crowd on 14th Street.

Tony Pastor, the vaudevillian, was known as the Impresario of Fourteenth Street. Pastor was a living summation of nineteenth-century urban entertainment. An Italian born in 1834 (or thereabouts), the son of a grocer, Pastor was an uneducated urchin who sang at temperance meetings, played tambourine in a minstrel company at Barnum's Museum on lower Broadway in 1847, and knocked around through half a dozen circuses in the 1850s, working as a singer, clown, acrobat, tumbler, dancer, and horseback rider, often all in a single show. In the early years of the Civil War, Pastor began a career as a balladeer in "concert saloons," descendants of the English music hall where the acts were often flimsy excuses for the alcohol, and the "waitress girls" considered the serving of drinks the beginning rather than the end of their job. Pastor became a beloved figure, famed for a stock of 1,500 tunes, and for his good-humored ribaldry. He sang about soused Irishmen and farcical Negroes and avenging wives and long-suffering husbands.

For all his knockabout life, Pastor was a rough-hewn gentleman, gracious and accommodating as well as thoroughly good company, his assiduously maintained mustache always waxed to fine points. Pastor understood that so long as variety was presented in the riotous, blowsy atmosphere of the concert saloon it would remain a minor adjunct to male carousing. He recognized that decency could be good for business; his goal, as he put it in one of the innumerable interviews he later granted as the grand old man of Broadway, was "to make the variety show successful by dissociating it from the cigar-smoking and beer-drinking establishment." Pastor opened a variety house of his own on the Bowery in 1865, and ten years later moved to the more respectable location of 585 Broadway, in what is now SoHo. There some of the great figures of the late-nineteenth-century stage, including Lillian Russell and May Irwin, made their debuts. At 585, drinking was permitted in an adjacent saloon, but not in the auditorium.

Pastor moved northward with the theater district, finally settling at 14th Street in 1881, just as the area was becoming New York's entertainment capital. The location alone signified a new level of prestige for variety. Pastor charged as much as $1.50 for a reserved seat, then the priciest variety ticket in town, and he secured the best acts. The bill of fare for one typical evening included Ryan the Mad Musician, "who plays on the xylophone without looking at the instrument"; the Sisters Hedderwicke, "character duettists and dancers"; Clark and Williams in "a funny Negro sketch"; Martha Wren and Zella Marion in an Irish operetta called "Barney's Courtship"; and Professor John White, "with his mule, monkey and dog." Pastor himself often came out to sing one of his sentimental tunes, which almost invariably brought down the house. But the most distinctive feature of Pastor's was that no liquor was served. Pastor encouraged a family atmosphere; as one wag said, it was the kind of variety "a child could take its parents to." There was a Ladies' and Children's Matinee, where the management gave out bouquets and wax dolls; door prizes on other nights included barrels of flour and even dresses. And it worked: Pastor's became both the most respectable and the most popular variety house in New York. Pastor had raised the variety show almost to the level of legitimate theater, as he himself was wont to say. As a singer he was a traditionalist, but as a promoter and entrepreneur Pastor was one of the creators of early-twentieth-century Broadway.

A combination of competition from "continuous houses," in which patrons could come and go as they pleased in the course of an all-day show, and the further migration of the entertainment district, ultimately stranded Tony Pastor. By the mid-nineties, he was being consulted by newspaper reporters as a sage of Broadway, a graybeard who had graced the sideshow at Barnum's as a lad. He was stout and lovable, a Broadway character with his collapsible opera hat and the diamond solitaire that glittered on his shirtfront. But Pastor's remained an important stop on the vaudeville circuit. In 1905, a twelve-year-old Jewish ragamuffin named Izzy Baline got a job at Pastor's as a "song-plugger," a kind of itinerant marketer of new ballads. He sang "In the Sweet By and By" with the Three Keatons, the youngest of whom went on to become one of the greatest silent comedians. And Izzy Baline went on to become Irving Berlin.

—

BY THE LATE NINETEENTH CENTURY, the distinction between "legitimate theater" and popular entertainment, even the sort of relatively genteel popular entertainment that Tony Pastor offered, was growing sharper, a fact recognized in the city's geography. Downtown, where the poor immigrants lived in their squalid warrens, you could see Yiddish or Italian or Chinese or Irish dialect theater. The Bowery was chockablock with vaudeville houses, and there were more around Union Square. The neighborhood known as the Tenderloin, in the West Twenties and Thirties, was the city's most notorious den of vice: prostitutes openly strolled along Sixth Avenue, and both sides of 27th Street west of Sixth were lined with whorehouses, one side for white patrons and the other for black. The Tenderloin was home to many of the city's biggest and most notorious concert saloons.

The legitimate theater increasingly clustered around Madison Square, the next in the nodal points created by Broadway. Occupying as it did the space between Madison Avenue, a rapidly developing upper-class district, and Fifth Avenue, which already enjoyed that status, Madison Square was a far grander and more glamorous setting than Union Square. It was here that the Gilded Age's nouveaux riches went to preen their feathers in public. On weekend afternoons, society gathered among the flower beds and fountains in front of the great, pillared Fifth Avenue Hotel, at 23rd and Fifth. Madison Square was less a rialto than a *faubourg*, with the city's finest jewelers, furriers, florists, and haberdashers. In 1876, Delmonico's, the most famous restaurant in the country and perhaps the only one with a celebrity chef, the famous Charles Ranhofer, moved up from downtown to 26th Street, two blocks north of the Fifth Avenue Hotel. Ward McAllister, Mrs. Astor's social secretary, was a regular patron, as were many of the other members of the Four Hundred. In this refined and clublike setting, men of wealth and standing could gather with their own kind, and eat, drink, and spend with abandon.

Many of the new theaters that sprang up around Madison Square catered to this elite. At the socially exclusive Lyceum, the electric lights had been personally installed by Thomas Edison. The Madison Square Theatre, on Fifth Avenue, enjoyed an equal cachet; at a special benefit performance there in 1884, "pretty ladies of the most exclusive social circles of New York posed, elaborately garbed, in tableaux illustrative of Tennyson's Dream of Fair Women." The better theaters sometimes presented Shakespeare—though often in bowdlerized form—and one of the sensations of the age was the 1884 visit to Broadway by the company of London's Lyceum Theatre, led by the great Ellen Terry, who showed Americans how to perform the classics. For the most part, "refined" drama meant translations of contemporary French and German farces. (The German variety was considered less indecent.) These were often presented as if they were original English-language plays. The most respected theatrical manager of the day, Augustin Daly, kept a steady stream of these productions going at his theater on Broadway and 30th. Most of them were, despite a surface air of sophistication, extremely creaky affairs. According to a plot summary of *The Undercurrent* of 1888, "the one-armed messenger (he is also one half-sister's father) is tied to a railroad track by the villain (a wicked uncle), but the scheme is foiled by the heroine, the daughter, who luckily happens to be in a blacksmith's shop nearby."

The drama of the time was cartoonishly stylized, with a first old lady and a second old lady, a first comedian and a second comedian, a juvenile lead, and so forth. The gifts of the Gilded Age lay more in the direction of consumption than of production. And yet, for this very reason, Broadway became an increasingly delightful, pleasure-filled place. In 1883, the Casino Theatre opened at the corner of 39th and Broadway, at the time an extremely remote locale. The Casino was a giant piece of Moorish whimsy, with a great circular tower terminating in an onion-shaped dome; it was modeled on a Newport clubhouse designed by the famous architect Stanford White. The Casino was intended to be a sort of theatrical clubhouse, with all sorts of amenities provided for the wealthy patrons who would pay for membership. The theater had a street-level café and a gallery where theatergoers could enjoy refreshments while gazing down through big windows at the street. And on top of the Casino, gathered around the Moorish dome, was a facility unheard-of on Broadway— a roof garden.

The Casino was built by Rudolph Aronson, who, like Tony Pastor and many another Broadway impresario, began his career as a performer and left his mark as an entrepreneur. Aronson's background was very different from Pastor's. Born in 1856, Aronson was a classical pianist, composer, and conductor who traveled to Europe as a young man for further musical training. In Paris, he passed many a happy hour at the "concert gardens" that lined the Champs-Elysées. He dreamed of opening up just such a spot along Broadway, but was thwarted by the high price of land. Then he had a revelation, which he later recorded in his memoirs: "Why not utilize for garden purposes the roof of the building I hope to erect, and thus escape the enormous cost of valuable ground?" He even dreamed up the expression "roof garden."

The Casino Roof Garden consisted of a circular open-air promenade trimmed in blue, white, and gold, like the theater itself. A tiled arcade, running from the tower to the corner of the building, allowed patrons to watch the pedestrians on Broadway's blazing pavements. The roof garden featured a rustic theme, with embowered hideaways and shrubbery and plants scattered among the café tables; hidden gas jets cast a romantic glow over the scene, while the colored lights of the Casino lit up the street below. Patrons could listen to the orchestra up on a stage, or watch the performance downstairs through an opening in the theater roof. On opening night, July 8, 1883, the orchestra presented Johann Strauss's operetta *The Queen's Lace Handkerchief* while patrons enjoyed coffee, ice cream, and light beverages brought up from a restaurant downstairs. For New Yorkers accustomed to baking helplessly in the summer heat, it must have been a transporting experience. An obviously delighted critic for *The New York World* wrote, "It is now possible to sit at a table and drink your beer or wine fanned by the night breeze and at the same time look down upon the performance of a comic opera or listen to the music of Mr. Aronson's orchestra."

Within a decade, the city was said to be "roof-garden daft," with theaters up and down Broadway offering entertainment beneath the stars. And as the roof garden became more popular it became less elegant and constrained, more democratic and informal; both men and women wore shirtsleeves, and many of the customers were out-of-towners treating themselves to a night on Broadway. The entertainment became far more populist as well. The roof gardens began offering variety shows, specializing in "dumb acts" like jugglers, acrobats, and animal performers, acts that could be enjoyed perfectly well amidst the noise of drinking and talking. There was a rage for "skirt dancers," women who wore calf-length skirts and long underskirts and struck balletic poses and made sweeping gestures which showed off their bodies. Aronson himself lost control of his theater in 1892 but hung on to the roof garden, making a success of a high-class Parisian-style "revue." The following year he lost control of the roof garden as well, and spent much of the rest of his life traveling the world, hobnobbing with the great composers he so much admired. He himself left behind no music of any importance, but he had invented something more important in the history of Broadway: a new and charming way of experiencing life. The roof garden was a delightful setting that put people at their ease, and that helped define the dreamy pleasure-world of Broadway for the next thirty years.

By the later years of the century, the whole experience of being in Broadway was becoming more open and fluid—more modern. Broadway was lined with electric streetlights, and all night long patrons and theater people, clubmen and chorus girls and gawking tourists, strolled up and down. The stretch between Madison Square and 42nd Street had come to be known as the Upper Rialto, and, as the author of *The New Metropolis*, a portrait of the city published in 1899, notes, "The best and worst of it is to be met here—stars, supers, soubrettes, specialists and managers alike. . . . The life of the street is as active at midnight as at noon, for the theatres create a constant patronage for the restaurants, which are crowded up to the early hours of the morning."

And Broadway was becoming sexy—not crude, like the Tenderloin, but racy and suggestive. Popular theater revolved increasingly around the charms of nubile young women. By the nineties, a vogue had set in for "light opera," an early form of musical comedy with only the sketchiest plot fleshed out with comic bits and elaborately costumed chorus girls. Carrie Madenda, the heroine of *Sister Carrie,* Theodore Dreiser's great, bleak novel of 1900, is an aspiring actress who begins her career in an unnamed production at the Casino, at that time the reigning temple of light opera. Carrie's role is to march at the head of a column of twenty girls in the "ballet chorus," wearing a white flannel outfit with sword dangling from a silver belt. When the run of Carrie's show ends, she finds another job in the chorus line of *The Wives of Abdul* at the Broadway Theatre, where she is assigned to "a group of oriental beauties who, in the second act of the comic opera, were paraded by the vizier before the new potentate as the treasures of his harem."

Indeed, in 1900, just when Dreiser's novel appeared, the Casino played host to a drama of giddiness and gratification that defined the culture of Broadway at the turn of the century. In keeping with its usual fare, the Casino offered a frivolous concoction called *Floradora*, a tale about a beautiful heiress cheated out of her inheritance. The play received poor notices, insofar as it was noticed. In one scene, however, six chorus girls, who had plainly been chosen for their beauty rather than their talent, paraded around the stage carrying parasols while their male partners did most of the dancing. A group of Yale men began coming to the theater in order to give the girls a standing ovation. Soon a cult developed over the "Floradora Sextette." Diamond Jim Brady and Stanford White, boon companions and two of the leading celebrities of Broadway, ordered standing tickets for the show; within days, every playboy and clubman in town was gathering to worship before the altar of pulchritude. Broadway had never seen such a craze before. The Floradora Girls were inundated with flowers, gifts, and expensive dinners; each of them ultimately married a millionaire, the most famous match being that of Evelyn Nesbit to Harry K. Thaw. Six years later, Thaw murdered the man he believed was carrying on an affair with his wife: the casino's architect, Stanford White. The Floradora Girls were the first chorines to go platinum, as it were. And yet these incarnations of the Platonic ideal of female beauty averaged five feet four inches in height, and 130 pounds. The Broadway ideal of female beauty was still evolving.

Something new was emerging as the city's entertainment culture began to lap at the edges of 42nd Street—and yet it was still only a dim shadow of the place that would come to be called Times Square. The word "Broadway" didn't conjure up anything like the magic, or the wickedness, that it soon would evoke. There are no novels of Broadway from this era; *Sister Carrie*, which does seek to anatomize this new world, was published just as Madison Square was giving way to Times Square (and, indeed, contains perhaps the first reference in literature to the gay life of 42nd Street). The cardinal points of New York's literary geography in the 1880s and 1890s were Fifth Avenue; Washington Square, redoubt of old money; Wall Street, with its thrilling casino of speculation; and, for socially conscious writers like Stephen Crane, the Bowery, where misery raged. Winston Pierce, the main character of *His Father's Son: A New York Novel*, written by the society author Brander Matthews in 1896, actually lives in a brownstone on Madison Square, yet neither Pierce nor any of his friends or family members takes the slightest note of the square or its environs. The only reference to theater occurs when the protagonist takes his wife, Mary, to 14th Street to see *The Black Crook,* a famous, if already venerable, production featuring an enormous troupe of scantily clad chorus girls. Mary is scandalized—and rightly so. Winston is tumbling rapidly down a moral slope that leads to adultery, drinking, gambling, and theft; his fascination with chorus girls in tights is a warning sign of his degeneracy.

THE FOUR HUNDRED
MEET THE FOUR MILLION

THE FIRST CROWD in the history of Times Square gathered on the east side of Broadway between 44th and 45th Streets on November 25, 1895. That night, Oscar Hammerstein's Olympia Theatre was opening up, and Hammerstein, the first of Times Square's masters of shameless hyperbole, was going only slightly overboard when he billed the Olympia as "the grandest amusement temple in the world." Perhaps he used that quaint expression because no word had yet come into the language to describe the vast miscellany that was the Olympia—music hall, concert hall, and theater, all spread out over an entire city block. The entire range of culture, from the most popular to the most refined, would be housed under a single roof. The Olympia bore some resemblance to a Coney Island amusement park, and some resemblance to Madison Square Garden, the leviathan on 26th Street; but it is safe to say that the first theater ever built in Times Square looked like nothing the world had ever seen before. It was a bad idea on a monumental scale.

Hammerstein was himself as various and as contradictory as the Olympia: an orthodox Jew, a practical joker, a reckless plunger into dubious enterprises. He was a short, portly character who always waved a cigar and wore a silk hat tipped back on his head. Hammerstein earned his first fortune inventing gizmos for cigars—a roller, a header, a cutter, a device that molded twelve stogies at once. He was an incessant tinkerer and inventor. But he was also a cultured man with a real love, and a modest gift, for music, which he once demonstrated in characteristic fashion by composing an opera in twenty-four hours on a bet. Hammerstein seems to have plowed his entire fortune into Broadway without a second thought. In 1892 he built the Manhattan Opera House on 34th Street, a populist rival to the aristocratic Metropolitan Opera. He and his partners split after Hammerstein loudly booed a singer he hadn't wanted to appear, and then got into a fistfight with the woman's paramour, which landed them both in the precinct house. Hammerstein then cashed out of the opera house, spent $850,000, most of it borrowed, to buy the property along Broadway, and commenced to build his immense, portholed palace of culture.

The Olympia was situated squarely in terra incognita. At the time, the electric lights that ran up Broadway stopped at 42nd Street. The corner of 42nd and Broadway was already a bustling commercial area by the end of the century, thanks to the convergence of north–south and east–west trolley lines, as well as the Ninth Avenue el to the west; but the area north of 42nd consisted mostly of cheap boardinghouses, tenements, factories, whorehouses, and dance halls. The neighborhood would also have smelled very strongly of horse: with Central Park just to the north, the West Forties were full of stables and of shops that sold and repaired carriages. The area was popularly known as Longacre Square, after a similar district in London. The eastern side of Broadway, which then centered on the 71st Armory building, was known as the Thieves' Lair.

Hammerstein's Olympia—it was never just "the Olympia"—was a work of pharaonic ambition. The Music Hall had 124 boxes ascending in eleven tiers, while the Theatre had eighty-four boxes (more than the Metropolitan). The color schemes of the three houses were red and gold, blue and gold, and cream and gold. Hammerstein was said to have spent $600,000 on his folly. No theater opening had been so eagerly awaited in years, and that November night, Hammerstein had sold ten thousand tickets; unfortunately, the Olympia had only six thousand seats. So, half the crowd gained entrance, while the other half, in the first recorded fiasco in Times Square, "slid through the mud and slush of Longacre back into the ranks of Cosmopolis," according to *The New York Times*. Later that evening, the crowd of swells, in crinoline and patent leather, formed themselves into a giant flying wedge and broke down the doors. It was not a good portent: Hammerstein had never really figured out how he could make back his immense investment, and within two years he had lost control of the Olympia; in 1898, he declared bankruptcy. But for Hammerstein, as for so many of the men who would come after him, disaster was a mere inconvenience; he bounced back almost as soon as he hit the pavement.

NEW YORK CITY in 1900 was, to a degree unimaginable today, the imperial capital of turn-of-the-century America. As J. P. Morgan and a handful of other New York financiers concentrated corporate power in their own hands, New York came to occupy the commanding heights of the emerging twentieth-century economy. By the early years of the century, 70 percent of corporate headquarters and 69 of the 185 trusts, or combines, being forged by Morgan and his colleagues were based in New York City; two-thirds of imports and two-fifths of exports flowed through its docks. Wall Street financed the growth of the nation's railroads and industries—and, increasingly, those of other nations. New York became a city of millionaires as well as a magnet for the millionaires of the Chicago stockyards and the Colorado mines and the Texas oilfields.

At the same time, the city was undergoing a radical physical transformation. Immigrants had been pouring into New York since the early 1880s, filling lower Manhattan and pushing existing residents uptown and into Brooklyn. On December 31, 1897, at midnight, Greater New York was born—a new city joining Manhattan to Brooklyn, Queens, the Bronx, and Staten Island. In the wake of "consolidation," as this process was called, the population of New York, which until that moment had consisted only of Manhattan, more than doubled, to 3.4 million. New York was now three times the size of Chicago, its nearest American rival, bigger than Paris, and gaining rapidly on London for the title of the world's largest city. New York was suddenly every bit as great in fact as its citizens had always thought it to be.

The astonishing array of public works and private projects unleashed by consolidation forged the new city into a single great metropolis and bound it far more tightly to the larger world. In the first decade of the twentieth century, the city built the Queensboro, Williamsburg, and Manhattan Bridges to link Manhattan with Brooklyn and Queens; financiers built Penn Station as well as the colossal tunnel under the Hudson that brought trains directly from New Jersey. (Travelers until then had had to dismount and board a ferry.) Beginning in 1907, a new and grandiose version of Grand Central Terminal began to bring commuters to the heart of Manhattan; by 1913 the trains and the terminal had been converted from steam to the far cleaner and more efficient electrical power. And, most important of all, in 1904 the city completed the first stage of its monumental subway system, which enabled New Yorkers to go from one end of the city to the other in scarcely more than an hour.

City planners had talked about building an underground rail line almost from the time of the advent of elevated trains, in the late 1860s. By the time the idea had become practicable, in the mid-nineties, it was clear that the new transit system would have to link the downtown business district with Grand Central, and then carry passengers to the new residential areas of the Upper East and West Sides. Since Grand Central was already on the East Side, the subways would need a transverse line to serve the West. Thanks to an 1857 municipal ordinance forbidding the use of steam power below 42nd, Commodore Vanderbilt had located his original commuter rail terminal, built in 1869, just north of that street. What's more, 42nd Street was one of the broad crosstown streets designated by the 1811 plan, so it already served mass transportation, with a trolley line running east and west. For these reasons, the transverse line would run across 42nd to Broadway before heading uptown. And that is why, in October 1904, when the underground system began to operate, the new subway station at 42nd and Broadway became one of the twin pivots or junctions at the heart of the subway system—indeed, of the much larger system of bridges, tunnels, train stations, and roadways that was just then beginning to allow millions of people to move swiftly and efficiently into, out of, and around New York.

Urban geography, real estate dynamics, and public transportation all worked together to make Times Square the city's latest rialto; but the fact that it became so much more probably has a fair amount to do with *The*

New York Times. In 1902, Adolph Ochs, the *Times*'s owner and publisher, purchased the tiny triangular plot of land at the point where Seventh Avenue and Broadway cross at 42nd Street. He bought the property from his friend and financial backer August Belmont, who was then in the midst of building the subway under contract to the city. Ochs's decision to locate a burgeoning enterprise inside such a skinny structure was almost as absurd as Hammerstein's—the *Times* would be forced to move again in 1913— but Ochs may well have understood that the new subway system would turn 42nd and Broadway into the center of town. The Times Tower was the second-tallest building in New York, a 375-foot marble-and-limestone needle based on Giotto's campanile for the Duomo in Florence. The building was said to be visible from eight miles away—an "X" that marked the center from which the great, growing city radiated. As the building was going up, Belmont, who had a financial interest in the *Times,* proposed to Mayor McClellan that both the neighborhood and the subway station be named for the newspaper, as Herald Square already was. And it was done: on April 8, 1904, the mayor proclaimed that Longacre Square would henceforth be known as Times Square.

Ochs, like Hammerstein—and like Rudolph Aronson, for that matter—was a German Jewish immigrant with a flair for ballyhoo; he became the very first entrepreneur to market his Times Square location. That first year, Ochs held a giant outdoor New Year's Eve party featuring a fireworks display at the Times Tower. The account of the festivities in *The Times* the following day emphasizes the symbolic importance of the event: "From base to dome," the paper reported, "the giant structure was alight—a torch to usher in the newborn, a funeral pyre for the old, which pierced the very heavens." The crowd, pouring in through the new subway system, was estimated at 200,000, and the tremendous roar they made at midnight with their rattles and noisemakers could be heard miles away. Three years later, the fireworks display having been banned, Ochs dreamed up the idea of dropping an electric ball from the top of the building, an ingenious bit of publicity that swelled the New Year's Eve crowd yet further. Times Square quickly became New York's agora, a place to gather both to await great tidings and to celebrate them, whether a World Series or a presidential election. In the minds of New Yorkers, Americans, and people all over the world, Times Square became associated with a particular kind of crowd—a happy crowd, made up of merrymakers rather than troublemakers.

THE OLYMPIA HAD BEEN a folly, a giant ocean liner moored in a remote backwater. Hammerstein's next move showed a much shrewder sense of the emerging market. In 1899 he scraped together $80,000 to build the Victoria Theatre, a slapdash structure of secondhand bricks and scavenged lumber on the northwest corner of 42nd and Broadway. Hammerstein stuffed rubbish in the empty spaces between floors or within walls, and bought carpeting from a defunct liner for 25 cents a yard. For the first few years, he offered high-minded drama such as Henri Bataille and Michael Morton's *Resurrection,* based on the novel by Tolstoy. But with such fine new theaters as the New Amsterdam, the Lyric, and the Liberty suddenly surrounding him on 42nd Street, he decided to explore the lower reaches of the market. In February 1904, Hammerstein announced that he was going vaudeville. It was an appropriate change, both commercially and symbolically. An estimated five million people passed through the Times Square subway station in its first year of operation. Those vast crowds were making Times Square radically different from any of its predecessors—more crowded, more turbulent and volatile, more democratic. Men and women, the middle class and the poor, were all flung together on the subway, as they were in the other rising institutions of the early part of the century—the department store, the office building. Barriers that had long seemed impermeable, and that had been treated as moral principles, were rapidly being lowered, if scarcely eliminated.

And then there were the facts of urban geography. Times Square could never be as genteel as Madison Square had been. Madison Square was, after all, a park, a grassy spot with fountains and flowers and tables, which in turn attracted the city's finest hotels and theaters and restaurants. Times Square, by contrast, was a great, eddying mass of people and vehicles, already, in the early years of the century, said to be the busiest street corner in the world. And so the ethos of Times Square always included a glorification of the inevitable mixing. The restaurateur George

Rector liked to say, only a little bit hyperbolically, that his establishment attracted both Mrs. Astor's Four Hundred and O. Henry's Four Million.

Oscar turned the Victoria over to his son Willie, who had learned the vaudeville trade from the famous agent William Morris. At first Willie featured top-billing vaudeville stars like Eva Tanguay and Nora Bayes. But Willie, who seems to have shared his father's gift for populist entertainment but not his loftier aspirations, continued further down the path of least resistance. Soon the Victoria, which charged 25 cents a ticket, was showcasing acts like Don the Talking Dog, the Man with the Seventeen-Foot Beard, and the Cherry Sisters, billed as "America's Worst Act"; Willie posted a net to catch the fruits and vegetables that audience members were encouraged to throw at the girls. Willie combined the roofs of the Victoria and the neighboring Republic Theater, which Oscar had built in 1900 (and which lives today as the New Victory Theater), to form the Paradise Roof Garden, which featured a "Dutch farm" with comely milkmaids and real cows. Later on, he installed "Mock's Corner," a jury of monkeys who provided a running commentary on the performers' work. Willie himself was a gloomy and apparently charmless character who was quite content playing cards with the stagehands, but he had a Barnum-like gift for inspired flimflam: in the hottest days of the summer he placed a thermometer conspicuously on top of a block of ice, its low temperature demonstrating the virtues of the theater's "air-cooling" system.

Willie understood that the daily newspapers, which were exploding both in number and in circulation, had created an insatiable appetite for scandal. He invented what was known as the freak or nut act, which the vaudeville authority Joe Laurie, Jr., describes as an engagement "made with the deliberate object of promotion, the financial profit being secondary"—the ultimate object being to expand the vaudeville audience by playing on the news of the day. Willie specialized in female murderers or would-be murderers, including two women who had shot a socialite and whom he billed as "The Shooting Stars." After Harry Thaw killed Stanford White, Willie hired Evelyn Nesbit at an unheard-of $3,500 a week to do some dancing. He booked the wife of Lord Hope, who owned the Hope Diamond, and then paid Lord Hope $1,500 a week to stand in the Victoria lobby during performances. Willie's greatest genius was in the manufacture of publicity. In 1905 he persuaded an itinerant Swiss sketch artist to pretend to be court artist to the Turkish sultan, hired three women as his wives, and then orchestrated a massive publicity campaign for *Abdul Kardar and His Three Wives;* Willie arranged to have the troupe detained by customs, and then furiously petitioned for their release. Three years later he repeated the gag, booking the famous Gertrude Hoffman to play Salome, and then arranging to have her arrested for indecency.

The Victoria was scarcely Times Square's only great experiment in popular culture; the Hippodrome, on Sixth Avenue at 44th, offered fantastic extravaganzas to six thousand spectators at a time. But the Victoria, located literally on top of the Times Square subway, offered entertainment that even an unlettered immigrant could enjoy—and it was identifiably American, unlike the Yiddish or Chinese or German theater downtown. You could teach yourself English at the Victoria, and you could keep up with the news of the day. Willie never lost contact with his audience. Joe Laurie, Jr., says that in its seventeen years of operation the Victoria grossed $20 million, of which $5 million was profit.

Almost directly across the street from the most tumbledown and loutish theater in Times Square lay the most beautiful and refined theater in Times Square—indeed, in the country. The New Amsterdam, designed by two gifted young architects, Henry B. Herts and Hugh Tallant, and completed in 1903, was the first example in the United States of art nouveau design, from the horticulturally accurate roses carved into the woodwork to the Shakespearean figures peering from jade-colored terracotta balustrades to the great mural over the proscenium illustrating the progress of the arts. The sinuous line and stripped-down ornamentation of art nouveau was the very look of modernity for the forward-thinking aesthetes of the early years of the century, and the New Amsterdam was considered a building of the first importance—a building that might well "mark an epoch in the history of art," as one penetrating if breathless account put it. This was also, of course, an era of opulence and show, and the New Amsterdam was intended to dazzle even the most blasé theatergoer. The gentlemen's retiring room featured a "fireplace of Caen stone, floor of Welsh quarry tiling, wainscot of nut-brown English oak," while that of the ladies was rendered "in tones of the tea rose, with decorations and carvings of conventionalized roses with leaves and stems entwined."

Opening night was a magnificent affair, with carriages disgorging a steady stream of men in top hats and tails and women in furs and long gowns. The New Amsterdam's owners, Marc Klaw and Abe Erlanger, two of the most powerful men on Broadway, had chosen to open with *A Midsummer Night's Dream*—an apt choice, for the architects had said that they intended to evoke that play's sense of magic. And indeed, one critic who attended the opening described the theater as "the most airy, fairy beautiful thing in the way of a playhouse that the New York public has ever seen." The play, on the other hand, received fairly poor reviews, and gave way after three weeks to *Mother Goose*, a Christmas pantomime. Soon the New Amsterdam was showing dopey musicals like *Miss Dolly Dollars*. In fact, nothing produced at the New Amsterdam during the first decade of its existence demonstrated anything like the creativity and daring of the building itself. Franz Lehár's *The Merry Widow* was a huge hit in 1907–1908, and set off a waltz craze that lasted for several years; but their other big successes were mostly harmless froth.

By 1910, the passion for playgoing had reached such a pitch that forty first-class theaters were operating in and around Times Square; and yet few, if any, of them showed more distinguished fare than the New Amsterdam. A combination of stifling Victorian respectability and the absence of a sophisticated urban culture ensured an endless tide of mediocrity. Though figures like Dreiser and Howells, Henry James, Edith Wharton, and Stephen Crane were forging a new kind of American literature at the time, Broadway showed no interest in their work. The art of playwriting, and for that matter the etiquette of theatergoing, remained stuck in the high artifice of the Gay Nineties. Audiences hissed the villain and shouted warnings to the endangered hero. Though Klaw and Erlanger had the courage to show *Peer Gynt* at the New Amsterdam, Ibsen, like Shaw and Strindberg, was generally considered either too difficult or too wicked for Broadway. Probably the most important theatrical development of those early years was the rise of George M. Cohan, a veteran of vaudeville who turned out the first truly American musicals—*Little Johnny Jones, George Washington, Jr.*, and others, which featured rousing, foot-stomping tunes, among them "Give My Regards to Broadway," "Yankee Doodle Boy," and "You're a Grand Old Flag."

Broadway in the early years of the century was a factory, just as Hollywood was to become several decades later. Theater—whether vaudeville, operetta, or melodrama—was the popular culture of the day, and people all over the country demanded performers and productions "direct from Broadway." In the 1890s, managers of theaters from across the country would sit in the saloons of Union Square dickering with producers for the rights to put on shows. Often, to be on the safe side, they would book two shows for the same period; or the producers would promise the same troupe to two different managers. Out of this chaos came a centralized booking organization known as the Syndicate, a partnership among six of Broadway's leading producers. The Syndicate's members owned theaters in New York and elsewhere, but its real power came from its control over the contracts of Broadway performers. If you wanted to book a Broadway show, you had to pay court to Abe Erlanger and Marc Klaw, who dominated the organization, and thus much of American theater, from their offices in the New Amsterdam. By 1905, Erlanger and Klaw were said to control 1,250 of the country's 3,500 theaters, including almost all the first-class ones. Thereafter, a group of brothers from Syracuse, the Shuberts, began to build up a rival chain of their own, forging alliances with powerhouses like the producer David Belasco. Small-town theaters would "go Shubert," or "go Syndicate," until the twenties, when the Shuberts gained dominance (just in time to see the movies and radio degrade the value of their monopoly). The one thing that didn't change was Broadway's control over "the road."

Broadway exercised a similar, but even more all-encompassing, control over vaudeville. In 1906, two vaudeville operators, B. F. Keith and E. F. Albee, incorporated the United Booking Office in Maine, which operated according to the same principles as the Syndicate. The Keith-Albee combine soon came to control virtually the entire vaudeville circuit east of Chicago. A rival circuit, the Orpheum, dominated vaudeville in the western half of the country. In 1913, Martin Beck, who ran the Orpheum circuit, built the Palace, Broadway's vaudeville house nonpareil. Keith and Albee almost immediately wrested control of the Palace from Beck and moved their office to the theater's sixth floor, which for many years thereafter remained vaudeville's epicenter. The UBO's bookers manned twenty desks on the floor, each responsible for a group of theaters in a particular part of the country. It was the bookers who composed the actual lineup of acts for the theaters, so vaudeville agents would hop from desk to desk, peddling their talent. In its own domain, the UBO exercised a supremacy no less complete than that of the steel trust. Vaudeville acts that declined a salary offer, or played at rival houses, or even played at Keith-Albee theaters through rival booking offices, put their careers in mortal peril. On the other hand, the Keith-Albee monopoly ensured that theatergoers in Kankakee or Altoona would see honest-to-God Broadway vaudeville.

TIMES SQUARE WAS, from the very beginning, a "theatrical" environment—a place that not only had theaters but was a theater. It was lit up by electric lights, and it throbbed with life until the early hours of the morning. It was vastly bigger, grander, and gaudier than Union Square, vastly more vivid and heterogeneous than Madison Square. The area was choked with actors, chorus girls, street urchins, newspapermen, gamblers, Wall Street barons, first-nighters in silk hats, and Fifth Avenue ladies in long gowns. Theater people gathered on the sidewalk in front of the Knickerbocker Hotel on the southeast corner of 42nd and Broadway, and at the Knickerbocker's famous bar. The side streets to the east and west of Broadway were jammed with saloons, cheap hotels, and whorehouses, which serviced both the longshoremen who worked and lived in Hell's Kitchen, to the west, and the tourists who poured in from all over. Times Square offered something for everyone.

In many ways, the most thrilling environments on Broadway in the early years of the century—the most theatrical ones—were not theaters, but restaurants. These were the "lobster palaces" of Times Square: Rector's, Reisenweber's, Bustanoby's, Murray's Roman Gardens. The lobster palaces were temples to the god of conspicuous consumption, where the freshly minted millionaires of the age went to flaunt their wealth by eating staggering meals and leave staggering tips; a headwaiter might clear upwards of $15,000 during the holidays. The settings were strictly Gilded Lily. The downstairs dining room at Rector's, which accommodated one hundred tables, featured floor-to-ceiling mirrors and Louis XIV furnishings; both the table linen and the cutlery bore the "Rector griffin." The Café Maxim, at 38th and Broadway, clad its waiters in its own version of Louis XIV: ruffled shirts, black satin knee breeches, silk stockings, pumps with silver buckles. Most of the dining rooms were below ground level, so that the patron reached his table via a grand stairway. The producer and impresario Florenz Ziegfeld had popularized the triumphal entry, with huzzahs and bravos and trumpet flourishes and bowing and scraping. Here the man about town with the actress of the day on his arm, or the budding plutocrat and his wife, could make just such an entrance, usually accompanied by the house orchestra. Here every man could be the star of his own drama.

This was an era of epic eating, when the plutocrat, like the Hawaiian prince, demonstrated his wealth by the dimensions of his belly. Diamond Jim Brady became one of the great celebrities of the age simply by out-eating everyone around him. Brady once explained his philosophy of dining by saying that he started each meal with his stomach four inches from the table and ate until the two made contact. When Diamond Jim returned from Paris with a mania for *filet de sole Marguery*, George Rector's father sent him off to France to learn how to prepare the dish. When Rector returned two years later, a virtuoso of sole, he was met at New York harbor by Diamond Jim and Rector's Russian orchestra. Whisked directly to the kitchen, he prepared perhaps the single most famous meal of an age famous for its meals. Diamond Jim was joined by Sam Shubert, the theatrical impresario; Marshall Field, the department store magnate; Adolphus Busch, the brewer; and the composers Victor Herbert and John Philip Sousa. Diamond Jim pronounced himself ecstatic.

The Rectors had made a fortune running the only restaurant permitted at the Chicago Exposition of 1893; the family was already well established by the time it opened its ornate palace, in September 1899, on the east side of Broadway between 43rd and 44th, immediately south of Hammerstein's Olympia. Rector's was the first, and the greatest, of the lobster palaces. (Rector claimed to have been the first to actually serve lobster, their signature dish.) Despite the magnificent setting, Rector's offered a vastly headier social milieu than the stodgy world of Delmonico's.

Everyone who mattered dined at Rector's—the Floradora Girls and their cattle-baron escorts, O. Henry and Stephen Crane, Oscar Hammerstein and the Whitneys, Diamond Jim and Lillian Russell. There was gambling in the private dining rooms in the rear, and manic stock speculating—it appears to have amounted almost to the same activity—at the tables upstairs and down. Whatever news there was on Broadway could always be gleaned among the tables at Rector's. In his memoirs—for restaurateurs then were at least as celebrated as ours are today—George Rector says, "It was the cathedral of froth, where New York chased the rainbow, and the butterfly netted the entomologist. It was the national museum of habits, the bourse of gossip, and the clearing house of rumors."

At a time when the theater itself was almost absurdly stylized, dining was a kind of free-form drawing-room comedy; and as the hour drew later, the drama became more intimate and more risqué. The light posttheater supper came to symbolize the sophistication, and the nocturnal habits, of the Broadway crowd. The stage door Johnny, the young swain or incorrigible roué besotted with an actress or chorus girl, was expected to preen with his catch in the racy setting of the Broadway restaurant. This late meal was widely known as the Bird and a Bottle, the "bird" standing both for the meal and the young lady. Chorus girl was, in fact, the principal dish served at the lobster palaces, at least late at night. Many of the restaurants kept rooms upstairs so that the gentleman need not suffer the inconvenience of a hotel. Murray's Roman Gardens, a palatial setting that would have made Nero blush, offered "24 luxuriously furnished and richly appointed bachelor apartments."

This entire world of gargantuan meals, corpulent men, and stolen kisses would come to seem thoroughly archaic to the next generation, who scarcely felt the leaden hand of the Victorian past. And yet the very publicness of these pleasures, the variety of the crowd, was something quite new. Back in the Gay Nineties, Stanford White had held private orgies in the damask-draped splendor of his private aerie in the tower of Madison Square Garden. Now the man of means could satisfy his appetites in full view of the world (if not of his wife). A new, unashamed morality was brewing in the democratic and ungoverned climate of Times Square.

NOTHING
BUT GIRLS

TIMES SQUARE WAS ALREADY the sex capital of New York by the early years of the twentieth century. The brothels of the Tenderloin had moved north along with the restaurants and theaters: in 1901, vice investigators identified 132 sites where prostitutes plied their trade in the area bounded by Sixth and Eighth Avenues and 37th and 47th Streets. In many of the hotels around 42nd and Broadway, including the celebrated Metropole, where the old gunslinger and newspaperman Bat Masterson held forth at the bar, prostitutes and their pimps controlled dozens of rooms. Forty-third Street between Broadway and Eighth, where *The New York Times* was to move its office, was known as Soubrette Row, for most of the brownstones on the block functioned as brothels. A man could scarcely walk a few blocks in the area at night without being propositioned. As a form of commerce, sex could scarcely have been more open and unabashed, despite constant attempts at suppression.

As a form of culture or entertainment, on the other hand, sex, or rather sexuality, remained largely taboo. The more degraded forms of popular culture, like the concert saloon, were essentially prostitution in the form of entertainment. The high culture of theater, on the other hand, remained largely starchy and histrionic. Between these poles lay the frolicsome light operas in which Dreiser's Carrie made her living and the more risqué burlesque-type shows, like the venerable *Black Crook*, where voluptuous women danced the cancan and trafficked in heavy-handed double entendre. What Broadway lacked, at the turn of the century, was a figure who could fuse the naughty sexuality of the streets and the saloons and the burlesque show with the savoir-faire of lobster palace society—someone who could make sex delightful and amusing. What it lacked was Florenz Ziegfeld.

Ziegfeld was an upper-middle-class figure with refined tastes and lowbrow instincts—a much improved version of Willie Hammerstein. Ziegfeld's father, a German (but not Jewish) immigrant, was a classical musician who ran a music school in Chicago. Ziegfeld absorbed his father's standards, and his dignified bearing, but from an early age demonstrated a Barnum-like aptitude for promotion and flimflam. While still a teenager in the 1880s, he bought a huge bowl, filled it with water, and charged admission to an exhibit of "Invisible Brazilian Fish." The fish flopped, but Ziegfeld then toured with the Great Sandow, a celebrated strongman. Ziegfeld understood that Sandow was not just a power lifter but a sex symbol: he substituted a pair of skimpy shorts for his star's circus-era leopard-skin cloak, and then persuaded several society ladies to feel the biceps of this near naked Apollo—thus causing, as he had intended, a tabloid sensation.

But Sandow was only a way station. Ziegfeld began dabbling in theater, and in 1896 he sailed to London in search of affordable talent. There he became utterly smitten—professionally and personally—with Anna Held, an adorable, toy-sized creature who had no great gifts as a singer or dancer, but whose tiny waist (eighteen inches), insinuating manner, impressive embonpoint, and dark, flashing eyes had made her the darling of the stage in both London and Paris. Wresting Anna away from Europe, and from her managers, with a combination of fabulous gifts and equally fabulous promises, Ziegfeld arranged a triumphant arrival in New York. Anna's ship was met by Diamond Jim Brady, Lillian Russell, a thirty-piece band, and a large contingent from the press. (Much the same welcoming committee was to reassemble several years later for the arrival of George Rector, Jr., and the recipe for *filet de sole Marguery*.) Once he had established Anna in a magnificent suite at the Savoy Hotel, Ziegfeld concocted a preposterous tale about the restorative milk baths she allegedly took that somehow held the newspapers of the day transfixed. Anna became the most celebrated beauty of the age—a new, hummingbird type as against the beloved but lumbering Valkyrie Lillian.

Ziegfeld created a series of flimsy vehicles designed to exploit Anna's famous charms, including *Mam'selle Napoleon,* in 1903, and the more daring *Parisian Model* of 1906. These were negligible works of theater. One New York reviewer wrote of *The Parisian Model:* "Real merit the concoction has none, the music being reminiscent, the humor bewhiskered and hoary, and the plot imperceptible." The same critic described one of Held's dances as "quite the most disgusting exhibition seen on Broadway this season." But that was more or less the point. In that number, called "A Gown for Each Hour of the Day," Anna ducked behind a screen composed of taller chorus girls for each of the many costume changes. Those girls themselves disrobed behind painter's easels in a number called, with typical Ziegfeldian lubriciousness, "I'd Like to See More of You." And yet Ziegfeld had a finely calibrated instinct for opening the floodgates of appetite so far, and no further; he was always saved by his sense of taste. In the words of one of his biographers, Marjorie Farnsworth, "Ziegfeld knew the subtle line between desire and lust, between good taste and vulgarity, and never crossed it. He came close a few times, but he never quite crossed it."

Ziegfeld was not a director, and certainly not a writer. His proper title was "producer," but this barely does justice to the influence he exercised. Ziegfeld's own life was a very conscious work of theater, intended to be consumed by the public through the medium of the newspapers, and to keep a gorgeous sense of luxury, romance, and inspired recklessness washing back and forth between the life and the stage. Ziegfeld was a handsome, dark-eyed man who dressed impeccably; and he understood how to stage-manage his serial romances in a way that Donald Trump could only envy. He fell in love with Anna, and then with an endless succession of beauties; these liaisons ensured that both he and they remained in the spotlight. Ziegfeld plied his beloved, whoever she was, with an endless stream of sable coats and diamond pins and hotel suites and private railroad cars; everything in their lives was the best, the biggest, the shiniest. The love was real, but the display was calculated. Ziegfeld was such a shameless promoter that when Anna's $250,000 jewelry collection was stolen, she suspected he had done it to create a sensation; and when the same thing happened to the actress Billie Burke a decade or so later, she lodged the same accusation.

Ziegfeld was said to be coldhearted and selfish—his principal biographer seems to have loathed him—but he was also a magnificent character. His plays made him fantastically rich, but his recklessness kept him perpetually teetering on the verge of bankruptcy. His insouciance was legendary. P. G. Wodehouse and Guy Bolton, who wrote the book for several of Ziegfeld's plays, describe him at a casino in Palm Beach: "Ziegfeld was standing by a table with a handful of the costly green chips, dropping them carelessly on the numbers and turning to talk to the woman next to him without watching the wheel. He won, but went on talking, leaving the chips where they lay. . . . Only when his companion squealed excitedly and pointed to the piled-up counters did he motion languidly to the croupier to push them towards him." An awestruck Bolton says, "You feel that hundred-dollar bills mean no more to him than paper matches to a cigar store"; to which Wodehouse responds, "And half the time he hasn't enough to buy a waistcoat for a smallish gnat." This was Ziegfeld's life; but it was also a myth—or what we would now call a lifestyle—every bit as potent as the dreams of giddy passion Ziegfeld retailed in his plays.

Ziegfeld's own art was the presentation of female beauty. He sought, he said, "the embodiment of every man's dream of the ideal woman." And this was no vaporous ideal. He once explained that "in a really beautiful face, the height of the forehead should equal the length of the nose, the length of the nose equal the distance between the septum of the nose and the chin, the distance between the eyes equal the length of one of them." He considered the "Titian beauty" the rarest of all; preferred the temperaments, if not the legs, of short girls; abhorred the knocked knee; and insisted that "thighs to be beautiful should exactly touch each other." It is somewhat shocking to read that Ziegfeld's ideal choral novice should be no more than sixteen, though of course at the time not many girls remained in school beyond that age. Ziegfeld taught these teenagers how to walk—breasts out, shoulders back, chin up—how to dress, how to talk, how to behave in public. Once he had turned them into Ziegfeld beauties, he added costumes, lighting, makeup, music: the magic of the stage.

Ziegfeld really hit his stride with the *Follies* of 1907. The *Follies* was hardly an innovative production: it was a remake of the popular Parisian "revue," a series of skits and songs poking fun at the leading figures of the day, the shows, the crazes, the stars. And yet the show exuded a sense of cosmopolitan refinement, of dash and wit, that made it a tremendous success. It was also short—forty minutes—and moved at a head-spinning velocity that only added to the sense of excitement. The *Follies* were widely imitated but never eclipsed. Ziegfeld rechristened the show *Ziegfeld's Follies*, turning it into a kind of branded product. He used the show to introduce his new beauties, as well as rising stars like the singer Fanny Brice. Every year the girls' dresses grew more revealing and their headgear more fantastically involved; and every year the show became faster, more elaborate, and more polished. In 1909, Ziegfeld featured Lillian Lorraine, whom he had proclaimed "the most beautiful woman in the world," and with whom he was then conducting a clandestine affair. Lillian appeared as a replica of Maxfield Parrish's famous cover girl from *Life* magazine and sang "Nothing but a Bubble" from what appeared to be the inside of a soap bubble; later she appeared at the controls of a prop airplane hanging from the rafters as she sang, "Up, Up, Up in My Aeroplane." The first act closed with "The Greatest Navy in the World," in which the girls pressed lights attached to their costumes, went behind a screen, and produced the effect of forty-eight illuminated battleships riding on the waves of New York harbor.

The *Follies* was not wholly a matter of delivering up chorus girls under conditions of high velocity and precision engineering, for Ziegfeld employed the leading choreographers, lyricists, writers, and performers of his day. He provided a home for many of the great vaudevillians of his time, including brassily Jewish singers like Fanny Brice and Sophie Tucker. And Ziegfeld brought the *Follies* to a much higher level of sophistication after the show moved in 1913 from the Jardin de Paris, the roof garden of the New York Theatre, to the main stage of the New Amsterdam—a major step up in prestige. Indeed, it took Ziegfeld to bring to the New Amsterdam a sense of glamour in keeping with the theater itself. The great impresario often presented stars like Will Rogers, W. C. Fields, and Eddie Cantor in a single show. And as designer—one might almost say "cinematographer"—Ziegfeld hired Joseph Urban, a Viennese émigré who was the leading set designer of his day and an artist of very great talent. Urban turned the giddy *Follies* into a unified work of art. For the 1917

Follies, according to Ziegfeld's biographer Charles Higham, "Urban created a Chinese lacquer setting, which dissolved in showers of colored water, followed by three sets of crossed red and gold ladders. Sixty girls in Chinese costumes climbed up and down in unison while the ladder rungs glowed in the dark. . . . An opalescent backdrop was laced with what seemed to be thousands of pearls."

All the great cultural critics of the day felt called upon to anatomize the Ziegfeld revue; it was, like the Berlin ragtime song, a central piece of cultural property. Edmund Wilson found its air of mechanical perfection frigid. On the other hand, it was just this air of polish that delighted the essayist Gilbert Seldes, who took the position that mechanical perfection was our destiny whether we liked it or not. The revue, Seldes wrote in *The Seven Lively Arts,* was the foremost expression of the "great American dislike of bungling, the real pleasure in a thing perfectly done." And Ziegfeld was its foremost exponent. "He makes everything appear perfect by a consummate smoothness of expression," Seldes wrote. "It is not the smoothness of a connecting rod running in oil, but of a batter where all the ingredients are so promptly introduced and so thoroughly integrated that in the end a man may stand up and say, This is a Show." Ziegfeld didn't aim at greatness; he aimed at delight. He was, in this and so many other respects, the very incarnation of Broadway.

THE LIGHTNESS, THE SPEED, the wit that Ziegfeld infused into his shows, and that his rivals supplied to their own revues and that sparkled in the roof gardens along Broadway, began to alter the climate of Times Square. The lobster palace came to seem increasingly formalistic, even dull. Julius Keller, the owner of Café Maxim, wrote in his memoirs that he realized some time around 1909 that customers would no longer be satisfied with lobster thermidor served on gilded platters. They needed action. Keller recalled the waiters who used to bawl out tunes at the German dive in the West Twenties where he had worked as a young man. And so, he says, one evening he planted two male and two female performers, dressed in evening clothes, like the rest of the clientele, at a table near the Hungarian orchestra. "At a prearranged signal," Keller writes, "they broke into song." Keller knew that he was onto something when his customers burst into applause. From that moment, he says, "Maxim's never suffered from ennui"—the one fatal ailment of all Broadway establishments. When the customers tired of popular tunes, Keller hired "dark-eyed señoritas with their castanets and Spanish dances," Russians with "their quaint native costumes," Hawaiians with ukuleles, and "beautiful girls who wove their way among the tables and with adoring eyes poured forth their ballads of love."

Thus was born—or by some other means was born—the cabaret. Soon almost all the great restaurants of Broadway had cleared out space for performances. The Folies Bergère opened its doors in 1911 as New York's first full-time cabaret, a theater with strolling orchestra, circulating waiters, a balcony promenade, and a series of shows mounted on a stage. But the Folies didn't last out the year, for the whole power of cabaret lay in its intimacy. Keller's innovation, if it was his, of stationing the performer among the diners was essential, because in erasing the footlights that had traditionally separated entertainer from audience it engaged the fantasy that the diner was part of the intoxicating and risqué world of the entertainers. The most desirable tables were right on the edge of the cabaret floor, where you could see and touch and talk to the performers. The cultural historian Lewis A. Erenberg has described the sense of liberation brought on by the "action environment" of the cabaret and the café: "Seated among the fast crowd, women of the town, ethnic entertainers, and guests from out of town, respectable urbanites were open to the flux of public life that the city offered. . . . Instead of letting gentility define the limits of their public lives, respectable urbanites were realizing they could enter a wider world of spontaneous cosmopolitan gaiety and experience 'the whirl of life' itself."

A passage in Rupert Hughes's 1914 novel *What Will People Say?* summarizes the astounding velocity with which the habits and mores of Broadway changed in the years after 1909 or so. A party has gone to the upstairs room of the fictitious Café de Ninive, and a middle-aged woman reminisce about very recent history:

> A few winters ago we thought it was amusing to go to supper at a
> good restaurant after the theater, have something nice to eat and
> drink, talk a while, and go home to bed. We thought we were very

devilish, and the preachers railed at the wickedness of late-supper orgies. . . . Then somebody started the cabarets. And we flocked to that. We ate the filthiest stuff and drank the rottenest wine and didn't care so long as they had some sensational singer or dancer cavorting in the aisle. . . . But it has become so tame and stupid that it is quite respectable. At present we are dancing in the aisles ourselves, crowding the professional entertainers off their own floors. And now the preachers and editors are attacking this. Whatever we do is wrong so, as my youngest boy says, "What's the use, and what's the diff?"

The really shocking thing about this passage is that a woman of mature years is adopting both the slang and the morals of her youngest son; it indicates how drastically the revolution in entertainment upended settled forms of behavior. It all began with cabaret, which mixed respectable urbanites with the fast crowd of Broadway, leaving respectability much the worse for wear. Cabaret was still a passive experience, like theatergoing. But almost immediately, restaurants and what were known as café-cabarets began encouraging diners to get up off their seats and get onto the floor. And this proved an even more dizzying sensation than the cabaret itself. Dancing in couples was still a new and quite daring phenomenon; nineteenth-century American dances such as the Virginia reel had been performed by groups, in a ballroom. Yet the dance craze spread so rapidly that early in 1911 Irving Berlin wrote "Everybody's Doin' It," a celebration of dance fever. ("Everybody's Overdoing It," the columnist Franklin P. Adams groaned.)

Berlin was a principal agent of this dismantling of Victorian mores along Broadway, and far beyond. Only a few years earlier he had been an urchin belting out tunes in Tony Pastor's, but in that extraordinary year of 1911, when he was all of twenty-three, Berlin wrote "Alexander's Ragtime Band," a song that, like "Everybody's Doin' It," was both about a craze—for ragtime—and the most vivid popular expression yet of that craze. "Alexander" was the most popular song ever written to that time, selling a million copies of sheet music in a few months. The song had a thrilling urgency to which everyone seemed to respond. Berlin himself wrote, "Its opening words, emphasized by immediate repetition—'Come on and hear! Come on and hear!'—were an *invitation* to 'come,' to join in, and 'hear' the singer and his song." That invitation, Berlin said, became part of the song's "happy ruction." The wild public reaction to "Alexander" changed the musical world, for the tunesmiths of Tin Pan Alley gave up their sentimental ballads and dialect songs for the more modern, urban, and black sound of ragtime. The music scholar Philip Furia goes so far as to say that "Alexander" "crystallized a crucial cultural moment as well, one when people fully realized that they were living in a truly modern age."

The overnight success of "Alexander," "Everybody's Doin' It," and other ragtime tunes created an insatiable demand for danceable music; and the dance craze changed Times Square from one moment to the next. The essayist and flaneur Julian Street wrote *Welcome to Our City,* a gimlet-eyed delineation of Broadway, in 1912; the following year he was forced to add a preface to a new edition because he had failed to take account of dancing. Broadway, he wrote ruefully, "changes faster than the main street of a mining town." By 1913, virtually every big restaurant in Times Square offered dance lessons, afternoon *thés dansants,* and revolving dance floors; or elaborate cabaret performances; or both. Indeed, Claridge's, the fine restaurant of an elegant hotel, made a lonely plea for the remaining sedentary diners: "We prefer to believe that there are some people in this city who would rather dine in silence and dine well than dine to music and go hungry." But probably there weren't many. When Harvey Forbes, the southern military officer who is the hero of *What Will People Say?,* comes to New York and takes a room in a 42nd Street hotel— this is also in 1913—he falls in with a crowd of well-bred fun-lovers who invite him to go "turkey-trotting." Forbes gasps with shock. "Do nice people—" The beautiful young socialite Persis Cabot cuts him off to say, "We're not nice people, but we do." And another friend adds, "That's all we do."

Persis and her crowd *were* nice people, but nice people wanted to be naughty. The dance craze always involved a balance, which teetered first one way and then the other, between the idea of erotic abandon and the idea of aristocratic restraint. The first dance celebrities were Vernon and Irene Castle, who had made a career teaching social dancing to the children of Fifth Avenue until the all-important year of 1913, when they opened up Sans Souci at 42nd and Broadway. The Castles were impeccable in matters of dress and deportment, and their aristocratic style had the effect of shielding dance from its lower-class associations and its black and Latin origins. Indeed, Irene's way of talking about freshly arrived dances gave the impression that she and her husband operated a laboratory for the neutralization of virulent dance germs. "We get our dances from the Barbary Coast," Irene once explained, using a euphemism for the black world. "Of course, they reach New York in a very primitive condition, and have to be considerably toned down before they can be used in the drawing room." A particularly low item called "Shaking the Shimmy" had "just arrived," and Irene said that "the teachers may try and make something of it."

The social hierarchy remained perfectly undisturbed in the mansions and the clubrooms of Fifth Avenue, but the Corybantes scrambled whatever was left of the old order in Broadway. As Julian Street wrote, "Practically any well-dressed person who is reasonably sober and will purchase supper and champagne for two may enter" a restaurant that offered dancing. "This creates a social mixture such as was never dreamed-of in this country—a hodge-podge of people in which respectable young married and unmarried women, and even debutantes, dance, not only under the same roof, but in the same room with women of the town." They might, in fact, dance with each other. Restaurants and cabarets provided men, typically of dubious background, as partners and dance instructors for the unescorted women who appeared at the afternoon *thés dansants*. This practice provoked scandalous rumors and much public debate; even *Variety*, the unofficial trade publication of Times Square, warned about the dangers of "tango pirates."

And no amount of Castling could disguise the erotic abandon encouraged—almost compelled—by dance. Even the names of the dances implied a new openness toward the body and toward touch: the turkey trot, the black bottom, the bunny hug, the tango. These steps typically required the partners to lock in a tight embrace and to fling themselves around the floor in wild gyrations. In "Everybody's Doin' It," a "ragtime couple" "throw their shoulders in the air," "snap their fingers," and shout, "It's a bear, it's a bear, it's a bear." Julian Street described a performance by Maurice ("the French pronunciation, please!"), the dance master at the rooftop cabaret of Louis Martin's, a traditional lobster palace: "Suddenly, the man flings the girl away from him violently, as a boy throws a top. Holding to his hand, she spins until their arms are outstretched. Then with a jerk, he draws her back again, revolving, to his arms." Faster and faster they go, until the climax: "With a leap, she alights astride her partner's hips and, fastened to his waist with the hooks of her bent knees, swings outward and away from his whirling body like a floating sash."

One can judge the impact these dances had on received moral principles from the reaction of the courtly Lieutenant Forbes in *What Will People Say?* Early in the evening, he is already disgusted by the spectacle: "Motherly dowagers in ball costumes bumped and caromed from the ample forms of procuresses." By the end of the evening, with exhaustion erasing inhibition, he concludes, "There was no mistaking the intention of some of these dancers. It was vile, provocative and, since it was public, hideous." And yet Forbes eventually becomes perfectly inured to the idea of locking knees, arms, shoulders, with a woman whom he wishes to place on a pedestal and worship. The pedestal thing, he understands, is gone with the wind.

The city ultimately tried to control the passions unleashed by dance by passing an ordinance—this is still 1913—requiring cabarets to close at two A.M. But the law was no match for unleashed appetite. Cabaret owners simply opened up private "clubs," which came to be called nightclubs, and which could remain open all night long. One could dance at Castles in the Air, the rooftop cabaret of the 44th Street Theatre, to which the Castles moved in 1914, and then go down to the "Castle Club" in the basement for still more drinking and dancing, perhaps with Vernon and Irene themselves. And so before long the old lobster palaces had spawned not only cabarets and dance floors, but nightclubs as well.

In 1915, Florenz Ziegfeld, still very much the patron saint of the sexual frisson, created a companion to the *Follies* known as *The Midnight Frolic,* staged on the New Amsterdam's terribly glamorous roof garden. This was the ne plus ultra of Times Square nightlife. The "garden" was an immense enclosed space, perhaps forty feet high, with great windows running up the sides and a skylight set into the roof. It accommodated as many as six hundred people, and featured a special roll-away stage that allowed the whole crowd to dance before and after the *Frolic.* It was a select crowd: the cover price of $5 kept out the pikers and the college freshmen, and the late hour attracted that part of the Broadway set which prided itself on never going to bed before dawn.

This was not the shirtsleeved rooftop crowd of 1892; the women wore narrow, clinging dresses and the men wore top hats and tails. They drank champagne and ate pistachio nuts while the masterful Ziegfeld ran his sparkling parade of beauties across the stage and into the crowd, including Sylvia Carmen and Her Balloon Girls, who sang "I Love to Be Loved" while they invited gentlemen to pop their balloons with lit cigars. The show, with admirable candor, was called *Nothing but Girls;* it featured songs like "My Tango Girl," "My Spooky Girl," and "My Midnight Girl," as well as the wild gyrations of Mlle. Odette Myrtill, "Apache Violinist." A glass ramp led up to a glass parapet lining three walls; sometimes the girls would march up the ramp, cast lines over the edge and go "fishing" for gentlemen; once they were on the parapet, their undergarments could be plainly seen from below. The sexiness, the frivolity, and above all the liberating sense of silliness that Ziegfeld had mined in the *Follies* reached its zenith in the midnight revels atop the New Amsterdam. Each table came equipped with wooden mallets, and patrons were encouraged to bang the mallets and rattle their silverware in a merry din; revelers could use telephones to call one another. The tables also included dolls and funny hats and other toys. It is safe to assume that many of the patrons got merrily plastered. Here was a setting in which not just conventional morality, but adulthood itself, had been temporarily suspended.

The Times Square of 1915 would have been practically unrecognizable to the denizen of 1905. The rules of self-restraint and delayed gratification—that is to say, the Protestant ethic—that had been drilled into generations of Americans had been lifted, if not quite obliterated. Barriers that had governed relations between men and women, the rich and their "inferiors," high and low culture, tottered and often toppled. A new subculture of cosmopolites had appeared; Julian Street called them the Hectics. These were the terribly fashionable, giddy young men and women who raced from restaurant to theater to cabaret to roof garden. "He has a golden cigarette case," Street writes acidly, "she a gold-mesh bag; receptacles in which, it is believed, they carry their ideals."

If one looks back even further, to the Broadway of 1895, the difference is even more drastic. "Broadway" barely appears in the upper-crust literature of the 1890s; in novels like Brander Matthews's *His Father's Son,* mentioned earlier, the reader has, in fact, almost no sense of street life, of crowds, of a "public," for the action is largely confined to parlors. But Broadway is a topic of never-ending fascination for the New York writers of twenty years later—for Julian Street, for Rupert Hughes, and for George Bronson-Howard, the author of *Birds of Prey: Being Pages from the Book of Broadway.* For these writers, Broadway is life itself—the speed, the lingo, the cynicism, the brittleness, the desperation. Bronson-Howard, for example, writes story after story about the relationship of mutual exploitation between chorus girls and the men who pursue them. The only moralists on Broadway—the only people who think like the characters in a Brander Matthews novel—are fools. It's a cold, glittering, gorgeous world. "Remember," Julian Street writes, "New York is the national parlour for the painless extraction of ideals; get a new set made of gold."

SKY SIGNS

IN THE CLIMACTIC SCENE of *Sister Carrie,* Hurstwood, Carrie's luckless consort, having spiraled downward into beggary and despair, trudges south on Broadway to 42nd Street and sees the "fire signs" blazing in the snow. This is Dreiser's portentous term for the electric signs that announced restaurants and theaters up and down Broadway, a technology too new to have a proper name. Hurstwood pauses before a restaurant— Shanley's, perhaps, or the Café de l'Opera—and there, too, a "fire sign" illuminates the giddy whirl of merrymakers. The snow in front of the Casino, where Carrie is starring, and which in fact had the biggest and shiniest electric sign of all the Broadway theaters, is also "bright with the radiated fire." Here is something new in the world, a glowing, glittering kind of speech that attracts nighttime revelers with a promise of excitement and warmth (and repels the likes of Hurstwood, who proceeds to trek through the darkness to a flophouse, and to suicide). The lighted sign, which came into being just as Times Square did, was quickly established as its visual signature and the symbol to the entire world of its dazzling nightlife.

At the time Dreiser was writing, in the last years of the nineteenth century, electric lighting was only twenty years old; Edison had perfected the incandescent lightbulb in 1879. The ability to turn night into day seemed miraculous. The world's fairs that were in such vogue in the last decades of the century were essentially festivals of light, with an Electric Building, or Electric Tower, their featured attraction. At many of the fairs, an anthropological exhibit designed to feature the evolution of the arts and sciences ended with a dazzling display of light. Electric light was not the home convenience we think of it as today, but rather a spectacle, used to illuminate streets, restaurants, theaters, and fairgrounds, and to draw country folk into the city.

Electric streetlights began to line Broadway almost as soon as they became commercially available, in the early 1880s; they reached 42nd Street in 1895. Theaters had long used gas lamps to light their marquees; now they began to switch to electricity. Advertisers at first continued to favor billboards, which were plastered over every available space on major thoroughfares and often stacked one atop another. And so the first electric signs were essentially billboards made of light. In 1892, the president of the Long Island Rail Road hired the Edison General Electric Company to erect an electric sign at the wedge-shaped corner of 23rd Street and Fifth Avenue beguiling passersby to "BUY HOMES ON LONG ISLAND SWEPT BY OCEAN BREEZES." The sign, located at what was then the absolute center of New York, was a sensation—a brilliant, almost three-dimensional ad leaping out from the drab two-dimensional signs around it. The food magnate H. J. Heinz often looked out over the sign from his Madison Square hotel; in 1898, Heinz took over the space and hired New York's leading billposter, O. J. Gude, to make a new electric sign for Heinz. The sign featured a fifty-foot-long pickle in pickle-green lights against an orange and blue background, a giant white "57," and the names of Heinz's most popular products: Sweet Pickles, Tomato Ketchup, India Relish, Tomato Soup, and Peach Butter. Advertisers had learned how to incorporate flashers into signs, so the pickle, the numerals, and the product names flashed on and off in the night sky of Madison Square. A new medium, and a new maestro, were born.

O. J. Gude belongs alongside figures like Adolph Ochs, Oscar Hammerstein, and Florenz Ziegfeld in the pantheon of promotional geniuses who created Times Square—or, rather, the idea of Times Square. Gude was a New Yorker who dropped out of school at seventeen, made a living posting signs, and then over time became the equivalent of an account manager for the food and beverage companies that then dominated outdoor advertising. Gude founded a company of his own in 1889 and soon became one of the leading admen in New York. He was the first to understand the power of the billboard. In a brief essay entitled "Art and Advertising Joined by Electricity," Gude wrote: "Practically all other advertising media depend upon the willingness or even cooperation of the reader for the absorption of the advertisers' story, but the outdoor advertising sign asks no voluntary acquiescence from any reader. It simply grasps the vantage point of position and literally forces its announcement on the vision of the uninterested as well as the interested passerby." It is the mark of a true adman that "literally forces" is meant to express a virtue, not an unfortunate side effect, of the new medium. And of course electric light brought this act of buttonholing to a pitch of aggressiveness unimaginable in the era of the two-dimensional poster. An electric sign was a billboard raised to the power of hypnosis.

Indeed, the earliest accounts of electric signs stress the awestruck reaction of viewers. According to a contemporary description of one of the very first signs on Broadway, "little knots of people used to gather nightly in newly christened Herald Square to watch the glowing eyes in the head of The Herald's owl wink solemnly at each minute as it crept by, and if you stopped and listened, you could hear little cries of satisfaction go up from the watchers at each repetition of the miracle." The power of the sign was the power of electricity itself, a force that compelled awe. And the need to compel that sense of awe pushed the signmakers to ever more miraculous acts of creativity. Around 1905, Gude spent $45,000 to erect a sign for the Heatherbloom company in Times Square. As Tama Starr, the author of *Signs and Wonders,* a history of the electric sign in Times Square, describes it, "The incandescent Miss Heatherbloom walked delicately through a driving rain—depicted in slashing diagonal lines of lamps—concealed by a shell-like umbrella. The gale behind her whipped at her dress, revealing her shapely outline and, above her high-topped shoes, a daring glimpse of stockinged calf." A few years earlier, men had gathered in front of the new Flatiron Building at 23rd and Fifth (the former site of that first electric sign) to see how the winds swirling around the building whipped up girls' petticoats. Miss Heatherbloom was a giant, glowing, endlessly visible version of that girl; and men gathered in the street below to watch her, again and again.

The Heatherbloom petticoat girl was the first Times Square "spectacular," to use the word that quickly came into vogue among sign men to describe a big, colorful, crowd-stopping sign. The history of the spectacular and the history of Times Square are utterly bound up with each other, for the spectacular, like the New Year's Eve celebration, came to define the way people thought about Times Square, while Times Square became the setting for the biggest, brightest, and most innovative signs. The spectacular became the one art form that Times Square, and Times Square alone, gave to the world—to the world, that is, of popular and commercial culture. The reasons for this are principally economic. As the most densely populated crossroads in the world, Times Square offered to advertisers the same commodity that network television later did: eyeballs. An adman writing in 1925 in *Signs of the Times,* the trade magazine of the sign industry, noted that a million people were said to pass through Times Square every day. "The willingness with which advertisers invest huge sums in long term contracts for this Times Square publicity can be understood when it is stated that this circulation is procured at a cost ranging from one cent per thousand for the illuminated displays to fourteen cents per thousand for the splendid spectacular 'electrics.' " Many of the people seeing those displays were visitors from foreign countries and other American cities; all the buyers from the big department stores passed through. Thus Times Square functioned as a national or even international advertising medium. As another writer for *Signs of the Times* observed in 1920, "The primary purpose of the large electric sign of the Broadway type is to send its message on a national scale rather than to try to influence the individual to stop at once and buy a new suit of underwear."

Times Square also provided the ideal geographic site for this new commercial art form. The triangle whose base was defined by 42nd Street, with corners at the western and eastern edges of Broadway, and its apex at 47th, where the two streets first joined, formed the perfect setting for viewing signs, with unobstructed sight lines in all directions. The low buildings that predominated in Times Square offered an ideal platform for signs. Times Square was poorly suited for practically everything— especially for functioning as a square—but as an amphitheater for the viewing of spectaculars, it was matchless. Perhaps the sidewalks were too narrow to accommodate a crowd of gawkers; then the gawkers simply overflowed into the street. Advertisers realized early on that, thanks to the combination of sight lines and the size and shape of buildings, certain sites had tremendous value: the west side of Broadway at 42nd, the east side between 43rd and 45th, and the point of the triangle, at 47th; they would be occupied by splendid signs for decades to come.

By 1910, more than twenty blocks along Broadway bore electric advertisements. The most astounding and inventive was without doubt the giant sign raised that year on the west side of Broadway at 38th Street—one of the few sites in the Times Square area not controlled by O. J. Gude. The sign featured a Roman chariot race in the style of *Ben-Hur*, at the time a beloved spectacle of the stage. Seventy-two feet wide and ninety feet high, it was the biggest electric sign ever built. As a crowd in an amphitheater looked on, one chariot raced into the lead while others chased behind, whips cracking and wheels kicking up dust. "The galloping effect," one historian writes, "was produced by outlining the legs of the horses in eight different positions and using flashing sequences of more than thirty times a second, far faster than the eye can follow, rendering their gallop perfectly." The effect of naturalism was greater than anything the nascent technology of the moving picture could offer, and far beyond anything ever seen on an electric sign. The race lasted thirty seconds, and then came a wait of thirty seconds before the next race. "Few spectators were content to watch the race only once. When the sign was first turned on, crowds halted traffic, and for weeks a special squad of police was detailed to handle them."

The sign was not only an aesthetic but a commercial breakthrough. The sign itself was framed by a "curtain," which acted as an internal frame; above the entire scene was another screen that offered space for commercial messages. Each message lasted fifteen seconds, so that an entire cycle of 150 messages would repeat about every forty minutes. In other words, the chariot race was a "show" intended to attract viewers to commercials, which would run simultaneously—television *avant la lettre*. The new sign failed as a medium—perhaps the commercials should have run during breaks in the programming, as on TV—but it raised the bar of spectacularity to heights unimaginable only a few years earlier.

By the mid-teens, Times Square, when captured at night by a photographer looking north from an upper floor of the Times Tower, already had the mind-boggling look that has long been its trademark: two merging paths of white phosphorescence flanked by innumerable glowing signs for theaters, restaurants, tires, cigarettes, and underwear. O. J. Gude bestrode this narrow world like a colossus. It was Gude who is said to have coined the term "Great White Way," around 1901. (Broadway was also known for many years as "the Gay White Way.") A 1907 article in *Signs of the Times* noted that "there was a time a few years ago when prospective outdoor advertisers were almost if not entirely at the mercy of the O. J. Gude Co., which concern has succeeded in securing control of, or an option on, about every available location that was at all desirable." Gude had signs up and down Broadway; Gude's sign for Trimble Whiskey occupied the single prime location in Times Square proper, at the 47th Street apex. Gude not only had the most signs, but the best signs. On the west side of the avenue, at 41st, he built a sign for Corticelli silk that was a masterpiece of playfulness as well as a genuine narrative. A kitten, gamboling on the Broadway side of the sign, became entangled in a length of thread, leaped around the corner to a giant sewing machine, caught up the thread, jumped back to Broadway, and brought the machine to a halt. "The kitten's tail wagged," Tama Starr writes, "its ears twitched, and its paws pummeled, pulling the silk off the turning spool in a blur and tangling the kitten in the loops."

These gigantic, ingenious and blatantly commercial narratives in the sky came to be understood as a new kind of public theater, a theater that was the special province of Times Square. When Harvey Forbes, the hero of Rupert Hughes's *What Will People Say?*, sits in his room at the Knickerbocker Hotel at 42nd and Broadway, and gazes out into the night, his view is of "the electric signs working like acrobats—the girl that skipped the rope, the baby that laughed and cried, the woman that danced on the wire," and "the kitten that tangled itself in thread." Foreign visitors to New York almost invariably mentioned the fantastic light show of Times Square. "Fabulous glow-worms crawl up and down," wrote a British visitor in 1917. "Zig-zag lightnings strike an acre of signboard—and reveal a panacea for over-eating!" The English novelist Arnold Bennett described for readers back home "the mastodon kitten playing with a ball of thread, an umbrella in a shower of water," and then delivered himself of this mighty apostrophe: "Sky signs! In Europe I had always inveighed manfully against sky signs. But now I bowed the head, vanquished. These sky signs annihilated argument."

Gude himself cited Bennett's declaration as evidence that even the most majestic arbiters of the traditional media had given their imprimatur to this new one. What Bennett was expressing, in fact, was resignation, not approval. Bennett understood that the marshaling of immense technological, economic, and cultural forces represented by the spectacular made the question of acceptance utterly irrelevant, for the culture of literary judgment suddenly looked like a very small thing next to the raw power of popular culture. Bennett didn't despise popular culture; he was delighted at the George M. Cohan play he saw during his visit, preferring it vastly to the wooden renditions of classical drama he otherwise watched. He was probably one of the first literary men to experience that profound ambivalence—that mingled sense of awe, horror, and inevitability—which Times Square has inspired in cultured citizens ever since.

The poet Rupert Brooke came to New York in 1914 and described "the merciless lights" of Times Square in accents Theodore Dreiser would have understood very well. "A stranger of another race, loitering here, might cast his eyes up, in a vague wonder what powers, kind or maleficent, controlled or observed this whirlwind," he writes. And the terrible, ludicrous answer is that the gods of the heavens have retreated before the gods of commerce. A "divine hand" writes its "igneous message to the nations, 'Wear _____ Underwear for Youths and Men-Boys.' " And then "a youth and a man-boy, flaming and immortal, clad in celestial underwear, box a short round, vanish, reappear for another round, and again disappear." Nearby, Orion "drives a sidereal golfball out of sight through the meadows of Paradise." Here, in Times Square, modern man had orchestrated the sky itself, the region that teems with the divinities of Western mythology, to sell toothpaste. This was a death of the gods which Nietzsche had not anticipated. Brooke could still summon a deep sense of dread at the thought; but Arnold Bennett's shrug was soon to become the more familiar response.

The great threat to the electric sign, however, came not from partisans of Olympus but from advocates of the city beautiful. The Municipal Art Society, a civic organization consisting of many of New York's leading citizens and dedicated to preserving the city's beaux-arts elegance and decorum from the depredations of popular culture, began a campaign against billboards as early as 1902. By 1912, public outcry had led Mayor William Gaynor to establish the Mayor's Billboard Advisory Commission. The commissioners turned Gude's arguments for the virtues of outdoor advertising against the industry, noting that the billboard or electric sign "thrusts itself upon unwilling and offended vision by day," and "glares and winks and radiates its often uninteresting messages" by night. The commission proposed an ordinance that would prohibit large electric signs in residential neighborhoods and regulate their hours elsewhere, limit the height of roof signs to ten feet, and prohibit virtually all outdoor advertisements on or near parks, squares, public buildings, schools, and boulevards and streets of exceptional character (that is, Fifth Avenue). In short, it would have crippled the sky sign.

It was O. J. Gude, more than anyone else, who came to the industry's defense. By this time, Gude was one of New York's leading business figures, wealthy and respectable, an art collector, a horseman, and a clubman in good standing. He was a broad-shouldered man with thick hair, a clipped mustache, rimless spectacles, and a solemn mien. Promoter though he was, Gude was neither a cynic like Willie Hammerstein nor, certainly, a libertine like Ziegfeld. He seems genuinely to have viewed advertising as a source of moral and aesthetic improvement, and he had the gift of using the late-Victorian language of uplift without abandoning commercial candor. He once paid tribute to "19 centuries of the most effective outdoor advertising that the mind of the greatest advertising genius could conceive," by which he meant the church steeple. When he testified before the mayor's commission, he unfurled from the balcony an early public-service ad: a poster showing children going off to church, with the caption "Take your children to church, give them the right start."

Gude believed that the solution lay in the promotion of high aesthetic standards among sign men. He believed that beautiful signs were more effective than plain ones, and he argued that outdoor advertising had "felt and shown the effects of the awakening of the artistic spirit in the people of this country"—a claim that he, at least, had every right to make. In 1913, Gude had the inspired idea of joining the Municipal Art Society and getting himself placed on its Committee on Advertising. There he made a raft of improving suggestions: that some prominent billboard locations be used as outdoor art galleries, that the Gude Company and the society jointly sponsor a sign design competition, that leading artists lecture Gude employees with the goal of "making advertising displays less offensive and more artistic." None of this got him anywhere, and he soon quit. Nevertheless, the outdoor advertising industry, with Gude's leadership, fought the forces of regulation to a draw; the city fashioned a much less restrictive ordinance in 1914, and then incorporated its principles into the new zoning ordinance of 1916. The zoning rules declared many areas of the city off-limits to electric signs, but otherwise placed few limits on their use. Times Square thus became New York's electric light district, as the Ginza was later to be in Tokyo, or Piccadilly in London. The brilliance and beauty and technical daring of the signs that Gude and others raised along the roofline of Broadway more than justified the city's ruling.

Gude's most stupendous achievement came in 1917, at the very end of his career as Times Square's master spectaculator. One of Gude's prize locations was the space atop the Putnam Building, on the west side of Broadway between 43rd and 44th Streets. William Wrigley agreed to pay $100,000 a year to lease the space, and Gude designed for him the largest electric sign on the face of the earth, two hundred feet long and almost a hundred feet high. Here is the indispensable Tama Starr on the Wrigley's sign: "Twin peacocks faced off on a tree branch, their tails forming a feathery canopy over the central portion of the display." Beneath were the Wrigley's logo and the actual ad copy. On either side of the text were six "Spearmen" in pointy hats. "Brandishing spears, they comprised a drill team that went through a series of twelve calisthenics the populace quickly dubbed the Daily Dozen. Flanking them were fountains spraying geysers of bubbling water, and the whole spectacle was framed in vinelike filigree."

Gude, who was in poor health, sold his business in 1918, gave his art collection to the Lotos Club, went off to Europe, and died in Germany seven years later, leaving an estate worth a million dollars. He was much eulogized as "the creator of the Great White Way," a title he deserved not simply because he lit up Times Square—that would have happened anyway—but because he combined art and commerce to forge the new form known as the spectacular, and thus gave Times Square the look for which it has ever after been known. Gude seems to have left no record of his own process of creation, but this astute and tough-minded businessman devised some of the most whimsical and fantastic works of art ever seen in Times Square. And he *was* a businessman, and a promoter, like Ochs and Hammerstein and Ziegfeld. In other parts of New York City—in Greenwich Village, for example—the motto may well have been "Art for art's sake." Not in Times Square. The motto of Times Square was, and always has been, "Keep the turnstiles clicking."

"BUY 18 HOLES AND SELL ALL THE WATER HAZARDS!"

O N AUGUST, 13, 1921, *Dulcy*, a play written by George S. Kaufman and Marc Connelly, opened at the Frazee Theatre. *Dulcy* was a satire—a genre familiar in European theater from the time of Molière, but quite novel, and even shocking, on Broadway, where authors were not wont to mock their own main characters. Most of *Dulcy*'s cast of characters either mouth stock inanities or nod sagely at the humbug of the others. Leach, who writes movie scripts, insists on reciting to the guests of a dinner party the ludicrous plot of his latest work, "Sin," which begins with Noah's Ark and then proceeds through world history: "And to keep the symbolism at the end, just as Jack kisses Coralie there in Chicago, Marc Anthony kisses Cleopatra in Ancient Egypt"—Leach speaks in capital letters—"And George Washington kisses Martha Washington at Mount Vernon." The hostess, Dulcy, is modeled on a preposterous character invented by Franklin P. Adams; her speech consists entirely of the clichés that pass for conversation among the stupid rich. If someone praises a book, Dulcy is sure to say, "My books are my best friends." Dulcy is, at bottom, a thoroughly lovable meddler, in the spirit of Austen's Emma, and she reduces the play's genteel suburban setting to a shambles before she and her husband are implausibly rescued by the gods of comedy.

Dulcy is a largely—and not unfairly—forgotten play, but in its breezy irreverence and its witty contempt for mediocrity it broke through a cultural crust and left Broadway a slightly different place. James Thurber later said that it was *Dulcy* that showed him how to wield his own satirical weapons. *Dulcy* reproduced in narrative form the urbanity, the irony, and the wit of the best of the revues; in retrospect, it turns out to have been the first ripple from the mighty torrent of witty and urbane plays and movie scripts and radio programs and magazine articles that was to come roaring out of Broadway in the burst of creativity that began in the years after World War I, and that ushered American culture out of the Victorian hinterlands and into the modern age. The 1920s on Broadway was, above all, the era of wit, and of the wits. If there was a wit-in-chief, it was George S. Kaufman, a beanpole who scrutinized the world from beneath a great, shocked thicket of hair, an ironist with an allergy to sentimentality, a neurotic perfectionist driven by a dread of failure. One of Kaufman's biographers writes that when *Dulcy* opened in Chicago, Marc Connelly discovered Kaufman, between acts, "huddled against a rusty pipe in the dusty, deserted scene deck . . . staring blankly at the floor and running his fingers through his thick hair." He could only mumble abject apologies while Connelly assured him that the play was, in fact, a hit.

IN "MY LOST CITY," an elegiac account of the accumulating wreckage of his own life, F. Scott Fitzgerald recalled Manhattan in 1920. Already, he wrote, "the feverish activity of the boom" had fired the city with life, but the "general inarticulateness" of the moment, its raw novelty, denied it any larger sense of meaning. Here was energy without voice.

> Then, for just a moment, the "younger generation" idea became a fusion of many elements of New York life. . . . The blending of the bright, gay, vigorous elements began then, and for the first time there appeared a society a little livelier than the solid mahogany dinner parties of Emily Price Post. If this society produced the cocktail party, it also evolved Park Avenue wit, and for the first time an educated European could envision a trip to New York as something more amusing than a gold-trek into a formalized Australian Bush.

In those years immediately after World War I, the country appeared to be shedding its old, familiar ways like a dried-up skin. Indeed, the very fact of drastic change, the widespread consciousness of it, was a central aspect of the new. American culture was rapidly taking on the jazzed-up, fragmentary rhythms of urban life. The census of 1920 showed that for the first time more Americans lived in cities than in the country. New York was the nation's colossus, and the world's. The city's population swelled almost to eight million. Economic growth was stupendous. Between 1918 and 1931, the number of cars registered in New York leaped from 125,101 to 790,123—more cars than in all of Europe combined. New York was the factory of the new at the moment when novelty itself had become a craze. The emerging cultures of fashion, design, advertising, and magazine publishing were all centered in Manhattan. It was as if the city were inventing the idea of urbanism, and then retailing it to the rest of the country. As the urban historian Ann Douglas writes, "Trendsetter to the nation and the world, New York finds its job in the commercialization of mood swings: the city translates the shifting national psyche into fashions of all kinds, from ladies' frocks and popular music, to Wall Street stocks, ad layouts and architectural designs, on a yearly, monthly, weekly and daily basis."

Only rarely does the national life change this fast. It did so in the late teens and early twenties because so many things happened at once—the stock market boom, which showered sudden wealth in all directions, and especially in the cities; a large-scale urban migration; the creation of a national culture through the new media of radio and the movies; the arrival of modern ideas, and above all those of Freud, who reduced the great edifice of Victorian morality to the status of drawing-room comedy; and the return of several million young men and women from World War I, an event which for many of them had proved at least as liberating as it had been disillusioning (or perhaps disillusion itself had proved liberating). Not only had they saved Europe, but Europe had taught them a thing or two about life. Some had been exposed to what were delicately known as Continental moral codes; the intellectuals among them had been exposed to Continental ideas.

It was a world that the young had seized from the old. In *Only Yesterday,* a retrospective account of the Roaring Twenties, Frederick Lewis

Allen describes the era in language that would be familiar to anyone who lived through the 1960s, another era when mass prosperity freed children from their parents' routines while a radical shift in values inspired young people to use that freedom in ways that horrified their elders. "Fathers and mothers lay awake asking themselves whether their children were not utterly lost," Allen writes, "sons and daughters evaded questions, lied miserably and unhappily, or flared up to reply that at least they were not dirty-minded hypocrites." In a 1927 magazine article entitled "A Flapper Set Me Right," the theatrical impresario David Belasco recalled receiving a visit several years earlier from a young and possibly fictitious woman who explained to him, "The old folks call us 'flappers'; we call them 'old-timers' and worse. They sit back and roll the cud of Victorian virtue under their musty old tongues, and never once have they tried to realize what it is we are demanding." The demand, she said, was for "honesty." Girls had had it with feigning "a sweetness and innocence totally foreign to their natural impulses." They would make themselves the equal of men in word and in deed.

Of course, the seeds of this epochal change had been sown in the years before World War I, when Persis Cabot and her merry friends were turkey-trotting the night away in various dives and nightspots. As New York City was the mother lode of national trends, so it was in Times Square that New York first broke in its new habits. Another way of explaining the spirit of the twenties is to say that it took about a decade for the abandon, the heedlessness, that first showed itself along Broadway to become a national phenomenon.

By the early twenties, the cosmopolitan nonchalance toward the proprieties that Florenz Ziegfeld had championed had become the stock-in-trade of Broadway. It was the era of girls in rhinestones—and not many rhinestones, at that. The theatergoer of the day could almost always choose from among three, four, or five revues in the manner of the *Follies*. There was *George White's Scandals,* and *Earl Carroll's Vanities,* and the Shuberts' *Passing Show,* and *The Garrick Gaieties,* and Irving Berlin's revue in the Music Box Theatre, which he had built expressly to showcase his own songs. Like vaudeville a generation earlier, the revue, with its unending appetite for material, offered a proving ground for the performers of the era—but these were performers of supreme gifts. Irving Berlin was writing songs not only for the *Music Box Revue* but for the *Follies;* George Gershwin was writing and performing songs for the *Scandals;* and Richard Rodgers and Lorenz Hart were turning out tunes for the *Gaieties.* The *Music Box Revue* of 1923 featured comic skits by Kaufman and Robert Benchley, soon to be one of the famous wits of the Algonquin Round Table and *The New Yorker.* The Paul Whiteman Orchestra, one of the first of the great jazz bands, performed in the *Scandals.*

The revues of the twenties were immensely more urbane than those of an earlier generation; they were also several orders of magnitude naughtier. At *Earl Carroll's Vanities,* by far the most shameless, hostesses in short skirts and sheer stockings danced with the customers, and show-girls were supplied to the better tables. The show itself adhered to the Ziegfeld principle of "nothing but girls," with seminude or thinly draped chorines posed, according to one authority, "against plume curtains, hanging gardens, gates of roses, swings, ladders, bejewelled ruffles, chandeliers, horns of plenty, the prehistoric, the futuristic . . . ," and so on. The Shuberts featured nude girls as lights in a chandelier and as fruits in a fruit basket. The skits were often just as transparent as the costumes. The Keith-Albee syndicate, which controlled many of the acts, eventually drew up a lengthy list of taboos, which included the stock joke of a girl walking onstage carrying an oar and announcing, "I just made the crew team." The 1923 edition of the show *Artists and Models* featured women nude from the waist up disporting themselves as "models." The market for sexual candor finally became so glutted that Ziegfeld himself began putting the clothes back on the girls. "This was not a moral standpoint on my part," as the Olympian one explained in a 1927 magazine article, "but an artistic one. I realized that a charming girl will not appear in public undressed."

A play like *Dulcy* could not have been presented on Broadway in an earlier age, both because sardonic wits like George S. Kaufman weren't writing for the stage—or perhaps didn't yet exist at all—and because the audience wasn't ready for such pitiless debunking. Everything made on Broadway, whether cafés or signs or plays, was, and still is, made with an audience in mind; and the audience of 1910 got the fun-loving but for-mulaic theatrical experience it craved. But the new generation, disgusted with received wisdom—and much enjoying its disgust with received wisdom—signaled an almost unlimited willingness to be challenged. The essayist and critic and wit-about-town Alexander Woollcott, who himself served in World War I and then lived briefly in Paris, along with many of the leading columnists and editors of his generation, observed in 1920 that "there has grown up an alert, discriminating, sophisticated public, numerous enough at last to make profitable the most aspiring ventures of which the theater's personnel is capable."

The bohemians of Greenwich Village had long scorned the overtly commercial culture of Times Square; but in 1918 a group of sophisticates from the Village established the Theatre Guild in order to bring serious English and continental drama to Broadway. In 1920, at a time when George Bernard Shaw was considered a rank immoralist both here and in England—he had condemned World War I as brutish militarism—the Theatre Guild mounted a famous and immensely successful production of Shaw's *Heartbreak House* on Broadway. The Guild staged Ibsen's *Peer Gynt* and Strindberg's *Dance of Death,* and virtually everything of Shaw's, as well as works by serious American and English writers like Sidney Howard and S. N. Behrman and A. A. Milne. Most of these works, presented in a spirit of brave artistic purity, found a Broadway audience. By 1925, the Guild had built its own theater, on West 52nd Street, and had traveling companies both here and in London; the Guild was supported by thirty thousand subscribers in New York, and thirty thousand more elsewhere in the country. Nor was the Theatre Guild the only source of high culture. Broadway audiences went to see plays by Somerset Maugham, Sean O'Casey, and John Galsworthy, as well as plays presented in Italian, German, French, Russian, and Hebrew.

Eugene O'Neill was not only a Broadway playwright, but a hugely successful one. His first full-length play, *Beyond the Horizon,* was staged at the Morosco Theatre in 1920. The play was so difficult and unsettling that initially it was seen only at matinees, when the regular play at the Morosco was not being performed. *Beyond the Horizon* told the story of two brothers on a farm: Robert, a poetic soul who dreams of the world "beyond the hills," and Andy, a creature of prose, wedded to the land. But their destinies are reversed, and their lives wrecked, by love. Robert, who had planned on going to sea, instead stays on the farm in order to marry the girl he loves, while Andy, in love with the same girl, bitterly renounces both farm and family and takes Robert's place aboard the ship. In the highly feminized and Christianized Victorian drama still then popular on Broadway, love had always been understood as the highest good, and home and hearth the final destination toward which the heart yearned. But for Robert, love is a terrible act of surrender, a betrayal of his deepest nature; and home quickly becomes a living hell as the farm collapses and his wife, Ruth, comes to despise him.

Beyond the Horizon is a resolutely un-Christian, uncomforting play in which only the tiniest scraps of human will escape the crushing force of fate. The most thoughtful critics immediately recognized the play as a work of genius. Alexander Woollcott wrote in *The New York Times*, "The play has greatness in it, and marks O'Neill as one of our foremost playwrights." Heywood Broun, an equally influential figure, hailed it as a breakthrough in drama. But what is more remarkable still, *Beyond the Horizon* was a genuine success, running for 111 performances. An audience that had been satisfied with bonbons was now eager for meat. As Brooks Atkinson remarks in his history of Broadway, after *Beyond the Horizon*, "hokum dramas like *The Easiest Way*, *Salvation Nell* and *The Witching Hour* became impossible." The demonically productive O'Neill would have nineteen plays produced on Broadway over the next fourteen years.

THE BROADWAY OF 1920 was a very different place from the Broadway of 1910, both physically and metaphorically. For one thing, "Broadway" was now effectively synonymous with "Times Square"; many of the theaters below 42nd Street had closed, while new ones were going up at a tremendous clip north of 42nd—twenty-eight in the second decade of the century, and seven more in 1921 alone. By the middle of the decade, well over two hundred new shows were opening on Broadway every year. Times Square now felt dense, complete, and self-contained. The empty spaces in the upper Forties had been filled, the rickety "tax-payers" (so called because they served to cover the developer's real estate taxes) had been replaced by substantial buildings, and skyscrapers, such as the Candler Buildings on 42nd Street, and the Putnam Building, on the west side of Broadway between 43rd and 44th (where the Paramount Building now stands), had given Times Square a new sense of modernity and power. And Times Square was filled with dazzling light and color, which blocked out the drab working world beyond its borders even more effectually than the tall buildings did. Times Square had become that pagan temple before which Rupert Brooke reeled.

But neither geography alone, nor buildings, nor even lights, accounts for the sense of ineffable magic with which the very word "Broadway" was hedged; for it was only in these years that Broadway had begun to tell a tale of itself. Every Saturday, newspaper readers all over the country— which is to say, virtually all literate adults—turned to Franklin P. Adams's syndicated column, "Diary of Our Own Samuel Pepys," to read about the doings of the Broadway crowd. Adams referred to himself as "FPA," and to all his pals by their own special monikers: there were "I. Berlin" and "J. Kern," and "G.S.K." for George S. Kaufman, and "H.B.S." for the publisher and gadabout Herbert Bayard Swope. *Variety*, the trade journal of the entertainment industry, was already ancient, having been founded in 1907, but by the mid-twenties *Vanity Fair, The New Yorker,* and *The Smart Set* were all anatomizing the Broadway life in a snappy new Broadway patois for the benefit of readers marooned in Dullsboro. The great dailies' theater columns, once a backwater for broken-down reporters, had become home to the most finely milled prose in the city, with the gifted Heywood Broun writing first for the *Tribune,* then for the *World,* and finally for the *Telegram,* and George S. Kaufman and Alexander Woollcott writing for the *Times.* In his memoirs, the writer and director Moss Hart recalled poring over Broun and FPA in his cold-water flat in the Bronx, dreaming of joining the immortals in Times Square; young people all over the country dreamed just such candy-colored Broadway dreams.

The frankly commercial art being pumped out of Times Square was taken seriously for the first time. Not only Broadway figures like Broun, Adams, and George Jean Nathan, editor of *The Smart Set,* but mandarin intellectuals like Edmund Wilson and Joseph Wood Krutch wrote about Irving Berlin and jazz music and the revues. The most ardent vindication of the new art forms came with the publication of Gilbert Seldes's *The Seven Lively Arts* in 1924. Seldes, erudite and grounded in the classics, nevertheless championed jazz, vaudeville, Ziegfeld, George M. Cohan, the Krazy Kat comics, and Mack Sennett movies. He referred to these topical and transitory forms, hell-bent on pleasing the customer, as the lively arts—what we would today call popular culture. These minor art forms, Seldes wrote, "are, to an extent, an opiate—or rather they trick our hunger for a moment, and we are able to sleep. They do not wholly satisfy, but they do not corrupt. And they, too, have their moments of intensity." Seldes went on to describe the ecstasy he found stealing over him in the presence of the great vaudevillians. This was Broadway in the twenties—the epicenter and apogee of the lively arts.

GEORGE S. KAUFMAN was a comfortably middle-class Jewish boy from Pittsburgh who, like so many clever and ambitious young men and women of the time, was magnetically attracted to Broadway. In an age of wits, Kaufman was the wisecracker-in-chief, a man whose lightning verbal reflexes would have served him well in an eighteenth-century salon. He once bumped into the playwright S. N. Behrman in the wilds of Hollywood and said, "Ah, forgotten but not gone." When Moss Hart, having catapulted to sudden wealth, appeared one day in a glittering cowboy suit, Kaufman hailed him with "Hiyo, platinum!" Kaufman began his career, as did many another aspiring wag, contributing funny items to FPA's column in the *Tribune,* and went on to write a humor column of his own.

Kaufman knocked around until age thirty, when he got a job in the drama department of the *Times,* working under the imperious Woollcott. In later years, Woollcott claimed to have been thoroughly intimidated by his brilliant and gloomy underling, who was wont to deliver devastating quips without so much as cracking a smile. Though Kaufman was more or less happily married, financially successful, and devoted heart and soul to his work, his deep discomfort with life was impervious to his external circumstances. "He was so nervous," a biographer writes, "that he veered between bursts of rapid speech and periods of shy and total silence." He was terrified of long elevator rides and hazardous street crossings, though his chosen mode of existence required that he confront both all the time. Phobic about germs, Kaufman shied away from all forms of physical contact, especially handshakes.

Kaufman's wit, indeed his whole temperament, was shaped around an intense aversion to uninflected emotion. Moss Hart, who as an untried novice collaborated with the already titanic Kaufman, describes addressing a heartfelt speech of thanks to the bundle of limbs that was the playwright slumped, apparently inert, in an armchair. "To my horror," Hart writes, "the legs unwound themselves with an acrobatic rapidity I would not have believed possible, and the figure in the chair leaped up and out of it in one astonishing movement like a large bird frightened out of its solitude in the marshes." Kaufman literally could not write love scenes; the love interest in *The Butter and Egg Man,* the only play he wrote by himself, is so perfunctory that the two young people seem almost to have been ordered to bond. Wisecracking protected Kaufman from having to peer too deeply into the human swamp, as O'Neill did. Plainly, he was not nearly so great a figure as O'Neill. But it was his very emotional astringency, his horror of the false—even of the heartfelt—that made him so representative a figure of this age of urbanity; for much of the drama, and much of the sensibility, of the twenties was based on a repudiation, whether comic or tragic, of the easy sentimentality of an earlier age. And this, in turn, explains why both Kaufman and O'Neill strike us today as "modern," though almost none of their predecessors do.

Kaufman was absolutely and utterly a creature of Broadway. He rarely strayed beyond walking distance from Times Square; almost all of his friends were show folk. He kept his job at the *Times* years after he no longer needed the measly salary, though it's hard to say whether this was owing to his love of the milieu or his ever-present fear of failure. And Kaufman wrote about what he knew; Broadway gave him his setting, his characters, and his language. The characters in *The Butter and Egg Man,* for example, speak an almost impenetrable vaudeville slang—"I done six clubs for the wow at the finish, and done it for years!" "Butter and egg man" was the Broadway pejorative for one of the freshly minted midwestern plutocrats who could be counted on to back stage productions; the play's main character is a starstruck rube from Chillicothe, Ohio, whom a scheming producer separates from his inheritance. (The play-within-the-play features a trial scene, a brothel scene, and a dialogue in Heaven between a rabbi and a priest who "talk about how everybody's the same underneath, and it don't matter none what religion they got.") Kaufman's *Beggar on Horseback* concerns a gifted young composer who agrees to marry a bubble-headed heiress in order to avoid having to write commercial dreck for the theater. *June Moon* takes up the same theme in reverse: the main character, Fred Stevens, is a sentimental dolt who makes a smash debut as a Broadway songwriter.

The surfaces of Kaufman's plays are so glittery, and the characters so busy amusing themselves and one another, that it's easy to miss the underlying ferocious disgust with the business ethic and middlebrow taste; in fact, Kaufman's contempt for the world of success is scarcely less bitter than that of his more notoriously sardonic contemporary, H. L. Mencken. Many of Kaufman's plays have a character like Fred Stevens, or like Leach, the movie scenarist from *Dulcy,* who has achieved commercial success through sheer force of mediocrity. Most of *Beggar on Horseback,* which Kaufman wrote with Marc Connelly, consists of a surreal dream sequence in which the bohemian hero, Neil McRea, is trapped in the bourgeois world of his in-laws as inescapably as O'Neill's Rob is on the farm. Neil's new father-in-law, dressed in golf knits, barks into the phone, "Buy 18 holes and sell all the water hazards!" while six corporate automata march about mindlessly repeating "Overhead," "turnover," "annual report." Neil is gradually driven insane by the cacophony of banalities; he murders the entire family, only to be subjected to a trial that turns into an antic musical comedy, in which he is pronounced guilty of writing unpopular music. Kaufman somehow managed to churn out one popular and meticulously crafted play after another without ever compromising his view that the marketplace demands craven pandering.

FOR ALL HIS MOODY silences and his tics, George Kaufman was a gregarious man who loved company and who seems to have hated to work alone. In an era when everyone worked with everyone, Kaufman was the arch-collaborator. He worked with fellow playwrights like Marc Connelly, novelists like Edna Ferber, even greenhorns like Moss Hart. And he was a charter member of the great floating cocktail party–poker game–mutual admiration and ridicule society of the day. Hart, still a wide-eyed observer of the Broadway scene in the late 1920s, records the guest list for a typical "tea party" (a comic euphemism for a drinkathon) at the Kaufmans': Ethel Barrymore, Harpo Marx, Heywood Broun, Edna Ferber, Helen Hayes, George Gershwin, Alfred Lunt, Alexander Woollcott, Leslie Howard, Dorothy Parker, Robert Benchley, Robert Sherwood, Herbert Bayard Swope. More or less the same group might have assembled another day at Woollcott's country place in Vermont, or the uptown studio of the artist Neysa McMein, or even at a rented place in the south of France. Theater is, of course, an inherently collaborative medium, but what is still remarkable about the circle of the 1920s is the extent to which they *were* a circle—a group of people who lived an almost collective life, and whose work was in many ways the record of that charmed, over-heated, fiercely competitive society. It was the special privilege and delight of the audience, both in the theaters and in living rooms across the country, to eavesdrop on this wicked and inspired conversation.

The wits of Broadway wrote with each other, for each other, and about each other. Dorothy Parker, the most mordant and perhaps the most heartbreaking of the whole circle, began her career as a theater critic at *Vogue* in 1916 and moved on to *Vanity Fair,* where she was edited by the playwright Robert Sherwood and his fellow Robert, Benchley, later a comic stage performer and then a mainstay at *The New Yorker;* she was ultimately fired after trashing Ziegfeld's wife, Billie Burke, in the *Follies.* Woollcott, in many ways the central figure of the group, as well as the presiding genius of the Algonquin Round Table, the famous lunchtime gathering of wits at a hotel just off Times Square, virtually made a career out of writing about his friends. Besides reviewing their plays, and often composing charmingly facetious prefaces for the plays' published editions, Woollcott wrote two magazine profiles of Kaufman as well as both a profile and a full-length biography of his friend Irving Berlin. In 1929 he began simultaneously writing a weekly column for *The New Yorker* and, more important, broadcasting a weekly radio show that told the world of Broadway doings and often featured Broadway stars. Woollcott played a Woollcott-like figure—a fat, indolent, waspish kibbitzer—in S. N. Behrman's *Brief Moment.* Much later, in 1939, Kaufman and Hart wrote a play about Woollcott, *The Man Who Came to Dinner.*

The effect of all this nonstop collaborating, chronicling, criticizing, lunching, and drinking was to push the art of the period in the direction dictated by the circle's collective sensibility: wit, speed, sparkle, savoir-faire. Irving Berlin, the peerless manufacturer of hummable, lovable tunes, was certainly the most mainstream, the most conventionally successful, of the figures who joined, or at least regularly visited, the Algonquin Round Table. But intimacy with Woollcott, Dorothy Parker, and the rest turned him in a different direction. Berlin's biographer describes him writing "What'll I Do?," a song that sounds as much like Cole Porter as it does like Berlin, in a setting that is sheer Cole Porter: arriving with a bottle of champagne at a party given by Parker and Neysa McMein, Berlin sat down at the piano and began composing. When Berlin first met the beautiful young socialite Ellin Mackay, who was to become his wife, she told him how much she admired "What'll I Do?"

The limitation of the Round Table was that it tended to inspire gag writing and brilliant buffoonery; but over time, Kaufman and his collaborators evolved a form of satiric drama that was rooted, more or less, in character. In 1929, Kaufman and Ring Lardner, the great and mordant sportswriter and essayist, wrote *June Moon.* In the play's prologue, two strangers on a train try so hard to make contact with each other that neither listens to the other, and each natters on about people whom the other couldn't possibly know. The situation is painfully human, though at the same time ridiculous; and indeed, Fred, the songwriting-star-to-be, is consigned to that special circle of hell Kaufman reserves for pandering success. "He's not a fellow that can think for himself," one hardened ex–chorus girl chirps. "They left that out." George Jean Nathan wrote in *The American Mercury* that *June Moon* "should assist greatly in putting the quietus on the mere phrase-makers, the wise-crackers, the apostles of the New Wit. Every word belongs to the situation, the milieu, the character who speaks it."

One of the running jokes of *June Moon* is the musical hack who predicts, "Gershwin will be a nobody in ten years," and then, when Gershwin actually shows up, complains, "He stole my rhapsody." Kaufman had in fact begun collaborating with Gershwin on the musical *Strike Up the Band,* which first appeared in 1927. The Broadway musical as it has since come down to us essentially dates from this year. As if by harmonic convergence, George and Ira Gershwin's *Funny Face,* starring Fred and Adele Astaire, also appeared that year, as did Richard Rodgers and Lorenz Hart's *A Connecticut Yankee,* adapted from Mark Twain, and *Show Boat,* the epic musical of black life on a Mississippi riverboat written by Edna Ferber, with songs by Jerome Kern and Oscar Hammerstein II, son of Willie and grandson of the original Oscar. What distinguished all these works from their predecessors was the sheer sophistication of the music and songs; they also began to move in the direction of integrating music, song, and narrative, rather than stitching together a patchwork of gags and skits and showstoppers, as Berlin, Kern, and others had largely done before.

Strike Up the Band is such a ferocious piece of work that it had to be withdrawn from the stage; it succeeded only after Kaufman and Gershwin had toned down its sarcasm. The main character, Horace K. Fletcher, is a butter-and-egg man on a monstrous scale, a cheese manufacturer who inveigles the dim-witted President Coolidge into declaring war against Switzerland in order to block imported Swiss cheese. The premise is vintage Kaufman, since its very ludicrousness has the effect of liberating the author's satirical imagination. Horace offers to pay for the entire war, and return a 25 percent profit, so long as the war is named after him. "It's a go!" cries the president's chief adviser. "Strike Up the Band," a typically ingenious Gershwin pastiche of patriotic tunes, is the musical device Horace uses to whip up war fever and thus further his shameless profiteering. Horace soon has the young men of America marching off to bloody the Swiss, who have the good sense to hide in the mountains, and ultimately to surrender. The Gershwins' score includes "The Man I Love" and "I've Got a Crush on You," as well as a Gilbert and Sullivan sound-alike in rhyming couplets and a ragtime tune celebrating the triumph of jazz. For all the virtuoso eclecticism, *Strike Up the Band* is generally considered the first musical in which the songs emerge directly from the narrative, just as *June Moon* was one of the first Broadway plays in which the humor is rooted in character.

Nineteen twenty-seven was an astonishing year. Broadway theaters staged an average of 225 shows a year during the decade; in 1927 the figure reached 264, a figure never equaled before or since. It was not only one of the greatest seasons in the history of Broadway, but the year of Babe Ruth's sixty home runs and Charles Lindbergh's successful transatlantic flight, a year of heroes and parades and headlines. The stock market was making everybody rich, elevator boys as well as bankers. "The uncertainties of 1920 were drowned out in a steady golden roar," Fitzgerald later wrote. "The parties were bigger . . . the shows were broader, the buildings were higher, the morals were looser and the liquor was cheaper." It was a moment of frenzy that was bound to spend itself, though you would think, from Fitzgerald's apocalyptic disgust, that the catastrophe of the Depression arrived as a biblical punishment for wantonness. Indeed, he writes, "The city was bloated, glutted, stupid with cake and circuses." Yet Broadway would never again be so entrancing as it had been in those dazzling and giddy years of Woollcott and Kaufman and FPA and chorus girls lolling naked in fruit baskets. And no one knew it better than Fitzgerald himself. "For the moment," he writes at the very end of "My Lost City," "I can only cry out that I have lost my splendid mirage. Come back, come back, O glittering and white!"

THE PADLOCK REVUE

FROM ITS EARLIEST DAYS, Times Square floated on a mighty ocean of alcohol—nickel beer, gin, whiskey, wine, and the fine champagne downed by the quart at Rector's and Shanley's. The artistic souls who passed their days and nights along Broadway—the actors and the hoofers and the chorus girls and the composers and writers and stage managers and agents and producers and ticket scalpers—soothed their frayed nerves and bucked up their faltering egos with nightly drafts from the local dives and taverns, the lobster palaces and the hotels. In *Mirrors of New York,* a thoroughly soused memoir dating from 1925, the essayist Benjamin de Casseres describes Times Square as the central depot of a "Grand Trunk Line of Booze" stretching down Broadway, and the bar at the Knickerbocker Hotel, on the southeast corner of 42nd and Broadway, as "the headquarters of the 42nd Street Country Club." "At the corner outside one heard for years only one phrase," De Casseres plangently recalls: " 'Let's have another.' " Nineteen twenty-five was, of course, the heart of Prohibition; and *Mirrors of New York* is a melancholy recollection of a vanished golden age. "The rapid fall of the booze forts around these corners and the rise of the chocolate and soda centers on their ruins is a matter of near history," De Casseres writes, in what is possibly the earliest account on record of Times Square ruined by the forces of modernization and propriety.

The Eighteenth Amendment took effect July 1, 1919, but the Volstead Act, which made Prohibition national law, only went into force on January 16 of the following year. It was a bitterly cold night; the temperature dropped to six degrees. The drinking crowd jammed into the old booze forts like condemned prisoners partaking of a final meal. Reisenweber's held a funeral ball; the waiters at Maxim's were dressed as pallbearers. For all the chin-up insouciance, the metaphor was no joke for the establishments themselves. Without alcohol, the great lobster palaces felt like overupholstered mess halls. Who would linger until the late hours over a carafe of ginger ale? Within three years, every single one of the great old Broadway restaurants had disappeared. And in their place came the hot dog stands and soda fountains and "coffee pots" that disgusted the likes of Benjamin de Casseres. Prohibition annihilated the splendid eating and drinking culture of Times Square.

What it could not annihilate, of course, was drinking itself; that was much too deeply ingrained in the life of the place. And so drinking changed, almost overnight, from a beloved pastime, like dancing or play-going, to a clandestine and fugitive act. Within a few years there were hundreds, if not thousands, of speakeasies in the area around Times Square. Most of them were located not in the grand open spaces formed by the convergence of the avenues, as the lobster palaces had been, but in brownstones, and above restaurants, and behind shops, on the cross streets of the Forties. Many of them were just underground versions of the cheap bars that had flourished in the area for years; the patron would show a familiar face or mention a familiar name, or even mumble a password through a sliding window or a barred opening in the door. Others were private homes, where drinkers would be escorted into what had once been the living room of an apartment. Some of these establishments—the kind you might read about enviously in *The New Yorker*—offered copies of the latest magazines, and soft armchairs, and legitimate Scotch highballs. Others—a great many more—reeked of yesterday's Welsh rarebit and watered their gin and padded their bills, and occasionally robbed a customer too drunk to notice. A. J. Liebling once wrote a story in *The New Yorker* about sign painters who had made a fine living during Prohibition instantly repainting nightclubs and shifting around the furniture, so that when outraged patrons returned the next day with the police the place was unrecognizable, and they doubted their own fuddled memories.

A speakeasy was a criminal establishment, like an opium den. The cop on the beat could usually be paid off to look the other way, but the more intrepid and relentless federal agents were raiding bars and nightclubs, smashing the bottles, padlocking the establishment, and carting off the owners and the staff to jail. Most patrons, and most owners, considered the raids a nuisance and an occupational hazard; Prohibition made absolutely no moral headway among the sophisticates and devout drinkers of Broadway. If anything, Prohibition had the effect of discrediting sobriety itself; the mild risk associated with drinking only made the act more chic. And the almost complete separation of eating and drinking probably also had the effect of promoting drunkenness.

But speakeasies rested on another and more serious species of illegality, for the trade in bootleg liquor was almost entirely controlled by organized crime. Rum-running essentially created organized crime in New York and Chicago, just as the rise of the drug trade in the 1960s and after fostered the rise of new criminal cartels. The great underworld figures of the day—Dutch Schultz, Owney Madden, Lucky Luciano—were first and foremost bootleggers. And they plowed their wealth back into Times Square in the form of nightclubs, which were speakeasies with entertainment. Virtually all the famous nightclubs of the day—the El Fey, the Silver Slipper, the Hotsy Totsy, the Parody—were partly or wholly owned by gangsters. "It was a setup made to order for mobsters," as Nils T. Granlund, the foremost producer of nightclub acts, writes in his memoir, *Blondes, Brunettes and Bullets.* The mobsters were already supplying the alcohol, they had access to enormous supplies of cash, and many of them loved nothing more than hanging out at the clubs.

"At its best," wrote Stanley Walker, the famous city editor of *The New York Herald,* "the night club, in all senses, was a poor imitation of the spacious, clean-aired cabaret; at its worst it was horrible—a hangout for thugs, cadets, porch-climbers, pickpockets, halfwits, jewel thieves, professional maimers, yeggmen, ex-convicts and, in its later days, adepts at kidnaping and 'the snatch racket.' " The nightclub was an underworld; that very fact made it deeply attractive to the newspapermen and ballplayers and chorus girls and instant millionaires who took a dim view of respectability, or at least wanted to dip their toes in the disreputable. And it was this mixed crowd, and this clandestine culture, that was the source of the raffish Times Square of the Roaring Twenties that the whole world came to know thanks to the writing of Damon Runyon, Walter Winchell, Mark Hellinger, and the other great newspapermen of the age. Not for nothing did Stanley Walker refer to the twenties as the Nightclub Era. The nightclub was the subterranean stage of this self-consciously theatrical age. While the cosmopolitan wit of Kaufman and Woollcott and Benchley played out on the public stage of the theaters, the ribaldry and hijinks and gunplay of the nightclubs created a private—and for that very reason glamorous—stage of its own.

NILS T. GRANLUND, who was in a position to know, opined that every nightclub on Broadway in the early years of Prohibition was essentially a bordello with music and dancing. The first generation of clubs, like the old concert saloons, catered to men who wanted to get stiff as a board and to men who wanted to buy sex; the waitresses were essentially on their own when it came to making money off the clientele. The clubs rarely had the resources to afford serious entertainment, and the gangsters who owned them were in the habit of aiming low. The first classy nightclub was the El Fey, which opened in 1924. The club's owner was Larry Fay, a bootlegger and taxi fleet operator who owned the taxi concessions at Grand Central Terminal and Penn Station. (It was widely understood that the second job required a good deal more ferocity than the first.) But the real force behind the club, and then behind a succession of clubs bankrolled by Fay and other gangsters, was a faded silent-movie star who called herself Texas Guinan. Tex, who at the time was forty, was a big, buxom woman perpetually swathed in diamonds and pearls, a florid, funny, loudmouthed, lovable character much like her near contemporary Mae West. And she was just about to become the whirling center of the new nocturnal culture—"the Queen of the Nightclubs."

Tex presented herself to the world as a cowgirl who found that she loved the lampposts of Broadway better than the stars of the big sky—a sort of Annie Oakley–turned–Sophie Tucker character. She said that she had been raised on a fifty-thousand-acre ranch in Texas, that she had run away with a rodeo circus, that she had knocked around the Colorado mining towns. A biographer, after much patient research, concluded that all of these claims were fabricated. Tex had a relatively genteel upbringing in Waco and Denver, and then around 1907 became a vaudeville performer and a second banana in light operas along Broadway. Trifling with the strict truth in such matters was considered, at the time, an entirely laudable proof of imagination, but the fact that Tex chose to invent a Wild West background for herself says a good deal about life on Broadway. In the demimonde, or perhaps hemidemimonde, that she occupied, certain western ideals—the ability to handle yourself with your fists, to spin a yarn, to live by your wits—became strangely mixed with the sybaritic nighttime world of the big city. A faint tang of the mining camp clung to the nightclub.

Tex perfected her two-gun persona in silent movies like *The Gun Woman.* She did all her own stunts and was known as "the personification of female daredeviltry." In 1921 she formed her own production company, planning to churn out a series of two-reelers—*Texas of the Mounted, The Soul of Tex, The Claws of Tex,* and so on. The venture never quite panned out, and Tex returned to New York, from which she had never been absent for long. Nils Granlund claimed that he discovered her emceeing a show at a club called the Beaux Arts, and introduced her to Larry Fay, an upwardly mobile gangster. In 1924 he opened up the El Fey—no one ever knew why he chose to misspell his own name—with Tex as hostess. The club, on 45th Street between Sixth Avenue and Broadway, was a tiny room located at the top of a narrow staircase and behind a door with a peephole cut into it. Most of the chorus came from the Ziegfeld Follies at the New Amsterdam; the girls came over after the show closed up at eleven. Some were as young as thirteen, and Tex served as their mother hen. There was no soliciting in either direction at the El Fey; some of the girls said later that they never heard so much as a cussword. The customers knew they would have to answer to Tex for any infractions of the rules.

Tex herself generally breakfasted some time before midnight, and arrived at the club around one. The girls would often come out and sing "Cherries," and while they sang they would pass through the crowd picking cherries from a basket and popping them into the mouths of customers, who would beg for a cherry. (The rule against soliciting did not extend to titillating.) Then Tex, who had a voice of brass, might get up on a chair and lead the crowd in a rousing version of an old standard, like "California, Here I Come." Thereafter, she would sit in the middle of the crowd, teasing and heckling her customers, inveigling the more demure among them into playing leapfrog and other silly games, and sometimes blowing on a police whistle to get attention. Arriving customers were greeted with the cry "Hello, sucker!," a tacit acknowledgment that they were about to be fleeced by Tex's ludicrous prices—$25 for a bottle of "champagne" that consisted of cider spiked with alcohol—and an act of welcome to the community of suckers, which included Tex herself. When a visiting dairy magnate spread his cash around particularly thickly, Tex shouted, "Here's my big butter-and-egg man!," coining the phrase that George S. Kaufman lifted for the title of his play—or so the legend goes.

Tex was a wisecracking, extravagant Dame of Misrule. Edmund Wilson described her as a "prodigious woman, with her pearls, her glittering bosom, her abundantly beautiful bleached yellow coiffure, her formidable rap of shining white teeth, her broad bare back behind its grating of green velvet, the full-blown peony as big as a cabbage exploding on her broad green thigh." With her gleeful contempt for propriety, her ready wit, her love of the rollicking good time, her world-weary wisdom, Tex came to be viewed as an incarnation of the age—a sort of one-woman Algonquin Round Table. Paladins of high culture like Wilson made pilgrimages to her throne, and the highest of nobility paid her court. Tex claimed Edward, Prince of Wales, as one of her dear friends, and said that when she was raided one time she told the prince to hustle back into the kitchen and start frying eggs; Lord Mountbatten, on the other hand, she disguised as a drummer. The battle for the high ground between Tex and the authorities was strictly no contest.

Tex never stayed in one place for long. The police closed down the El Fey in April 1925, and Tex reappeared at the Texas Guinan Club on West 48th Street. The club was busted after four months, and then Tex popped up again at the Del Fey, back in the old spot on 45th Street—a calculated act of insouciance. Later she moved on to the 300 Club, the Club Intime, and the Club Argonaut. *The New Yorker,* which chronicled Tex's doings, once noted that "the occasion of Texas Guinan's 3,465th opening occurred, this time at 117 West Forty-eighth Street, where she was two summers ago." Tex laughed at enforcement; and all New York, or so it seemed, laughed with her. When she was arrested in early 1927, the crowd spilled out onto the street while the band mournfully played "The Prisoner's Song," a big hit from 1924. When the city passed a draconian piece of legislation known as the Padlock Law, Tex put on "The Padlock Revue," and swanned around her latest club in a necklace of padlocks. Finally subjected to a sort of show trial in 1928, Tex insisted that she had never owned any of her places, that in any case she had no idea liquor was being served, that her good name was being trampled in the mud, etc. The trial was a tabloid sensation, and the unsinkable Tex was finally cleared of all charges.

Tex's various clubs were the Rector's of the Prohibition era—the spot where the life of the place was most intensely led, where the true denizens of Broadway passed their idle hours while awestruck out-of-towners enjoyed a taste of the real thing and collected an anecdote or two to bring home. Tex knew everyone and everything. Reporters found her a precious resource. Heywood Broun of the *World* would drop by, and Mark Hellinger of the *Daily News* came almost every night with his young friend Walter Winchell. Winchell was a former vaudevillian, like Tex, who had spent years knocking around small-town theaters with a song-and-dance act known as Winchell & Green. He had begun his writing career by tacking typewritten sheets in the lobby of a theater with news items about the performers appearing that night. Then he had landed a job with *Vaudeville News,* a bit of puffery published by the Keith-Orpheum vaudeville circuit from the company's headquarters in the Palace Theatre. Since virtually the entire world of vaudeville was concentrated in a two-block radius around the Palace, Winchell came to possess a microscopic knowledge of this knockabout, baggy-pants world. He did not, however, have much acquaintance with the beau monde, and in 1924, when the El Fey opened up, Winchell had just landed a job as a gossip columnist—a term that did not yet exist—at a dreadful little newspaper called *The Graphic.*

Winchell was, as Stanley Walker put it, "an astonishingly alert, electrically nervous little man," fast-talking, indefatigable, avid. His biographer Neal Gabler writes, "He smoked furiously, gabbed incessantly, scribbled quickly (usually with a stubby pencil on the back of envelopes or on a folded square of newsprint) and drummed the table with his fingers on the rare occasion when he wasn't talking." He would hang around the speakeasies, and if he heard a burst of laughter from a table he would race over and cry, "What's the gag? Is it anything for the column?" Tex was, in the early days, his mother lode. Winchell would often spend the entire night at one of her clubs, playing poker and swapping stories with her and Hellinger after the place closed up, at three or four in the morning. Later on, Winchell would say that it was Tex who gave him the idea to write about society folks, because she would point around the room and say that this one was having an affair with a chorus girl, and that one was about to get married, and the other one had just come back from Reno. And Tex knew the gangsters every bit as well as she knew the party girls.

Winchell's obsession with ephemera, his breathlessness, his hokey neologisms, made him something of a joke with the soigné crowd who hung around Neysa McMein's studio; but he would ultimately become a bigger figure than any of them. Winchell's education ran through sixth grade, and he aspired to nothing greater, or lesser, than to tell the secrets of Broadway, which he described variously as "The Main Stem," "The Street of Broken Dreams," "The Clogged Artery." A nation that was as besotted with Broadway as he was couldn't get enough of Winchell's news. By the late 1920s, when he had left *The Graphic* for the far more reputable *Mirror,* Winchell was one of the most famous newspapermen in the great age of newspapermen. And then his stupendously popular radio show, which he began broadcasting in 1930, lifted him to a level of celebrity all his own. Winchell became the Mayor of Broadway, the Bard of Broadway, the Boswell of Broadway. He described a world where everybody had something going on the side—an affair, a racket, a dark secret. And he defined as well the tough-guy ethos of a crowd that lived by its own rules. "At that other table is a horse from a different stable. The woman with him isn't his wife. . . . His wife is in a 46th Street hideaway right now with The One She Goes For. Got it? . . . Must be terrible to be found out. . . . And a guy is a sap to wise a pal, too, even when he knows he is being crossed. . . . They never appreciate the tip."

Winchell absorbed the gangster ethos, and the gangster language, of the nightclub world, and replayed it to America in his own peculiar patois—"a guy is a sap to wise a pal." Winchell knew that whole crowd, and was particularly close to Owney Madden, who gave him a Stutz Bearcat. Madden, who was also a friend of Tex's, owned one of her clubs along with his confederates Frenchy DeMange and Feets Edson. Winchell often passed along to his readers juicy bits of gossip about hoods that he picked up from Tex. In February 1932, he reported that "five planes brought dozens of machinegats from Chicago Friday" in order to rub out Vince "Mad Dog" Coll, a feared hit man who had been reckless enough to kidnap DeMange and extort a ransom from Madden. When Coll was murdered in a phone booth that very night, Winchell was targeted for revenge—the hoods feared he would be forced to talk to the DA—and it may only have been his relationship with Madden that saved him.

Winchell was at once a creature of Broadway and a student of Broadway. He loved the big names, but he was too much the ex-hoofer to have stars in his eyes. Broadway, he once wrote, "is a hard and destructive community, even for those who 'click.' " He would later become a baroque figure, a great friend of J. Edgar Hoover and a notorious red-baiter, less a teller of tales than himself the tale; but as a young man, hopping from one speakeasy to the next, he "caught the tempo of New York in the late twenties and early thirties," as Stanley Walker writes. "The tempo was brittle, cheap, garish, loud, and full of wild dissonances."

Texas Guinan ultimately became such a byword for Broadway nightlife that she starred in her own movie, *Queen of the Night Clubs,* in 1929, and enjoyed several stints as a celebrity journalist. Her column, "Texas Guinan Says," appeared daily in *The Graphic.* She put three dots between her items, just like Winchell, producing the same breathless, jazzy sense of experience caught on the fly. She tossed off a rapid-fire sequence of cracks and tough-guy asides: "There are far too many women who act like they were born in revolving doors—they are so dizzy and keep going around in circles." And she was a name-dropper to put anyone but Winchell in the shade, managing to include, in the space of about 250 words, Woodrow Wilson, Herbert Hoover, Benito Mussolini, Primo Carnera, David Belasco, Heywood Broun, and Ethel Barrymore—although, to be fair, it's unlikely that Wilson, who died in 1921, visited any of Tex's clubs.

Tex comes down to us today chiefly through the works of Damon Runyon, the other and more lasting bard of Broadway in the nightclub era. Runyon's girlfriend Patrice Gridier was in Tex's chorus in 1925, though it is safe to say that he would have gravitated to Tex's clubs in any case. Tex was a natural-born goddess of Runyon's scruffy Olympus. One of his most famous stories, "Romance in the Roaring Forties," written in 1929, concerns not only Tex but Winchell, whom Runyon normally treated as somewhat below his level of regard, but who served perfectly as a Broadway type. Runyon barely deigned to disguise his characters: "Romance in the Roaring Forties" opens in the "Sixteen Hundred Club" of "Missouri Martin," "an old experienced doll" known as "Mizzou" who "tells everything she knows as soon as she knows it, which is very often before it happens." The story concerns a gossip columnist named Waldo Winchester who falls in love with Billy Perry, the girlfriend of a gangster named "Dave the Dude," whom Jimmy Breslin, in his luminous but hallucinatory biography of Runyon, identifies with the Mafioso Frank Costello. The story's narrator treats Waldo as an unaccountable idiot for having placed his life in jeopardy over a girl; and Mizzou tells Billy that she is "a little sap" for falling in love with a starving newspaperman when "everybody knows that Dave the Dude is a very fast man with a dollar."

"Romance in the Roaring Forties" is, like so many Runyon stories, a kind of extended joke, because the violence for which the reader is being continually prepared not only never occurs but collapses into rank sentimentality. Rather than obeying his initial impulse to murder Waldo, Dave arranges for him to marry Billy because, he tells the narrator, "I love her myself so much that I wish to see her happy at all times, even if she has to marry to be that way." And then, when it turns out that Waldo is already very much married and was only trifling with Billy, rather than murdering Waldo a second time, Dave turns around and marries Billy himself. Dave has a heart of gold; and he is still, of course, a ruthless killer. The story never loses its hard-boiled edge because we know perfectly well that marriage will not "reform" Dave. And it probably won't reform Billy, either. But of course only a sap would suggest as much to either.

Runyon's Broadway, like Winchell's, was a comic rather than a tragic place, a place full of wild incident, a place where the normal human motives are much easier to read because the citizens prefer to do without the usual layers of hypocrisy. It is a very far cry from the Broadway of Julian Street or Rupert Hughes—not because the place has degenerated, but because it has become impossible to imagine a morally superior alternative. Some combination of Prohibition with the generational contempt for received proprieties has so completely discredited conventional norms of behavior that an honest cynicism, combined with the threadbare sentimentality of a dying hood who falls in love with a lame dog (another Runyon tale), has become the local ideal of nobility. A guy is a sap to wise a pal.

Runyon was, like Tex, a western migrant to the big city. He was born, by an amusing coincidence, in Manhattan, Kansas, and as a small-town newspaperman he had knocked around the western mining camps—usually reeling drunk—that Tex could only boast about. Runyon wasn't a florid person, like Tex; he was one of those devastatingly funny people who almost never smile, which is to say that he could be a very disconcerting person. His stoicism, his tough-mindedness, his contempt for the straight and narrow, and his storytelling gifts made him an appealing figure among the hoods and horseplayers and reporters with whom he invariably hung out. Runyon only arrived in New York in 1910, when he was twenty-six. In 1914 he landed a job at William Randolph Hearst's *American,* where he remained as sportswriter, feature writer, and columnist until 1928. When he wasn't in Florida for spring training, or in Chicago for a fight, he could normally be found within the confines of Times Square.

Though Runyon was at least as much a Broadway character as George S. Kaufman or anyone in his circle, one finds very little reference to him in their writings, or to them in his. They occupied different Times Squares, for by this time Times Square had become such a capacious, such a various, place that it could accommodate several very different cultures and could conjure up to the rest of the world a very mixed set of images and associations. There was a lighthearted, witty, and urbane Times Square, and a roguish, slightly sinister Times Square. And this truth was expressed geographically, for Runyon's Times Square, both the one he wrote about and the one he lived in, was a micro-neighborhood located well to the north of Kaufman's theatrical world, which was concentrated in and around 42nd Street.

A new Madison Square Garden had gone up in 1925 on Eighth Avenue between 49th and 50th Streets; and the sports fans and promoters and ticket agents and bookies who went to the Garden for prizefights and college basketball games and bicycle races and wrestling matches hung out at the hotels and bars immediately to the east. The sidewalk on the east side of Broadway between 49th and 50th was known as Jacobs Beach, because the fight promoter Mike Jacobs and his pals were wont to camp out there. Both Winchell and Runyon frequently dropped in on the crowd there for local tidings; both men also lived for a time in the rooms above Billy LaHiff's Tavern on 48th west of Seventh, as did Jack Dempsey and the columnist Bugs Baer. Runyon later removed to the Forrest Hotel, a block to the north, which also hosted the innumerable assignations of the boxer and heartthrob Primo Carnera. Texas Guinan's various clubs were never more than a few blocks away, and the other great nightclubs of the time, including the Hollywood and the Silver Slipper, were virtually next door. Here was a vast, teeming world that extended no more than a thousand feet in any direction.

If Walter Winchell was Broadway's town crier, then Damon Runyon was its griot and its folklorist-in-chief. Runyon gave the world a Broadway that was infinitely dense with incident, and yet scaled down to the size of a village. It was an intricate little place where people walked from here to there, saluting their friends and experiencing chance encounters that not infrequently led to their death. "One night," Runyon writes in "The Brain Goes Home," "the Brain is walking me up and down Broadway in front of Mindy's restaurant, and speaking of this and that, when along comes a red-headed raggedy doll selling apples at five cents per copy. . . ." In other stories, the narrator isn't even going anywhere; he's just standing outside Mindy's front door when the neighborhood characters come waltzing down the street, and soon another adventure has begun.

Runyon's geography was subtly different from Winchell's. With the help of guides like Tex, and thanks to his own burning ambition, Winchell had left behind the vaudeville shtetl of 47th Street for the beau monde of the clubs and cabarets. But it was just this side-street world, whose denizens gazed yearningly at the blazing lights of Broadway, that interested Runyon. For all his tough-mindedness, Runyon was a sucker for little people with hopelessly big dreams; he wrote about them with a pathos Winchell never could have mustered. In fact, he christened the block behind the Palace Theatre "Dream Street." There, he wrote, "you see bur-

lesque dolls, and hoofers, and guys who write songs, and saxophone players, and newsboys, and newspaper scribes, and taxi drivers, and blind
guys, and midgets, and blondes with Pomeranians, or maybe French poo-
dles, and guys with whiskers, and nightclub entertainers, and I do not
know what else." And all of them "sit on the stoops or lean against the
railings of Dream Street, and the gab you hear sometimes sounds very
dreamy indeed. In fact, it sometimes sounds very pipe-dreamy." It is no
coincidence that after this epic evocation, Dream Street Rose, the living
soul of the street, tells the narrator a tale about a young woman—herself,
in days gone by—in the mining town of Pueblo, Colorado, another burg
full of stranded souls dreaming of the big strike that will set them free.

It is a crucial part of Runyon's mystique that it is almost impossible to
say where life ends and literature begins. You cannot read the Broadway
stories without imagining Runyon himself as the all-knowing, deadpan
narrator—the fellow who modestly says he "gets about." Runyon, of
course, got about. Keeping approximately the same hours as Winchell or
Tex, he would emerge from LaHiff's or the Forrest in the early afternoon,
join the crowd at Jacobs Beach, and then wander inside to his table immediately to the right at the front of Lindy's, the "Mindy's" of his stories.
Lindy's was to Runyon what Texas Guinan's clubs were to Winchell: the
place where the stories he wanted to hear were told. Runyon would sit
there for hours with Nils T. Granlund, or with Carnera or Dempsey, or
with various small-time gangsters, or with Arnold Rothstein, the model
for the Brain.

Rothstein, who controlled the poker games and the floating craps
games along Broadway and elsewhere in the city, was a legendary figure
in Times Square, a soft-spoken and mysterious character who seemed ac-
countable to no one. In *The Great Gatsby*, Fitzgerald names him Meyer
Wolfsheim and recounts the widely believed tale—since discredited—that
he had fixed the 1919 World Series. Fitzgerald's Rothstein is a silken monster who proudly shows Nick Carraway his cufflinks: "finest specimens of
human molars," he brags. Indeed, the dark revelation at the heart of the
novel is that Jay Gatsby works as a bootlegger for Wolfsheim and owes his
entire fortune to him. In Rothstein are concentrated all the dark forces
that lie below the wild gaiety of Fitzgerald's novel.

Runyon, by contrast, was friendly with Rothstein, as he was with Al Capone, Owney Madden, Frank Costello, and virtually every other important hoodlum of the day; and he turned them all into "characters." Runyon knew very well what they were, but he had too dim a regard for legitimately constituted authority to judge them according to their deserts; besides, he had business transactions with several of them. Runyon and a few of his buddies were with Rothstein in Lindy's the night of his death—one of the great set pieces of the journalism of the day. Rothstein used Lindy's as his telephone booth, and one night in 1928 a call came in for him. Rothstein listened, nodded, put down the phone, handed his gun to a friend, and went out into the night. Everyone sitting there knew that he had become a hunted man after failing to pay a quarter of a million dollars in gambling debts. It was a moment of the kind of high stoicism Runyon cherished in his Broadway characters—a moment when Times Square turned into the O.K. Corral. Several hours later, Rothstein, riddled with bullets, stumbled out of the elevator of a Central Park West apartment building. He lived for several days, refusing to breathe a word about his assailant.

TIMES SQUARE IN THE Roaring Twenties was both the sparkling world of the Algonquin Round Table and the yeggs' kingdom of Owney Madden—"Owney the Killer." And though these may have been more parallel than overlapping worlds, each lent its atmosphere to the other. It was the sparkle of the age that made the gangsters so glamorous; it was the lurking brutality of the age that gave the drama its edge of menace. Perhaps the single most famous play of the decade was *The Front Page,* a story about gangsters, cops, killers, and reporters written by a pair of hard-boiled newspapermen. It was an era that thumbed its nose at authority and turned lawbreaking into a charming adventure. Even the city's mayor, James J. Walker, was a figure out of Runyon—a dandy, a wit, a barfly, a friend to all, a faithless husband, and a veteran of Tin Pan Alley who never missed a heavyweight bout or a new nightclub act. A biographer called him "the John Barrymore of the political stage." Walker ordered the police to stop enforcing Prohibition, and deprecated all forms of moral crusading with the sarcasm of a true New Yorker. Placing himself in opposition to a piece of censorship known as the Clean Books Bill, Walker famously declared, "I have never yet heard of a girl being ruined by a book."

And then the bubble burst. First came the Depression, though it would take several years of hard times before people stopped buying tickets to shows or peeling off twenties in nightclubs. And then came the repeal of Prohibition, in 1933. Repeal killed many of the clubs, just as Prohibition had killed the lobster palaces. And it forced the mobsters to find less glamorous precincts in which to ply their trade. Jimmy Walker finally had to resign in 1932 after an investigation documented his habit of exchanging city contracts for quite large personal gifts; the new mayor, Fiorello La Guardia, vowed to clean up the town, and did. Florenz Ziegfeld, whose career had begun in the previous century, died in 1932—penniless, of course. Larry Fay was murdered by the doorman of his latest club in January 1933. And Tex, whose star had been dwindling since the late twenties, died later that year in Vancouver. She and the girls had been booted out of Paris for indecency, and Tex had then mounted a show called *Too Hot for Paris,* which turned out to be too hot for the hinterland as well. She had then bounced around Chicago, and had died on a western swing.

Tex's demise received the kind of newspaper coverage once given to the deathwatch over J. P. Morgan. Her obituary appeared on the front page of many of the New York papers, and she was recalled as the very emblem of a world already receding into memory's mists. Walter Winchell did not stint on behalf of his old muse. "We learned Broadway from her," he wrote. "She taught us the ways of the Street."

"COME IN AND
SEE THE GREAT
FLEA CIRCUS"

On MARCH 9, 1933, the "42nd Street Special" came roaring into Grand Central Terminal after a ten-day trip across country. Bette Davis was on board, and Tom Mix, and many of the contract stars at Warner Bros., which had chartered the train and laid on the ballyhoo to promote *42nd Street*, its entry into the swelling sweepstakes of backstage Broadway movies. As many as a quarter of the early talkies—including, of course, the very first one, Al Jolson's *The Jazz Singer*—were backstage shows; it was the most obvious way of working songs into a movie, as well as capitalizing on the prestige of Broadway. Three of the four biggest movies of 1933 would be shows about Broadway musicals: *Gold Diggers of 1933*, *Footlight Parade*, and, of course, *42nd Street*, starring Dick Powell, Una Merkel, Ginger Rogers, and Bebe Daniels, and featuring the kaleidoscopic choreography of Busby Berkeley.

Coming at the moment it did, *42nd Street* symbolized the transfer of energy, and of glamour, from the stage to the screen, as if Hollywood had vampirically sucked the lifeblood from Broadway. The Times Square of 1933 had been ground down by the Depression and transformed by new forms of entertainment, above all the movies. Half of the street's ten theaters had been converted either to movies or to burlesque. The number of plays showing in Times Square, and the average number of weeks that the area's theaters were open, had both been dropping steadily since the glory days of 1927. *Variety* called the 1932–33 season "legit's worst year"; only 26 of the 117 shows either broke even or made a profit. To those who knew it well, 42nd Street itself had already lost its status as the fabled nexus where, as the movie put it, "the underworld can greet the elite." The elite had moved on, and Broadway was rapidly becoming a honky-tonk world of burlesque and dance halls and pitchmen and hot dog stands.

The movie *42nd Street* arrived at precisely the moment when this tawdry new Times Square was taking shape. It was based on a novel by Bradford Ropes, a thoroughly wised-up twenty-eight-year-old ex-vaudevillian, a junior version of Walter Winchell. The novel, which the novice producer Darryl F. Zanuck bought for $6,000, a very ample sum at the time, contains only a few hints of the Depression: the boys and girls in the chorus are starving, but only in the immemorial way of the Street of Broken Dreams. *42nd Street* describes a world that is as pitiless and all-consuming as a meatpacking plant: when an old actor dies onstage in rehearsal, the producer's only concern is how to hide the misfortune so as not to delay opening night. Everyone from the chorus girls to the starlet is scheming and sleeping her way to the top. Even the ingenue and heroine, Peggy Sawyer, agrees to serve as the beard to a popular homosexual dancer in order to raise her status. Peggy extenuates her hypocrisy to herself by saying, "Pardon me while I climb a few rungs on my ladder!" By the end, Peggy's few scruples are altogether forgotten, and she is as self-important, and as hard, as everyone else in the company. But this is a familiar story: Ropes's book is essentially a grimly de-sentimentalized version of the Kaufman-style Broadway satire of the late twenties, as if too many years and too many shows have leached all the delight out of the form, and out of Broadway itself.

The movie version of *42nd Street* is a much stranger piece of work, a giddy extravaganza about economic desperation. While the play familiar to today's theatergoers is the story of those plucky kids in the chorus, and the novel was the story of the implacable Show, Zanuck's movie, which he described as a "musical exposé," is chiefly the story of the director Julian Marsh, who has emerged from retirement despite fragile health because he has lost his entire fortune in the Crash. Marsh is a desperate and bitter figure, a screamer and a slave driver; commanding the chorus girls to hike up their skirts, he shouts, "Higher, higher, I want to see the legs!" The girls are in no position to argue, since the show is their only shot at a square meal. When Peggy at first declines the chance to step in for the show's fallen star, Marsh cries, "Two hundred people, two hundred jobs, two hundred thousand dollars, five weeks of grind and blood and sweat depend on you! It's the lives of all these people." The characters are playing for much higher stakes than they had been in the world of George S. Kaufman and Ben Hecht and Irving Berlin.

But of course this is Hollywood, and the movie fantasticates its Depression setting into something every bit as delightful and improbable as the Broadway of Damon Runyon. (The Runyon stories themselves were then being rapidly converted into movies.) When the chorus sings "We're in the Money" after one of them finds a nickel, hard times seem about as overwhelming as a toothache. Like the other Broadway movies that Hollywood churned out in a great flood in those years, *42nd Street* capitalized on a national romance with Times Square that had been building for decades. The combination of crime and Depression had given this 42nd Street a darker hue. But that, too, was part of its appeal; *42nd Street* is in love with 42nd Street, just as were the *Broadway Melody*s (*1929, 1936, 1938*) and the "Gold Diggers" series and all the others.

But if *42nd Street* is a love note to the tough-hearted Times Square of the Depression years, it also, almost unconsciously, serves notice that Broadway's star is fading. *Pretty Lady,* the play-within-the-movie, is hopelessly hokey and stilted; the jokes are stale, the dances are drab, and even the singing has the stiff elocution of an earlier age. The feel of the movie abruptly shifts halfway through when Busby Berkeley arrives, and his inspired cinematic effects launch the action into the realm of fantasy. The girls are mounted on a rotating table—a classic Ziegfeld touch—and a camera, high above, shows them weaving some stretchy material into fantastic geometry. The girls form a row, and the camera guides us through an endless A-frame of long, perfectly tapered gams. Here is an effect that even Ziegfeld himself could never match; here is beauty closer than you've ever seen it before. Although *42nd Street* celebrates the raffish life of Broadway, underneath, it marks the ascendancy of film and the decline of theater, and thus of that very world of Broadway.

The advent of talkies tilted what had been a close match between a classic and an upstart medium into a one-sided battle. A Broadway show in a movie was so much bigger, brighter, and dreamier than the show itself, and so much cheaper to present. You could fit two or three times as many people into a cinema house as into a theater, and you could turn that audience over two or three or four times in a day. The iron law of Times Square, and of the entertainment districts that preceded it, is that real estate is turned to its most profitable use; even in an earlier generation, it had become plain that economics favored film. The first movie theater had appeared on 42nd Street in 1910, and movie houses began replacing theaters in Times Square as early as 1914, when Vitagraph Studios turned the Lyric Theatre in Hammerstein's Olympia into the Criterion. That same year the Strand became the first theater on Broadway built expressly for the movies, with a thirty-piece orchestra, three thousand seats—and no stage. It was there, in fact, that *42nd Street* opened, for the converted theaters of 42nd Street itself, mostly dating from the first years of the century, were far too small to accommodate a blockbuster movie. By the mid-twenties, both sides of Broadway were lined with impossibly opulent movie palaces—the Rialto, the Rivoli, the Capitol, and, above all, the Roxy, with 6,214 seats, the 110-piece Roxy Symphony Orchestra, the corps of dancers known as the Roxyettes, and, of course, the Roxy ushers, whom Cole Porter was later to immortalize as the acme of swank. In 1930, the Palace, the sun around which the vast universe of vaudeville had once revolved, was wired for sound—and all Broadway mourned.

The movies very swiftly displaced theater as America's chief form of popular culture. As the folks in Altoona decided they wanted to see movies rather than plays, those splendid theaters in every downtown in America were converted to movie houses, just as they were on 42nd Street. The number of legitimate theaters nationwide plummeted from 1,549 in 1910 to 674 in 1925; the number of touring companies dropped even more drastically. It had been the insatiable demand for real Broadway shows in towns all over the country that had provoked the theater-building spree in Times Square; with the decline in demand, Broadway had more theaters than it could fill. By the early thirties, plays were shown almost exclusively in Times Square's side streets; the great public places of Broadway and 42nd Street showed movies.

Times Square was in many ways the movie capital of the country. As the center of the entertainment world, Broadway had the grandest movie houses in the country; as the favorite source of Hollywood's material, it served as the eastern headquarters for virtually all the big film companies. But Broadway didn't make the movies; Hollywood did. And so Broadway didn't matter as it had before; the expressions that Americans had on the tips of their tongues, their favorite characters, their jokes, and their gossip, no longer issued from Times Square. The beloved stars moved to Hollywood. The glossy magazines glorified the sun-shot world of Hollywood, not Tin Pan Alley or the Main Stem.

And just as the movies were displacing 42nd Street from the center of the universe, the rabble was laying siege to the street's fabled charms. The street, and Times Square itself, had long lived in a fine balance between the mob and all that was inaccessible to the mob—between the lobster palace and Hammerstein's Victoria, between the dance hall and the roof garden. But gradually the elite had begun to exit Times Square in favor of the more sheltered precincts of Fifth Avenue; and the masses increasingly filled the vacuum. The decline of 42nd Street can be dated to as early as 1925, when Murray's Roman Gardens, a relic from the age of the lobster palaces, closed up and was quickly replaced by Hubert's Flea Circus, a Coney Island–style dime museum with sword swallowers and freaks and, of course, trained fleas. But it was the Depression that really killed the old elegance, because cheap and crude forms of entertainment like the dime-a-dance hall and burlesque quickly replaced more expensive and refined ones.

Burlesque traced its lineage back to *The Black Crook* and Lydia Thompson's Blondes, and then forward to the hootchy-kootchy dance that made "Little Egypt" the sensation of the Chicago World's Fair of 1893. Burlesque was a world of dirty songs, crude jokes, and women in frilly underthings shaking whatever they had (and that was usually a very great deal). Irving Zeidman, a historian of the form, crisply sums up its place in the galaxy of the arts by noting that "while variety became vaudeville and aligned itself with talent, burlesque became itself and aligned itself with dirt." Burlesque gradually moved northward from the stews of the Lower East Side to Union Square, and thence to Harlem. And then, in 1931, Billy

Minsky, the Ziegfeld—or perhaps the Hammerstein—of burlesque, breached the final barrier when he took over the Republic Theatre, which Hammerstein himself had built, and which for many years had served as the headquarters of David Belasco. The arrival of burlesque on 42nd Street was as shocking a proof of decline as the conversion of the Palace to a movie house.

By this time, the erotic dance had given way to the striptease; the girls stripped down to a G-string, and nothing else. Artists of the strip like Gypsy Rose Lee and Sally Rand hadn't yet come along to give burlesque its air of tawdry glamour. *Variety,* no nest of prudes, described the girls at Minsky's opening as "too inelegant, too dumb and too dirty to be called a troupe," and called the show "the cheapest dirt, the dirtiest coochers ever forced upon a stage or platform." Minsky's was actually considered high-class burlesque; the dearth of both plays and vaudeville meant that he could feature actual Broadway talent in the chorus and charge as much as $1.50 for seats. But when the Eltinge, at the other end of 42nd Street, began to offer four-a-day shows with cheap seats, Minsky was forced to follow suit. And then the Apollo went burlesque, and then the Central, at 48th Street, and the Gaiety, at 46th. Times Square seemed to be returning to the lubricious men-only world of early vaudeville.

The Times Square of the mid-1930s still had glamorous nightclubs and black-tie openings and giant spectaculars lighting up Broadway in a hundred colors; but the character of the place, and especially the character of the place in the harsh light of day, had become irretrievably tawdry. The Depression had burst, and burst forever, the glittering bubble blown by Ziegfeld and Hammerstein and George Rector and the Castles. And this collapse, so sudden and so sweeping, wrung the heartstrings of Broadway's leading citizens. A new form of literature came to flourish in Times Square—the dirge, the woeful lament of "O tempora!, O mores!" In 1933, the great George M. Cohan, a child of Broadway if ever there was one, wrote an impromptu and thoroughly disgusted ditty:

It means the increase in honky-tonk joints,
The blast of the radios from the amplifiers hanging over dance-hall
    doorways,
The pedlers and the barkers shouting at the top of their lungs:

"Buy a balloon an' act natural";

"Come in and see the great flea circus";

"This way for a good time, folks";

"No tights in this show";

"Plenty of seats in the first balcony; 'She Kissed Him to Death' just
   starting";

"Magnificent love story; bring the children."

The decline of Broadway provoked Stanley Walker, hard-boiled city
editor, into a mighty blast of dismay. The street, he wrote, "has degenerated into something resembling the main drag of a frontier town. . . .
There are chow-meineries, peep shows for men only, flea circuses, lectures on what killed Rudolf Valentino, jitney ballrooms and a farrago of
other attractions which would have sickened the heart of the Broad-
wayite of even ten years ago." The great old chophouses had given way to
penny restaurants, "where a derelict just this side of starvation may get
something known as food for as little as one cent." The very faces on the
street had become grotesque: "cauliflower ears, beggars, sleazy crones,
skinny girls who would be out of place in even the cheapest dance hall,
twisted old men, sleek youths with pale faces, the blind and the maimed."

   Broadway had, in short, turned into Coney Island, a street carnival
staged for the tourist and the boob. Runyon had adored and immortalized
the Broadway street life, but by the early thirties Runyon was spending
more time in Miami than at Lindy's. Where were the hoods of yesteryear?
This new world was a ceaseless yammer of religious nuts and self-styled
magicians and novelty salesmen—itching powders and exploding cigars—
and hot dog vendors and con artists and even, late at night on the east side
of Broadway, dope peddlers. Runyon's Dream Street, the block behind the
Palace, was no longer, just as the Palace itself was no longer. The gossip
columnists Jack Lait and Lee Mortimer wrote, "Its 200 yards are lined almost unbrokenly by cheap hotels and rooming houses sheltering all manner of strange characters: retired vaudevillians, down-and-out horseplayers,
dope fiends, grifters and grafters, pickpockets, derelicts (male and female),
drunks, stage widows, miserly recluses, tars and their tarts, crap-game-
steerers and bottom-dealers." Here, by the way, was a subspecies of the new
literature of decline: the epic enumeration of depravity.

Nowhere was the change more drastic than on 42nd Street, increasingly the home of shooting galleries and peep arcades and dumb movies. As the theaters passed into the hands of the banks, they emerged with very different owners. In 1931, William and Harry Brandt, who had made a living in movies and low-grade vaudeville in the city's more humble neighborhoods, bought the Lyric Theatre, tried a diet of four-a-day vaudeville, and then switched to second-run movies. The Brandts took over the Apollo in 1932, and then the Times Square, the Selwyn, the Eltinge, and the Republic—the block of theaters that would later form the core of the porn empire of the 1960s. The Rialto, which had been showing movies at the northwest corner of Broadway and 42nd since 1916, was torn down in 1935 to make way for the New Rialto, whose first feature was *Fang and Claw*. The New Rialto was open all day and well into the night, and charged as little as 25 cents a ticket. These theaters, like the burlesque shows and the dime-a-dance halls and the penny restaurants, brought a very different kind of customer to 42nd Street: the lowlife whose many faces Stanley Walker had catalogued.

Burlesque actually had a very short life span in Times Square. Here was a species of show so crude that many of the critics found it as deplorable as the moralists did. But what killed burlesque was not so much dirt as menace. The burlesque theater spilled out into the street in the form of barkers and steerers who tried to whip the customers inside; giant posters of half-naked girls blared from under the marquees. The burlesque theater seemed to degrade the street in the same way as the sex shop and the porn movie house would in the 1960s; it posed, in effect, an ecological danger. At hearings in 1932, the New York City license commissioner, James F. Geraghty, said that the lobbies of the burlesque houses served as "loitering places for men who trade on the shady side of night life." A *New York Times* editorial complained, "The alleged obscenity of the burlesque shows is exceeded by their external frowsiness. The neighborhood of such theaters takes on the character of a slum."

The crusade against burlesque, later mocked and memorialized in *The Night They Raided Minsky's,* was fueled by fears that Broadway was sinking beneath a mighty wave of trash. Fiorello La Guardia's license commissioner, Paul Moss, whose brother B. S. Moss was an old nickelodeon operator who had become a producer and movie house owner, devoted himself to cleaning up burlesque; when that proved hopeless, on May 2, 1937, he revoked the licenses of all fourteen of the city's burlesque houses. "This is the beginning of the end of incorporated filth," said the mayor. And it was—for the nonce. The houses were reopened under regulations prohibiting the striptease. Clean burlesque was, of course, a contradiction in terms, and by 1942 the brief reign of burlesque had come to an inglorious end.

As burlesque waned on 42nd Street, so did legitimate theater. By the mid-1930s, the only house still showing plays on 42nd Street was the redoubtable New Amsterdam. In January 1937, Walter Huston starred in *Othello;* and that would be the last play mounted on 42nd Street for over forty years. In July, the New Amsterdam reopened under new ownership as a movie theater. The first feature was *A Midsummer Night's Dream*—the very same show which, in a different medium, had inaugurated this art nouveau castle in 1903.

IT SEEMS A STRANGE irony that the quality of theatrical writing improved markedly as the cultural power of theater declined; but perhaps it's no irony at all. As Broadway lost its status as the proving ground for national culture, where plays were hatched to be distributed to the hustings, theater became an increasingly local medium, needing to please only a local, and of course, sophisticated audience. Movies took on the burden of suiting the lowest common denominator. And as the grip of Broadway culture on the national imagination weakened, or perhaps as viewers counted on the movies to glorify that magic world, dramatists began to look far beyond the confines of Times Square for their subject matter. Few of the leading playwrights of the thirties were themselves Broadway figures, as George S. Kaufman and Marc Connelly and Moss Hart were; they were biographers, essayists, advocates, novelists, and whatnot. Some of them, like Elmer Rice, professed to despise the theater as a thoroughly compromised medium of expression, while others tried their hand at plays to earn their keep while doing something they deemed more important, like crusading for justice. The 1930s was the era of Depression and the onset of war, and thus of intense ideological mobilization, at least within the intelligentsia; the drama of the time was exalted, and sometimes banalized, by those profound concerns.

There can be little question about the difference in quality. Very few plays from the 1920s or earlier have made it into the semiofficial canon of school anthologies and beloved revivals, but at least a dozen Broadway shows from the 1930s have achieved that status. The list includes, but is scarcely limited to, Maxwell Anderson's *High Tor*, William Saroyan's *The Time of Your Life*, Clifford Odets's *Golden Boy*, Thornton Wilder's *Our Town*, Lillian Hellman's *The Little Foxes*, John Steinbeck's *Of Mice and Men*, Cole Porter's *Anything Goes*, and George Gershwin's *Porgy and Bess*—almost certainly the greatest musical work mounted on Broadway up to that time. In the 1933–34 season, when *42nd Street* was stealing Broadway's thunder and the number and profitability of shows was dropping like a shot, theatergoers could attend O'Neill's *Ah, Wilderness!*, Sidney Howard's *Yellow Jack*, Gershwin and Kaufman's satirical musical *Let 'Em Eat Cake*, and *Tobacco Road*, Jack Kirkland's adaptation of Erskine Caldwell's bleak novel of sharecropper life, which ran for 3,182 performances.

The best plays of the thirties were both more serious and more literary than the drama of the previous generation. Plays like *Of Mice and Men* and *Tobacco Road* exposed theatergoers to a world of rural immiseration utterly foreign to them. In *They Shall Not Die*, John Wexley bluntly condemned the police, attorney, and judges responsible for locking up the Scottsboro Boys, nine young black men who had been falsely, and sensationally, charged with raping two white women in 1931. In *There Shall Be No Night*, of 1940, Robert Sherwood, who in previous works had denounced militarism and declared an equal pox on all the houses of Europe, reversed himself and urged his listeners to accept the necessity of war to defend democracy against totalitarianism. Meanwhile, the protean Orson Welles was shocking audiences with a haunting voodoo version of *Macbeth* set in Haiti, as well as a modern-dress interpretation of *Julius Caesar*.

As Kaufman, the master satirist and wit, was the prototypical playwright of his age, so Clifford Odets, the inflamed pamphleteer, was the emblematic figure of Broadway in the thirties. Odets was a struggling actor who in the early thirties had joined the Group Theatre, a cooperative that brought together actors like Lee J. Cobb, John Garfield, and Franchot Tone; directors like Elia Kazan; and instructors like Sanford Meisner and Stella Adler. Though the Group Theatre was not originally politicized, many of its members, and above all Odets, were deeply marked by the growing radicalization of the time. In 1934, Odets, who had never had a play produced, wrote *Waiting for Lefty*, an anticapitalist tract barely disguised as a drama. In a thrilling *coup de théâtre*, the actors turned to address the audience directly, turning the theater into a union hall and the spectators into fellow workers; at the climax, when word arrived that the heroic Lefty had been murdered by company goons, first the actors, and then the patrons in the seats, took up the cry "Strike! Strike! Strike!"—and the identification was complete. *Waiting for Lefty* ran for 168 performances on Broadway and was subsequently performed by special troupes all over the country, several of whom were dragged off to jail by outraged local authorities.

Odets turned out to be a gifted playwright who knew how to reproduce real feelings and real speech; he quickly learned to embed the doctrine in the narrative. Jacob, the embittered patriarch of *Awake and Sing!*, views capitalism as legalized theft and is given to such stony pronouncements as "If this life leads to a revolution it's a good thing. Otherwise, it's for nothing." Odets seems to share Jacob's views, yet *Awake and Sing!* is far from the blunt agitprop spirit of *Waiting for Lefty*, which it followed by only a year. The play revolves around the struggle of a young man to break free from his all-consuming mother. *Awake and Sing!* has something of O'Neill's harsh realism, though it is at the same time infused with Odets's fervid romanticism about human prospects. The dialogue abounds with the Yiddish turns of speech—"You gave the dog eat?"; "He should talk to you an old man?"—that Moss Hart and S. N. Behrman must have heard at home every day, but would never have dreamed of putting into a play. The world of Broadway is all but invisible from the family's Bronx tenement; Jacob's son Myron absentmindedly picks his teeth as his daughter reads of the doings of Sophie Tucker. What matters, finally, is not political revolution but personal liberation—"Get-what-it-takes," as one character puts it. Myron doesn't have it; life has squashed him flat. But Ralph, Myron's son and the play's protagonist, just might. Jacob makes Ralph the beneficiary of his will and then, horribly, arranges his own death. And Ralph, finally independent, accepts the dreadful sacrifice with joy. "I saw he was dead and I was born," he declares, in the kind of melodramatic speechifying to which Odets was much given. "I swear to God, I'm one week old!"

The plays of the thirties were notoriously engagé, but they were also very often set at a great distance from the audience's place and time, in Lincoln's day or in that of Mary, Queen of Scots. They aspired, as literature does, to universal truths rather than to the kind of immediacy and familiarity that delighted the audience of *The Front Page*, not to mention *Earl Carroll's Vanities*. Theater traditionally depends on topicality to forge a bond with the audience. And yet Thornton Wilder, a novelist whose subject was almost always "the human condition" rather than any particular transitory state of affairs, devised in *Our Town* a form of drama wholly removed from the particular. The village in which the play is set, Grover's Corners, New Hampshire, has the generality of allegory; it could be—indeed, is—anywhere. Wilder even dispenses with incident itself, an act of daring and a conscious flirtation with tedium that few authors before Samuel Beckett even thought to attempt.

The stratum of life Wilder seeks lies below the busyness and turbulence of event. "This is the way we were," says the Stage Manager, who narrates the comings and goings of Grover's Corners: "In our growing up and in our marrying and in our living and in our dying." The prose itself aspires to a kind of stately, reverential quietude. *Our Town* has no wit, no politics, no "views." The small-town folk talk endlessly about the weather and express themselves in the kind of earnest aphorisms that would have marked them as oafs in the sparkling drama of an earlier generation. The play's faith in common wisdom is a rebuke to urbanity itself. But Wilder doesn't mean the rebuke: *Our Town* wishes to recall us to our common humanity, and to remind us that death settles all differences and stills all vanity. And the wiseacres of Broadway, to their great credit, recognized *Our Town* for what it was. Jed Harris, who had produced and directed many of Broadway's wittiest and most self-referential shows, directed the play with the softest of hands. And the work was hailed as "a gentle masterpiece" by that most prolix and noisy of critics, Alexander Woollcott.

Men like George M. Cohan and Stanley Walker and the columnist Jack Lait, who recoiled in horror before the new Broadway of dance halls and penny arcades, had been raised in, and in some cases had helped shape, the old Broadway of the lobster palace and the roof garden. But younger men could not share their nostalgia, or their horror. A. J. Liebling was born in 1904; the Times Square he knew as a rich kid growing up on Park Avenue was the Times Square of the speakeasy and of the fight crowd hanging out at Jacobs Beach. Liebling was an impudent and mischief-making character who loved the con artists and sidewalk mythologizers of Times Square. All forms of fabrication, so long as they were ingenious or at least preposterous, appealed to him; and as a young reporter on *The World-Telegram,* he returned again and again to the petty characters of Broadway. He covered Commissioner Geraghty's 1932 hearing on burlesque and quoted Geraghty heartily defending Professor Heckler's Flea Circus, the star attraction of Hubert's Museum, whose license was also up for renewal. Billy Minsky sniffed, "I will not tell my girls that they have been compared with fleas. They would be much offended." "Well," one of the lawyers cracked, "at least the fleas wear clothes."

Liebling yearned to write for the arch and saucy *New Yorker;* and in 1935, he got his wish. His already prodigious literary gifts were polished to a yet brighter sheen by contact with his fellow wags at *The New Yorker,* as well as by the opportunity to write at greater length and with greater leisure; but his subject matter, and his essential tone, changed not at all. Liebling wrote about the nobodies of Times Square, and especially about the nobodies in its northern reaches, which Damon Runyon had haunted the decade before. He wrote of Izzy Yereshevsky, the proprietor of the I. & Y. cigar store at 49th Street and Seventh Avenue and genial host to a free-floating late-night salon. Liebling delicately pumped Izzy and his patrons full of the hot air of mock-epic. He wrote, "Most of his evening guests—their purchases are so infrequent that it would be misleading to call them customers—wear white felt hats and overcoats of a style known to them as English drape. . . . Short men peer up from beneath the wide-flung shoulders of these coats as if they had been lowered into the garment on a rope and were now trying to climb out." (Is it any wonder that Liebling laughed out loud as he typed?) Each of these men, he wrote, "fosters a little legend of lost affluence; fifty grand dropped on the races in one day, twenty grand blown on a doll in a brief sojourn at Atlantic City. Never to have been in the chips marks one as a punk or a smalltimer. It precludes conversation in big figures."

Liebling was the bard of Times Square in its era of picturesque impoverishment. He wrote a long profile of Hymie Katz, a local virtuoso of the con who ran a racetrack "tipping service" in which he scammed out-of-town ministers and doctors. Hymie was a hero at the I. & Y. "Hymie is a man who knows how to get a dollar," said the habitués. Hymie had opened twenty-five nightclubs in his day, and took a view of them which precluded all forms of sentiment. "What is a nightclub?" he sneers. "Spit and toilet paper." Hymie explained how it was possible to open a nightclub with nothing more than a loan of $50, which was the figure required to retain a lawyer in order to draw up a lease for one of the innumerable basement rooms in the West Forties usable for nothing save a nightspot. Hymie would then flourish the lease, and a great deal of promotional and by no means credible nonsense, before a hat-check concessionaire who would front $3,000; use these funds to lease cut-rate supplies from a nightclub equipment supplier, and to buy liquor; and then sell jobs to waiters— $400 for the captain, $200 for the headwaiters, $50 for the rest of the staff. "Waiters like to work for Hymie because he lets them take whatever they can get," Liebling writes. He quotes Hymie as saying, "Most of the stealing they do is from the customers, so what do I care?"

Liebling was a famous gourmet and gourmand, but he rarely wrote about New York's fine restaurants; likewise, he considered the great clubs of the day unworthy journalistic material. He referred to the Times Square of the late Depression as a "famine area"; and it was life under famine conditions that stirred his imagination and provoked his humor. Liebling's masterpiece in this spirit of Daumier was a series of articles about the Jollity Building, a fictional office building formed out of several real-life low-rises on Broadway in the upper Forties. Liebling guides the reader through the many layers of the Jollity with the rapt attention of Dante surveying the Inferno; as his Virgil he recruits the Jollity's rental agent, Marty, "a thin, sallow man of 40 whose complexion has been compared, a little unfairly, to that of a dead robin." On the ground floor of the Jollity are eight phone booths manned by what Marty calls the "Telephone Booth Indians," "because in their lives the telephone booth furnishes sustenance as well as shelter, as the buffalo did for the Arapahoe and the Sioux." A Telephone Booth Indian who puts a few dollars together through, say, successful bookmaking may graduate to one of the tiny cubicles on the third floor, in which case he becomes a "heel." And if a heel can put together a down payment on an unfurnished office upstairs—say, through booking a few animals acts at a nightclub—he may graduate to the rarefied status of "tenant," though it tends to be a very transitory state. "A dispossessed tenant often reappears in the Jollity Building as an Indian," Liebling writes. "It is a life cycle."

A quarter of a century earlier, Julian Street, the Liebling of his day, had recoiled in disgust from the hedonism and heedlessness of Broadway. A decade after that, Damon Runyon hadn't blinked at hoods pumping bullets into one another, though he had sentimentalized street urchins like Dream Street Rose. But now that hedonism was itself a distant memory, and the remaining hoods were small change, Liebling neither excoriates nor sentimentalizes; he records, with anthropological care and journalistic zest, the innumerable, and only rarely legal, means by which the residents of the Jollity Building earn their precarious living. Liebling notes that in the precincts of the Jollity, a "promoter" is understood to be "any man who mulcts another man of a dollar, or any fraction or multiple thereof," and that the highest praise among the residents is "He has promoted some very smart people." Liebling's gallery of small-time promoters includes Hockticket Charlie, a booking agent who on the side sells pawn tickets enabling the holder to redeem objects that are, in fact, trash, and Lotsandlots, who sells phony land lots secured by phony deeds. But the noblest figure in the rogues' gallery is surely Maxwell C. Bimberg, known as the Count de Pennies, owing both to his waxed mustache and his reputation for tightfistedness. The Count is a publicity agent who cons everyone he comes across, including such otherwise unpromotable figures as strippers, bookmakers, and nightclub owners. After the Count steals several thousand dollars, he gambles it all away at the track and is soon back to begging nickels for phone calls. Even his marks admire the Count's bravado. "The Count de Pennies was never no good to nobody," says Marty, "but he was the champion heel of the Jollity Building."

It is Liebling's characters, not Liebling himself, who invent the nicknames and the slang that pepper his prose—or at least, he puts the words in their mouths. An exotic language seems to arise almost unconsciously from the exotic lives they lead in the sheltered village of Times Square. "I like the country," says Whitey Bimstein, a fight manager of ancient vintage. "It is a great spot." Times Square's language was a Yiddish, showbiz, midway patois; but not only that. Innumerable flavors made the Broadway stew. Liebling's only rival as a Broadway folklorist, his friend and *New Yorker* colleague Joe Mitchell, quotes the bearded lady of Hubert's Museum, an ex-Tarheel like himself, as follows: "When I was a young'un I taken the name Princess Olga. After I first got married I changed to Madame, but when every confounded swami-woman and mitt-reader in the nation taken to calling herself Madame So-and-So, I decided Lady was more ree-fined."

It was language that became Broadway's great cultural export when theater lost its salience. In the twenties, Damon Runyon and Walter Winchell and Ring Lardner and the staff of *Variety* began to reproduce the village slang of Broadway, and soon the knowing cosmopolites back in Evansville were talking about rats who got bumped off when they squawked. As the cultural historian William Taylor has written, "Press replaced theater as the voice of the area, a transfer of energy . . . from stage to page." But Runyonese, or Winchellese, was a cartoon language, a language more invented than overheard; it was a theatrical product every bit as much as what Kaufman was offering on the stage. Liebling and Mitchell, and Mark Hellinger and Ben Hecht and Myron Berger, were newspapermen, with a gifted reporter's ear for the peculiarities of speech and behavior. In their language, the reader could feel the strange combination of provinciality and cosmopolitanism that made Times Square.

It is from Mitchell, as much as from Liebling, that we receive the sense of Times Square in the years just before World War II as an enclosed garden in which the strangest, the most endearingly misshapen, flowers bloomed. Mitchell was a quiet and gracious Southerner, a meditative character who seemed to identify with the sadness of the oddballs he portrayed. His profile of Jane Barnell—Lady Olga—is an act of loving observation; the hyperbolic sense of dignity of this woman who carefully wraps her beard in a scarf when heading out for a cup of coffee is touching rather than absurd. "Some of Miss Barnell's less gifted colleagues are inclined to think that she is haughty," Mitchell writes, deadpan, "but she feels that a woman with a beard more than a foot long has the right to be haughty." A time would come, a few decades hence, when Hubert's was a dive; but Mitchell's Hubert's is the New Amsterdam of the dime museum. Professor Roy Heckler, maestro of the flea circus, drops his flock, one by one, onto his forearm, "where they browse for fifteen minutes," while he smokes, reads the paper, and shares a quiet moment with his friend Lady Olga. "Taciturn herself," Mitchell writes, "Miss Barnell does not care for talkative people."

Mitchell and Liebling created a Times Square that lives today—and not merely through the golden haze of memory. When we mourn the passing of a Broadway that once was and never will be again, few of us try to wish back the top-hatted and white-tied Broadway of Ziegfeld and the Castles, and Fitzgerald and his Princeton pals. Those images are not only too remote in time, they are, in a way, too contaminated by privilege and wealth. We are all populists now, and few of us would wish back a place so gaudy, so deluxe, so unattainable. That Times Square does not feel authentic to us in the way that the Times Square of Hubert's and the Jollity Building does. *That* Times Square is a populist place—the home of carny populism. People like Izzy and Marty and the Count de Pennies and Lady Olga have a kind of proprietary right to Times Square; what we most wish for Times Square is that it be hospitable to eccentrics like them. And we wish that because Liebling and Mitchell made these characters so very alive, and somehow endowed them with the life of the place, as if they were its indwelling genius. Most of us, had we been alive then, would have passed through Times Square without even noticing the I. & Y. cigar shop; Times Square would not have been to us what it was to Liebling and Mitchell. But we live with their Times Square, as surely as we live with the Times Square of *Guys and Dolls* or *Broadway Melody of 1929*.

We want to have a Times Square that is hospitable to Izzy Yereshevsky—even though Izzy's grandchildren probably now live in Westchester. In the debate over what Times Square should be, the pull of carny populism was, and remains, powerful. We can't help feeling inauthentic in the face of the vital, tawdry Times Square of 1938. But we cannot have it back; we cannot have a Times Square that Joe Liebling would have loved.

A WORLD
CONQUERED BY THE
MOTION PICTURE

A T 7:03 P.M., August 14, 1945, the words America had been waiting for flashed across the news ribbon running round the Times Tower:
"Official—Truman announces Japanese surrender." At that moment, according to a news account the following day, the half-million people
packed into Times Square sent up a mighty roar that surged across the
great open space for a full twenty minutes. Workers in the buildings
around the square unleashed a mighty shower of paper and confetti.
"Men and women embraced—there were no strangers in New York yesterday." And then something happened that seems yet more remarkable
to us today: people all over New York left their homes in order to flood
into Times Square. They certainly didn't need to read the news on the
Times Tower; they could have learned a great deal more by staying home
and listening to the radio. But they wanted to share this moment of sub-
lime emotion with their fellow citizens; and so they converged on the central spot of their world. By ten P.M., the crowd had reached two million,
the largest gathering in the history of Times Square, and possibly in the
history of the republic. The area from 40th to 52nd Streets, and from
Sixth Avenue to Eighth, was one solid mass of joyful humanity, kissing,
hugging, sobbing, or simply gazing in wordless relief and delight. And
they did not want to leave. Half a million people were still jammed into

Times Square at three A.M, which means that many had stayed on their feet for seven or eight hours.

It is hard to imagine any comparable event today, for we have lost the habit of congregating, and television has become our town square. But up until the age of mass suburbanization—which is to say, up through the end of World War II—urbanites were in the habit of gathering in central places at moments of high importance, and they derived comfort and re-assurance from the massed presence of fellow citizens (or, in the case of the mob, from the sense of massed fury). And Times Square was the agora of our greatest urban culture. Ever since the beginning of the twen-tieth century, New Yorkers had been collecting in Times Square not only for the festivities of New Year's but for the more somber business of pres-idential elections, and for the great prizefights, and for the seventh game of the World Series. The photographs of the time, with great seas of men in dark suits and gray fedoras, their necks craned up toward the "zipper" on the Times Tower, remind us of this moment of mid-century urban glory.

The photograph that memorialized V-J Day, and indeed the one picture of Times Square that occupies a secure, everlasting place in the national pantheon of received images, is the one the *Life* magazine photographer Alfred Eisenstaedt took of a sailor in his dress blues scooping up a white-clad and wholly unsuspecting nurse and planting an ardent kiss on her lips. What the picture is principally about is the historic moment—the immense relief, the jubilation, the abandon, the no-strangers-in-New-York. But it is also about a place. Eisenstaedt captured a *Life* magazine version of Times Square, a place of vast crowds, of incongruous meetings, of free-dom and expressiveness and cheap thrills—a kind of all-American urban playground. The Times Square of that era, as the writer Jan Morris re-marks, "had a frank and jolly air to it, and there was an impudent naivete even to its naughtiest activities."

A new, middlebrow Times Square emerged in the 1940s, a Times Square neither gracious nor derelict. Elegant nightlife had migrated to Fifth Ave-nue and to the East Side; the great clubs of the twenties and thirties had given way to shabby little basement boîtes, or to such giant emporia as the Latin Quarter or Billy Rose's Diamond Horseshoe, where a sailor could take his girl for dinner and a gaudy show. Ripley's Wax Museum had opened up on the west side of Broadway between 43rd and 44th. Forty-second Street was now lined with big late-night cafeterias and pinball arcades and gimmick shops and even a few bookstores selling girlie magazines. The great old theaters of 42nd Street had been converted to "grinder houses," showing cheap action movies (but not pornography) until deep into the night. The street hosted forms of naughtiness that passed far beyond impudent naïveté, including drug dealing and male prostitution, but visitors who weren't looking for the criminal underside rarely encountered it.

Times Square had become a place of benevolent eccentricity. America was a country on the move in the years after World War II, and the square came to be seen as the great junction point through which much of the vagrant population of the country passed, a place epic in its variousness and its sheer oddity. Jack Kerouac caught this spirit in his first novel, *The Town and the City,* published in 1950. Times Square, he wrote, "was the one part to which all the 'characters' eventually migrated across the land at one time or another in their lonewolf scattering lives." The young Kerouac, still very much in the grip of Thomas Wolfe, then looses a cataract of the incongruous: "The Broadway weisenheimer-gambler glancing at the old farmer with bundle wrapped in newspaper who gapes and bumps into everyone. . . . The mellow gentleman in the De Pinna suit headed for the Ritz Bar, and the mellow gentleman staggering by and sitting down in the gutter, to spit and groan and be hauled off by cops. . . . The robust young rosy-cheeked priest from Fordham with some of his jayvee basketballers on 'a night of good clean fun,' and the cadaverous morphineaddict stumbling full of shuddering misery in search of a fix."

That Eisenstaedt photograph captured a Times Square poised on a kind of pinnacle. The census of 1950 was the last one showing that more Americans lived in cities than in towns or the countryside; the suburbs were soon to change the balance. New York was holding steady at eight million people, most fully assimilated and middle-class or at least working-class; the "urban crisis" was somewhere over the horizon. Most of the country's wealth was still in the cities; most of its poverty was still in the countryside. Most cities were safe, clean, and orderly. And Times Square was the last word in seedy, thrilling urbanity at a moment when urbanity itself was still prized. Yes, it could feel dangerous, but usually just in the shivery way a funhouse did. As late as 1959, the cops in the fabled 16th Precinct, which covered 42nd to 50th from Fifth Avenue to the Hudson River, reported virtually no drug arrests (perhaps they weren't looking too much harder than the tourists) and relatively little serious crime. Their worst problem, they said, was street peddlers.

THE IRONY OF THIS booming, bustling, frank, and jolly postwar Times Square is that it no longer made a cultural product that the rest of the country really cared about. The cross streets between Broadway and Eighth Avenue were still lined with theaters, but the numbers both of playhouses and of plays continued to shrink in the years after the war. People went to the movies instead; and then, increasingly in the fifties, they were staying home to watch TV. Much of the theatergoing and nightclub-going population had decamped for the suburbs. And since old fire codes had prevented the building of skyscrapers on top of theaters, though not of movie houses, the theaters became increasingly poor competitors in the Darwinian struggle of real estate values. Along 48th Street, known as the Street of Hits, first one theater, then another, closed up. By 1948, 80 percent of Broadway actors were said to be unemployed; by the 1950–51 season, only eighty-one shows were mounted in Times Square theaters. Arthur Miller and Tennessee Williams were writing widely admired plays, and people were going to see them; but, as Brooks Atkinson remarked, "To go to the theater was like going to a minor, subsidiary social event."

Yet, at the same time, live entertainment retained its old prestige. The great stars established themselves on the stage before the new gods, Hollywood and radio and TV, swept them into the ether. What's more, the stars needed to reaffirm their bond with an adoring public through regular public appearances. And Times Square was still the capital of live entertainment. Ever since the twenties, the great movie theaters of Broadway—the Paramount, the Strand, the Capitol, the Rivoli, Loew's State—had been showcasing the comedians and dancers and divas and leading men in the elaborate shows they mounted between movies. Of these, the greatest was surely the Paramount, a lavish Xanadu that Adolph Zukor, the czar of the studio, had reared on the west side of

Broadway between 43rd and 44th, as a showcase for its talent. The theater, which opened in 1926 at a cost of $16.5 million, sat beneath Times Square's tallest office building, which in turn was topped by a glass globe twenty feet in diameter. The globe was intended to signify "the world conquest by the motion picture," a conquest soon to become all the more indisputable with the introduction of the talkie. A clock, facing in all four directions, had been incorporated into the globe, and it was well known that you could always tell the time in Times Square by looking up at the Paramount clock. The Paramount was a behemoth that seated almost four thousand patrons (proportions nevertheless rendered modest by comparison with the Roxy's 6,200), and was widely admired for its splendid acoustics. All the great stars under contract to the studio played there in the twenties and thirties—Maurice Chevalier, Gloria Swanson, Gary Cooper, Eddie Cantor, Fred Astaire, Mary Pickford, Ginger Rogers, Rudy Vallee, Ray Bolger, Danny Kaye, Jack Benny, Bob Hope. Bing Crosby's record-shattering ten-week engagement in 1931–32 vaulted him from stardom to superstardom. Like the other big Broadway movie houses, the Paramount was famous for immense, lavish productions. The theatre had its own corps de ballet, dancing chorus, choral group, and seventy-piece symphony orchestra. The two mighty Wurlitzer organs always cued the smashing finale.

In 1935, the Paramount began to regularly book the big bands, who had taken the nation by storm. Jitterbugging was said to have been invented when kids at a 1937 Benny Goodman concert began dancing up and down the aisles. There was no bigger gig than the Paramount; Tommy Dorsey, Glenn Miller, Paul Whiteman, Duke Ellington, and Goodman all played frequent engagements there. On December 30, 1942, Goodman featured an "Extra Added Attraction," a skinny kid who sang with Dorsey; he was, of course, Frank Sinatra. Sinatra stayed at the Paramount for eight weeks, and during that time he became an object of adolescent devotion such as no singer ever had before, nor would again until Elvis Presley, if then. He drove fifteen-year-old girls insane. The "bobby-soxers" would scream and faint and weep and hurl themselves at the stage; they came first thing in the morning, and left late at night.

At first, the Sinatra phenomenon was dismissed, at least by highbrow critics, as a momentary craze. But when Sinatra played a return engagement in October 1944, he sparked what became known as the Columbus Day Riot at the Paramount. Despite a curfew, kids began gathering at the box office the night before the first show. A line ten thousand teenagers long snaked down 43rd Street, up Eighth Avenue, and back down 44th. Twenty thousand more kids clogged Times Square. Hundreds of policemen were called away from the Columbus Day Parade to keep order. But to no avail: according to Arnold Shaw, one of Sinatra's biographers, "The ticket booth was destroyed in the crush. Shop windows were smashed. Passersby were trampled and girls fainted. When the first show finished, only 250 came out of the thirty-six-hundred-seat house. . . . A woman on line with her daughter told a reporter that the girl had threatened to kill herself unless she saw the show." It was an echt Times Square moment: mammoth crowds, unrestrained glee, more than a hint of danger, and, above all, the instant, irrefutable proof of public adoration.

In a world conquered by the motion pictures, Times Square still provided an indispensable stage for "legitimate" performance. But in a world conquered by television, performance itself became irrelevant. Why pay for the stage show at the Paramount when Ed Sullivan was dishing out the same fare for free? In 1950, 4.4 million American households owned a television set; by 1960, the figure had reached 60 million. And the great stages of Broadway went dark. The Paramount put an end to the shows in 1952 (though Sinatra played yet another sold-out engagement in 1956). The Capitol, at 51st Street, had long since shifted to an all-movies schedule. The Roxy, which had showcased Milton Berle and Jack Benny and Cab Calloway, gave up the stage show in 1948; in 1960, the theater, on the northeast corner of 50th and Seventh, was demolished to make way for an office building. The Capitol went soon thereafter.

Times Square had one last ratifying role to play for Hollywood. The blockbuster movies that Hollywood began to turn out in the forties and fifties—gorgeous Technicolor fantasies set in ancient Rome or Egypt or Hawaii or never-never land—may have been made in a studio backlot, but they almost all opened on Broadway. Movies like *Quo Vadis?* and *White Christmas* and *Around the World in Eighty Days* had spectacular openings in one of the great movie palaces, with red carpets, mega- and mini-stars, klieg lights, madly shoving photographers, and gawking fans. These events were minutely orchestrated by the studios, who knew that nothing generated better publicity than a boffo opening in Times Square. *Cleopatra,* which, thanks to the affair between the stars, Richard Burton and Elizabeth Taylor, arrived trailing glorious clouds of scandal, opened in June 1963 at the Rivoli Theatre, on 49th Street between Broadway and Seventh, with ten thousand fans straining at police barricades. "As each celebrity-bearing limousine arrived," a reporter noted, "the people at the curb, their necks craning and their cameras ready, stood on tiptoe and leaned over at such an extreme angle that at times it seemed they would fall on the cars." It was the crowd—the kind of crowd available only in the pulsing, borderline-lunatic world of Times Square—that proved the movie's mass appeal. The Times Square of the middle of the century retained tremendous power as a symbol not of refined consumption, but of all-American fantasies and preferences.

ONE SPECIES OF THEATER still exercised a tight grip on the American imagination: the Broadway musical. Here is a very brief list of musicals from the 1940s alone: *Pal Joey,* 1940; *Oklahoma!,* 1943; *On the Town,* 1944; *Carousel,* 1945; *Annie Get Your Gun,* 1946; *Brigadoon* and *Finian's Rainbow,* 1947; *Kiss Me, Kate,* 1948; *South Pacific,* 1949. The shows were incredibly popular; *Oklahoma!* ran for 2,212 performances. And of course every single one was made into a movie, usually within a few years, and then seen by ten or twenty times as many people. But musicals bulked large in American life not simply because they were more popular than straight plays but because they provided Americans with a common idiom: the show tune. This was the era before the rise of folk or rock music; pop music meant, to an extraordinary degree, tunes written for musicals. These were the songs heard on the radio, the songs the leading vocalists sang, the songs people played on the piano at parties. Think of just a few of the songs from the shows listed above: "Beautiful Mornin'," "June Is Busting Out All Over," "Too Darn Hot," "There's No Business Like Show Business," "A Wonderful Guy," "Old Devil Moon," "Almost Like Being in Love."

Only a few musicals took anything like the thematic risks associated with serious Broadway theater. Most of them were fantasies designed to reaffirm the conventional world of the viewer. Beautiful girls walk around unwed until the right man comes along, at which point the two fall in love instantly; the greatest tragedy, from which one is providentially saved at the last moment, is choosing the wrong spouse; and, as they say in *Brigadoon,* "If you love someone deeply enough, anything can happen"— including suspending the laws of nature under which the hamlet of Brigadoon operates. Virtually all musicals drive their way relentlessly to marriage; the obstacles along the way tend to be fashioned from balsa wood. A work like *South Pacific* is exceptional not only because it involves yearnings that summon a man away from duty—the siren song of Bali Ha'i—but because something terribly serious—unexamined, bone-deep racism—must be faced and overcome before the marriage rites can be enacted.

But who went to a musical for the story? The story was the framework upon which the songs were hung. Many musicals featured a song that had virtually no relation to the action or the characters, but had been shoehorned in because it was just too wonderful to exclude, like "Too Darn Hot" in Cole Porter's *Kiss Me, Kate.* Indeed, Ethan Mordden, an indefatigable student of the musical, writes that *"Kiss Me, Kate* is a show we love not despite its sloppy realism and irrelevant hunks of Shakespeare"—it is a Broadway retelling of *The Taming of the Shrew*—"but because the score is so good that the rest doesn't matter." The score, by the way, includes "Why Can't You Behave?"; "So in Love"; "Always True to You (In My Fashion)"; "Where Is the Life That Late I Led?"; and "Brush Up Your Shakespeare."

Perhaps the prototypical musical—not the best or the most innovative—is Irving Berlin's *Annie Get Your Gun.* It is worth pausing over the fact that this was the same Irving Berlin who had begun plugging tunes in Tony Pastor's in the first years of the century. When he wrote "Alexander's Ragtime Band" in 1911, Berlin introduced ragtime to America, and got the country up and dancing in an era when the group dances of the nineteenth century were still in vogue. During World War I, Berlin told a simple truth that delighted both soldiers and their loved ones when he wrote "Oh! How I Hate to Get Up in the Morning." In the jazz age, he presented some of the most artful versions of the musical revue in his own Music Box Theatre. Berlin conjured up an unsinkable answer to Old Man Depression in songs like "Let's Have Another Cup of Coffee" from

Face the Music, and evoked the suffering of black life in New York in "Supper Time." In the thirties, he wrote the songs for Astaire-Rogers vehicles like *Top Hat* ("Cheek to Cheek" and "Let's Face the Music and Dance") and *Carefree.* In the years just before and during World War II, he wrote "God Bless America" and "White Christmas," two of the most popular songs in American history. And then, after all that, still just shy of sixty, he wrote *Annie Get Your Gun.*

Has there ever been such a career in the history of popular entertainment? It is not Berlin's longevity that is astounding, but rather his ability to capture the sound, and the mood, of one era after another. He seemed, at all moments and in all settings, to retain his magical access to the hearts of his listeners. There was something almost mythological about Berlin, the unlettered Jewish ragamuffin who could barely read music but who had songs pouring from his fingertips—like the Shakespeare who had little Latin and less Greek. A misty-eyed patriot and a self-made American, Berlin was Broadway's chief entry in the national pantheon; as Alexander Woollcott observed as early as 1924, "The life of Irving Berlin is a part of the American epic."

Annie Get Your Gun, like *Kiss Me, Kate,* is a Broadway show about show business. The show opens with the rousing anthem "There's No Business Like Show Business," in which strolling stagehands offer a rapturous tribute to the world Berlin had known and loved for half a century—the world that was, for him, the center of the universe. *Annie Get Your Gun* is a backstage musical about the rise of a Broadway star and her quest for the summum bonum of all musicals—love. Annie Oakley is torn between her desperate, doglike love for her fellow sharpshooter Frank Butler and her skills in a field where women are not supposed to excel. Thus her lament in "You Can't Get a Man with a Gun," which, like so many great Berlin songs, is a complex mechanism built out of what feel like remarkably simple parts: "They don't buy pajamas for pistol-packin' Mommas, / For a man may be hot but he's not when he's shot. . . ."

Annie cannot bring herself to sacrifice one for the other. She celebrates her unquenchable competitive fires in "Anything You Can Do," an exercise in the kind of western braggadocio made famous by Mark Twain and Ambrose Bierce that somehow morphs into a meistersinger competition in which Annie—Ethel Merman, in the original cast—holds a note until she busts. "Anything You Can Do" is both a song about virtuosity and itself an astonishing display of virtuosity: the story goes that Berlin was asked to supply a new song for the two leads, and fifteen minutes later called the director, Josh Logan, and sang the entire first chorus. "Most amazing thing I ever experienced in my whole life," Logan later said.

When Fred, the songwriting sensation of George S. Kaufman's *June Moon*, is ludicrously praised as the next Irving Berlin, an otherwise cynical showgirl immediately demurs. "There's something behind his songs," she says of Berlin. "They're sympathetic." Berlin never lost sight of the fact—never had to be told, for that matter—that in popular entertainment, all the ingenuity in the world doesn't matter if you don't have the audience on your side. His songs were always sympathetic, even when they were busy doing something else. Annie Oakley wins us over by her artlessness and her ardor, and by the competitive fire that keeps getting in the way of her amorous designs. And she remains sympathetic even as she becomes a more worldly figure. The Annie who sings "Lost in His Arms," with its lush, jazzy orchestrations, or the euphoric "I Got the Sun in the Morning," is not the woman who belted out "You Can't Get a Man with a Gun"; but we root for her to win Frank, and to stay true to herself, every bit as much as we had before. Berlin was as beguiling as Cole Porter or George Gershwin; but he also knew how to hit you where you lived. He was the past master of what Gilbert Seldes called the lively arts—the art forms that seek to appeal to a mass public, that speak to concerns which are topical and local rather than universal, and which, nevertheless, at times transcend their own modest ambitions.

TIMES SQUARE IN THE forties and fifties, and even into the sixties, was a fabulously romantic place. The place showed its age, and its sores, in the daytime, but it was still glamorous and enthralling at night. The classy entertainment may have moved eastward, but in Times Square, and nowhere else, the night was charged with the glories of the spectacular. The giant bowl of Times Square, where Seventh Avenue merged with Broadway, was a great electrical circus. The theaters that lined both sides of Broadway had their names and their marquees picked out in lights;

even the Horn & Hardart Automat at 46th and Broadway was brilliantly illuminated. And fantastic signs, with ingenious special effects, perched atop the low buildings on both sides of the street, as well as at 42nd Street, facing north, and 47th Street, facing south. To visit Times Square, in this last moment of its glory, was to be bathed in light.

O. J. Gude was long gone, of course, but the title of Lamplighter of Broadway now belonged to the charming, mercurial, and prodigiously inventive Douglas Leigh. Leigh was, in his own soft-spoken way, one of those mythical figures of Broadway, like Tony Pastor and Oscar Hammerstein and Florenz Ziegfeld, whose artfully shaped story was told again and again in the popular press. The son of a banker in Anniston, Alabama, he had come to New York to work as an adman, grown bored and frustrated with his lowly post, quit in the heart of the Depression, sold his beat-up old Ford, and set out to build spectaculars in Times Square. It was the kind of crazy impulse that comes only to the implacably self-confident (or the crazy). Leigh kept his megalomania carefully hidden beneath a screen of southern politesse, unfailingly addressing the business executives with whom he dealt as "sir." He was slight, and dapper, and always sported a fresh boutonnière; a writer once compared him to "a Princeton freshman." He was, perhaps for this very reason, a salesman of the highest order. For his very first spectacular, Leigh imagined a giant coffee cup that would emit real steam from holes punched into the rim of the cup—a "special effect" none of his predecessors had ever tried. He then sold the idea to the A & P food chain and installed the sign at Broadway and 47th Street in late 1933. From this moment on, Times Square became Leigh's canvas.

Leigh was a peculiar fusion of artist and pitchman. He would wander around Times Square looking for virgin rooftop and then lease the space for signage. Then he would sit in his office and dream up ideas for signs, or play with images already used by advertisers. A 1941 profile by E. J. Kahn in *The New Yorker* noted that Leigh "judged it would be artistically and commercially pleasant to place a large penguin over Broadway with a blinking red eye that would flash on every few seconds. He was influenced in his thoughts by the fact that the manufacturers of Kool cigarettes had been featuring penguins in their magazine advertising." Leigh seemed to have a mind that naturally thought in advertisements. He lacked the technical expertise to make steam come out of coffee cups or make red eyes blink on and off, but he understood that the images would work, and he found engineers who could make them happen.

Leigh was, at least in his own mind, a visionary who dreamed in light, but not in light only. He was a great admirer of Henry Ford, and he spoke of going into politics, of starting a businessmen's party, of delivering lectures over the radio. He once described to *The New York Times* a Times Square with wind machines blowing trees and flags, artificial snow and fog, signs that emitted smells, live animals, three-dimensional signs—the kind of brilliantly orchestrated fantasy we would now expect from Disney, or Las Vegas. He had an instinct for the new. In the late thirties, he purchased the rights to a new lighting technology called Epok, which allowed him to stage five-minute animated cartoons on the gigantic dimensions of a Times Square spectacular; it was an early version of the LED technology that has increasingly come to dominate today's Times Square. Immediately after the war, he bought from the Navy dirigibles that had been scheduled to be cut up into raincoats; he attached rubberized fixtures lined with fifteen thousand tiny lightbulbs, and rented them to advertisers as spectaculars in the sky. MGM used one to promote *National Velvet*.

Leigh was also responsible for the most famous sign in the history of Times Square: the Camel cigarettes sign, atop the Claridge Hotel on the east side of Broadway between 43rd and 44th Streets. The ingenuity of the sign lay more in its conception than in its fabrication, for it consisted of a red-painted plywood billboard with a picture of a handsome, deeply contented smoker with a hole in place of a mouth. And through the hole, every four seconds, issued a perfectly formed smoke ring, made of steam, collected from the hotel's heating system and driven by pistons through a yet smaller hole. Perhaps the most ingenious thing about the sign was that it didn't depend on light. It was completed three days before Pearl Harbor, and six months before a blackout that switched off the lights in Times Square. But the smoker kept blowing his rings. Indeed, he continued until 1966, when, after a remarkable run of twenty-five years, the sign finally came down.

Leigh's last masterpiece, and arguably his greatest, was mounted atop the Bond Clothing store, one block north of the Camel smoker, in 1948.

Bond was the closest thing to an elegant haberdasher in Times Square, a place never noted for its stores. And what Leigh devised for his client was a block-long, ninety-foot-high montage of sex and swank, one of the most eye-popping tableaux ever seen in Times Square. Leigh ordered up fifty-foot-high plaster casts of heroically proportioned nudes, a man and a woman, with swags of golden neon draped across their torsos like togas. At night, they seemed to be wearing evening gowns of light, and nothing else. The statues were posted on either side of a real waterfall, 27 feet high and 132 feet across. Ten thousand gallons of water tumbled over the falls and was recirculated by pumps at the base, while the scene was illuminated by 23,000 incandescent lamps as well as neon tubes. In *Signs and Wonders,* Tama Starr, whose family firm, Artkraft Strauss, built the Bond sign as well as many other Leigh inventions, explains that the waterfall was meant to conjure up Niagara Falls, and thus honeymoons, and thus sex.

Like Irving Berlin, Douglas Leigh ultimately became one of the Methuselahs of Broadway. In the early 1960s, he bought the Times Tower, stripped off its marble cladding, and turned the building into a giant sign-board, which of course is just what it ultimately became thirty years later. In 1979, with Times Square in a state of what must have seemed like irre-versible decay, he sold his seventeen prize sites there to Van Wagner, a big national billboard firm, and embarked on an entirely new career doing ex-terior lighting for big buildings, including the Empire State Building. As late as the mid-nineties he was planning a light show for the 1996 Summer Olympics in Atlanta. Leigh died in 1999, at age ninety-two. He was like Berlin, too, in his combination of canny salesmanship, creative brio, and almost childlike access to the wellsprings of pleasure. He was a genius of the lively arts, and a demiurge of Times Square.

THE POKERINO
FREAK SHOW

IN HIS NOVEL GO, published in 1952, John Clellon Holmes describes a feverish visit he made to 42nd Street in company with his fellow Beats Jack Kerouac, Allen Ginsberg, and Herbert Huncke, in a fruitless search for marijuana. The time must have been 1945 or so, right around the moment when Alfred Eisenstaedt was capturing his frank and jolly image of Times Square. It is late at night, and the band of poets and junkies stops in at Lee's Cafeteria—Holmes's mild joke on the actual name, which was Grant's—at the corner of 42nd and Broadway. "The place," Holmes writes, "looked like some strange social club for grifters, dope passers, petty thieves, cheap, aging whores and derelicts: the whole covert population of Times Square that lived only at night and vanished as the streets went grey with dawn." The crowd at Lee's was a "confraternity of the lost and damned."

It is strange to think that the demonic Times Square of the Beats was the same place as the Times Square of the bobby-soxers and Irving Berlin. And yet it was. This is why Kerouac wrote that Times Square was home both to the gentleman in the De Pinna suit and the drunk in the gutter. Times Square was always so weirdly heterogeneous that you could choose what to make of it; but never more so than in the postwar period. It is to some extent true that the Beats focused their attention on 42nd Street and Eighth Avenue, while the Times Square of the De Pinna suit was Broadway and the theater district; but it is also true that the crowds at the Paramount were celebrating Times Square as it had been, while the Beats dwelled in the Times Square that was becoming. They were the last true celebrants of the great Times Square decay; after them, the decay passed beyond the capacities of literary celebration.

For a few brief years, essentially from 1945 to 1948, Times Square played a central role in the formation of the Beat mood, culture, and even language. The very word "Beat" was coined by Herbert Huncke, a hustler, drug addict, and petty thief who hung out in Times Square and then crashed on the floor of various Beat apartments. "The new social center had been established in Times Square," Allen Ginsberg later wrote, "a huge room lit in brilliant fashion by neon glare and filled with slot machines, open day and night. There all the apocalyptic hipsters in New York eventually stopped, fascinated by the timeless room." They gathered at the Pokerino arcade, and Bickford's cafeteria, and the Angle Bar, at 42nd and Eighth, where pimps and drug dealers and small-time crooks hung out. For the Beats, this tapped-out, phantasmagorical realm held the key to truths invisible to the "squares" in the upper world of success and sobriety. After describing the nightmare world of Grant's, the narrator of *Go* observes that Hobbes, the protagonist, "somehow was not repulsed, but rather yearned to know it in its every aspect, the lives these people led, the emotions they endured, the fate into which they stumbled, perhaps not unawares." Why, that is, would someone consciously choose so degraded a fate?

It was Beat dogma that you had to leave the suffocating world of normalcy behind, and pass through degradation, in order to find truth. Allen Ginsberg was the product of a liberal Jewish suburban home; only when he left for Columbia, in 1943, did he meet other people—Lucien Carr, Jack Kerouac, William Burroughs—who were seekers, to use one of his favorite words, as he was. Burroughs, an older man with a strange air that mingled breeding, erudition, and menace, introduced Ginsberg and Kerouac to writers who subverted the reassuring rationality of the Columbia English department: Rimbaud, Verlaine, Cocteau, and Spengler, with his apocalyptic sense of doom. Burroughs was himself a denizen of Times Square; he had first started haunting the local bars in 1944 when he was trying to fence a stolen tommy gun and some morphine, and now he went to keep himself supplied with drugs and to gaze on the mesmerizing scene. Ginsberg adopted Burroughs's preferences in literature, his view of the world, his taste for amphetamines, and his fascination with the lowlife of Times Square.

In 1945, he and Kerouac began accompanying Burroughs and Huncke, whom they all respected as a true denizen of the lower depths, on all-night trips to Times Square. They sat for hours in Bickford's, the giant cafeteria under the marquee of the Apollo Theatre, talking to the dead-end crowd that gathered there; Ginsberg even worked at Bickford's briefly as a busboy. They were interviewed about their sex lives by Dr. Alfred Kinsey, who had been fascinated by Huncke's polymorphous sexual experience. Stoked on Benzedrine, the Beats would float up and down 42nd Street with the strange human flotsam, entertaining splendid, Technicolor, end-of-the-world visions. Here was the hallucinatory landscape that matched their hallucinatory state of mind. The spectaculars held an entirely different meaning for them than they did for Douglas Leigh. The garish blues and greens and yellows of the neon lights penetrated human flesh and revealed the ghastly pallor beneath. "It was a hyperbolic spookiness all taking place in an undersea light of Pokerino freak shows of Times Square," Ginsberg later said.

The Pokerino was a 42nd Street pinball arcade filled with speed freaks who, as Kerouac's biographer writes, "were concentrating on the pinball machines with amphetamine intensity, gripping the tables, willing the ball to stay in play, while the crash and zap of the machine noises and the intense bright light made their heads spin." Here, Ginsberg concluded, at the heart of 42nd Street, at the heart of Times Square, at the heart of New York and thus of the world, the end of the American dream was being enacted and prefigured. In Kerouac's *The Town and the City,* Leon Levinsky, the Ginsberg stand-in, points into the heart of the Nickel-O— the Pokerino stand-in—and descries there "the children of the sad American paradise" reduced to zombies in the sickly light, "milling around uncertainly among the ruins of bourgeois civilization." Jumping up and down with excitement, Levinsky goes on to describe the inmates of the Nickel-O as geeks—and he means not just the speed freaks in the Nickel-O but himself, too, and others, all unclean and diseased and riddled with guilt. The mad monologue has that inspired lunacy the Beats prized as oracular wisdom. Reaching his wild peroration, Levinsky declares that this geekishness is, in fact, an "atomic disease," a modern form of plague. "Everybody," he declares, "is going to fall apart, disintegrate, all character-structures based on tradition and uprightness and so-called morality will slowly rot away, people will get the hives right on their hearts, great crabs will cling to their brains. . . ."

The apocalyptic hipsters soon moved to other visionary geographies—to the West, to Mexico, to Paris, to Morocco. But in their work, and in their lives, they had added another layer to the great archaeological site that was Times Square. Just as the Depression-era journalists like Liebling and Mitchell and Myron Berger had fashioned a Times Square of eloquent freaks and fading vaudevillians, so the Beats left behind them a Dostoyevskian underworld whose very degradation posed a challenge to pleasure-loving bourgeois culture. There was a peculiar form of romanticization in the way the Beats idealized, even lionized, figures like Huncke; perhaps it was the Runyonesque impulse of Times Square in a decadent key. But before long there would be nothing left to romanticize.

TIMES SQUARE DIDN'T get appreciably worse over the course of the next decade, but what had been largely subterranean became increasingly visible, and what had been the subject for surrealist evocation became, increasingly, a Problem. In March 1960, *The New York Times* ran a long front-page story under the headline "Life on W. 42d St. A Study in Decay." The reporter, Milton Bracken, noted that "it is frequently asserted" that 42nd Street between Seventh and Eighth Avenues "is the 'worst' in town." As evidence, Bracken adduced the ten "grinder" theaters on the block showing racy or violent films from eight A.M. to four A.M., and the "male perverts" who "misbehave" during the shows; the homosexuals and transvestites who gathered on the sidewalks; the arcades in the subway stations at either end of the block, whose pinball games and shooting galleries attracted drifters and runaways; the con artists bilking soldiers and unwary tourists, and the bookstores peddling "second-hand magazines featuring pictures of women stripped to the waist."

In the light of retrospection, of course, the dreadful depths of 42nd Street circa 1960 sound fairly innocuous. And in fact Bracken was at pains to distinguish between the street's increasingly noxious reputation and its daily reality. The youthful "deviates," he writes, may have been material for the psychiatrist, but not for the policeman. The drifters in the arcades could be counted on to comply when the officer on the beat shooed them away. The knives on display in the stores were for show rather than for battle. The jukebox in the IRT arcade was wholly devoted to opera. The police made relatively few arrests on an average night. Forty-second Street was an "enigma" in an otherwise healthy city; indeed, Bracken observed, "places that attract deviates and persons looking for trouble are interspersed with places of high standards of food, drink and service." And yet precisely because New Yorkers were accustomed to clean and orderly streets, 42nd Street's anarchy was shocking. "Respectable elements," Bracken noted, were "deeply offended and, in some cases, outraged."

The Times Square that the Beats had frequented, which is to say, 42nd Street as well as Eighth Avenue from the upper Thirties to the lower Fifties, had grown more scrofulous in recent years. The dirty bookstores had begun to proliferate in the 1950s. The merchandise, which in the past had run to joke books, war stories, westerns, and horoscopes, increasingly shifted to such standards of soft-core erotica as the "French deck"—playing cards with pictures of naked girls—calendars, paperbacks like *Sex Life of a Cop,* and those secondhand magazines. Prostitutes had patrolled the area since the late nineteenth century, but the opening of the Port Authority Bus Terminal, at the southeast corner of 42nd and Eighth, in late 1950, had vastly increased the numbers of both teenage boys and girls available to be conscripted into the trade, and probably increased the supply of customers as well. And by the early sixties, Times Square had become New York's capital of male prostitution, known as hustling.

The Times Square area had long been congenial to homosexuals, thanks both to its general air of laissez-faire and to the relatively high concentration of gay men in theater and the theater's ancillary professions, like costume and set design. Places like the bar of the Astor Hotel—or at least one designated side of the bar—were well-known gay hangouts as early as the 1910s, and then increasingly so with the influx of servicemen during World War II. Tourists often poked their heads into 42nd Street coffee shops like Bickford's, where they were likely to spot the flamboyant "fairies" who had made the street such an exotic slice of American life. Timothy Gilfoyle, the leading scholar of this subject, cites a tabloid in the early thirties to the effect that "The latest gag about 2 A.M. is to have your picture taken with one or two pansies on Times Square."

With the onset of the Depression, the hustling scene, according to Gilfoyle, became less theatrical and more grimly commercial. Forty-second Street became the center of "rough trade," forcing overtly effeminate gay men to Bryant Park, one block to the east. The unnamed main character of John Rechy's *City of Night,* published in 1963, arrives in New York determined to make a living with his body, and is immediately directed by a wiser hand to Times Square—"always good for a score." And indeed it is. Standing at the corner of 42nd and Broadway, he says, "I can see the young masculine men milling idly. Sometimes they walk up to older men and stand talking in soft tones—going off together or, if not, moving to talk to someone else." The signals are all terribly discreet, but nonetheless unmistakable, at least to the initiate. After taking in two "sexy foreign movies" at the Apollo, Rechy's narrator stands under the marquee until a middle-aged man approaches him and says, "I'll give you ten, and I don't give a damn for you." And so he is inducted into the life of 42nd Street.

This moment in the early 1960s marks a middle point in the downward spiral of 42nd Street. The street is not nearly as violent or degraded as it is soon to become; on the other hand, it has lost the gift for evoking a euphoric sense of liberation from social convention—the Baudelairean sense—that it had borne for the Beats. It is a place of melancholy epiphanies. *City of Night* opens with the line, "Later I would think of America as one vast City of Night stretching from Times Square to Hollywood Boulevard. . . . One-night stands and cigarette smoke and rooms squashed in loneliness." The operative word is "squashed," for Rechy's 42nd Street is a furtive, joyless world.

Much the same feeling of failure and constriction arises from the other important hustling novel of the era, *Midnight Cowboy,* written by James Leo Herlihy and published in 1965. Herlihy's knight-errant, Joe Buck, heads straight for the Times Square Palace Hotel when he arrives in New York from El Paso. The first thing he sees from his room is "an incredibly sloppy old woman sitting on the sidewalk under a movie marquee across the street" who "poured something from a bottle on to her filthy, naked feet, and rubbed them with her free hand." Here is a form of degradation he never saw, or even imagined, in Texas. Joe's tenure in New York is an unsentimental education. Despite his unsinkable enthusiasm, he suffers a string of mortifying failures: arriving in triumph as a stud, he is soon reduced to the status of hustler, and an unsuccessful one at that. He sleeps in the all-night theaters and dines on baked beans at the Automat. In the end, he leaves for Florida, as he must; the only permanent citizens of Times Square are grotesques like his sidekick, Ratso Rizzo, who dies before he reaches the southern promised land.

Just as Joe was climbing aboard that Greyhound, Times Square was taking another turn down the spiral of decay. Times Square had been a refuge for self-expression and self-gratification at a time when social conventions kept most Americans toeing the line of propriety; this was as true in 1950 as it had been in 1910. But in the sixties, when those conventions lost their moral force, and ordinary citizens began to live by the motto "If it feels good, do it," Times Square sank from impudent naïveté to genuine debasement. In 1966, a vending machine operator, Martin Hodas, purchased thirteen old film machines, outfitted them with stag films showing the kind of frontal nudity then commercially unavailable in New York, and distributed them to the Times Square bookshops that specialized in risqué material. At first the owners resisted, since this kind of thing had been a provocation to police action from the days of burlesque; but they soon found that the "video peeps" were the most popular items they carried.

Police enforcement might have eliminated, or at least suppressed, this new level of erotica, but starting in 1966, the Supreme Court issued a series of decisions extending First Amendment protections to explicit sexual materials. Real estate in Times Square had always adapted to the most high-profit uses; now, with remarkable speed, pornography became the boom industry of 42nd Street and Eighth Avenue. Martin Hodas was soon a major producer and distributor of hard-core material, allegedly in collaboration with the Mafia (claims he regularly denied). And he and others began buying up the leases on storefronts up and down 42nd Street and Eighth Avenue. The camera shops, gadget stores, delis, cafeterias, and pinball arcades that had lined the street, and that had accounted for what remained of its raffish feel, gave way to pornographic bookstores and peeps. Soon there were stores specializing in gay porn, kiddie porn, and S & M. Stores with forbiddingly blacked-out windows and kinky posters out front lined the street. Hubert's Museum, the last relic of the old honky-tonk 42nd Street, closed in 1975. Three years later, Peepland, a porn emporium, opened on the site, a change just as portentous in its way as the replacement of Murray's Roman Gardens by Hubert's had been half a century earlier.

The Supreme Court rulings also cleared the way for "massage parlors," which were storefront shops with booths where men could buy sex—in effect, street-level brothels. By 1967, Eighth Avenue was lined with massage parlors: the Sugar Shack, the Honey Haven, the Danish Parlor, the Love Machine. According to Josh Alan Friedman, the author of *Tales of Times Square,* a zestful romp through the neighborhood's lower depths, the first live sex act, where customers paid to watch a man and a woman have sex on a stage tilted toward the audience, was conducted at the Mine-Cine, on 42nd Street, in 1970. Friedman dates the first "Live Nude Girls" act, where customers could look through a slot as the girls touched themselves, to 1972. Within a few years, he writes, the partitions separating customer from performer came down, so customers could pay extra for quickie sex, or just a feel. The films became more explicit, and kinkier. At Peepland, a customer could rent, according to show cards cited by the unflinching Friedman, films in which "Two wild girls shove live eels up snatch and asshole," "Farmboy fucks cow," "Man fucks a hen," and "Girl takes on dog, horse and pig simultaneously." These are among the less baroque subjects Friedman lists.

By the mid-seventies, many of the 42nd Street movie theaters had switched to pornography, a change that further degraded the life of the street. Prostitutes often worked the aisles of the theaters, bringing johns to bathrooms in the basement, while thieves preyed on the derelicts who often camped out in the theaters all day, slashing open their pockets while they slept. Adam D'Amico, a New York police detective who worked in Times Square, recalls a time when a wall was torn out of a theater being refurbished, and forty to fifty wallets, some with identification dating back to the 1950s, came tumbling out; thieves had apparently tossed them there after removing the contents. D'Amico says that he spent several months staking out one fetid movie-house bathroom where gangs of kids would wait for a patron to go to the urinal and then grab his wallet, yank his pants down to his ankles, and run. Usually, he says, they targeted Asian men, who tended to carry a good deal of cash, speak little English, and feel too humiliated to report the crime.

In 1960, the decay of 42nd Street had seemed anomalous; but by the end of the decade, the downtown of virtually every old northeastern and midwestern city had begun to totter, or collapse. Suburbanization had robbed the department stores and the restaurants and the movie theaters of their customers; and as companies followed people, the cities' employment base had begun to dwindle as well. And just as middle-class whites were decamping, large numbers of blacks, most of them poorly educated and unskilled, were migrating up from the South—2.75 million between 1940 and 1960 alone. They were arriving just as the low-level manufacturing jobs they might have taken were leaving. It was a recipe for catastrophe. Crime rates, which had been remarkably low during the urban efflorescence in the middle decades of the twentieth century, began to surge. New York City had 390 murders in 1961; by 1964, the number had reached 637. In 1972, almost 1,700 New Yorkers were killed—a more than fourfold increase from barely a decade before. The number of reported robberies almost tripled from 1966 to the early seventies. Not only the volume but the nature of crime changed; knives and blackjacks gave way to the Saturday Night Special. Heroin hit the streets around 1964. The combination of guns, drugs, and enormous amounts of cash produced a lethal dynamic.

Times Square, which for generations had been understood to exemplify the freedom and the energy and the heedless pleasure-seeking of New York, now came to be seen as the emblem of a city deranged by those very attributes. The change can be measured in the difference between *City of Night* and *Taxi Driver*, released in 1976. Rechy's narrator says in *City of Night* that he "surrendered to the world of Times Square" like an addict mainlining junk; Travis Bickle, the enraged and delusional loner at the heart of *Taxi Driver*, does the same thing, but with far more deadly results. Travis's Times Square is the heart of darkness—his own darkness and the world's. He returns again and again to the surreal streets, dense with hookers and hustlers and crazed street people. Iris, the fourteen-year-old hooker, tries to climb into his cab, but is yanked out by her pimp—and then meekly complies. The casual cruelty drives Travis mad. "All the animals come out at night," he growls in an ominous voice-over as he prowls 42nd Street. "Someday a rain will come and wash all this scum off the street." Travis wants to be that rain; he dreams of a vigilante act of purification. Ultimately he takes all the insane violence of the city into himself and slaughters Iris's pimp and two confederates—for which a grateful city congratulates him.

By the time of *Taxi Driver,* the two precincts that covered Times Square, which not long before had recorded a relatively modest number of crimes, placed first and second in New York in total felony complaints; the next closest precinct, in Harlem, had about a third as many complaints. While they remained popular thoroughfares during the daytime, at night 42nd Street and the Eighth Avenue corridor had descended to an almost feral state. Here is Josh Alan Friedman on the area around the Port Authority Bus Terminal:

> A Puerto Rican pre-op transsexual stabs a trick in the eye with a sharp fingernail to grab his cabfare before he pays the driver. Brain-damaged evangelists rave aloud to themselves; 300-pound hookers flip out their hooters to stop traffic. . . . Near-dead human vegetation takes root in their own excretion in condemned doorways— most of them have slit pockets from scavengers searching for their wine-bottle change. . . . Fifteen ghetto guerrillas wearing Pro-Keds (what transit cops call "felony sneakers") swoop down on a victim, then scatter back into subway oblivion.

For the legitimate shopkeepers, restaurateurs, theater managers, pedestrians, and even police officers who worked in, frequented, or patrolled the area, Times Square had become a hellhole. Dale Hansen had left the small town of Wausau, Wisconsin, to become the minister of St. Luke's Lutheran church, on 46th Street just west of Eighth Avenue, in 1975. It is safe to say that nothing in Wausau could have prepared the Reverend Hansen for what he found in Times Square. In the course of his first year, five congregants were killed, one of them by being pushed onto the subway tracks. In the ensuing years, a prostitute was killed on the front steps of the church, a seventy-four-year-old congregant was mugged while delivering flowers to a shut-in down the street, and Hansen himself was knifed twice. Dozens of prostitutes solicited on the corner; dealers sold crack openly. The building next door was taken over by Cuban transvestites who had been released in the Mariel boatlift of 1980. "Stuff would come flying out the windows," Hansen recalls; "suitcases and garbage. They would break people's legs with a baseball bat."

The city had actually stepped up enforcement efforts in the mid-seventies. The mayor's Midtown Enforcement Project targeted massage parlors and other sex establishments, and succeeded in closing many of them down and even keeping some of them closed. In 1978, the police established a new substation on 42nd Street and increased the size of its force until nearly eighty uniformed officers, and twenty-five plainclothes officers, patrolled the area on a regular basis. But to the officers themselves, it still felt like King Canute ordering the sea to turn back. The prostitutes and the drug dealers were back on the street almost as soon as they were rounded up. The daytime crowd of con artists and three-card monte players gave way every night to pickpockets and "push-in" robbers, who would throw a victim into a dark doorway and make off with his or her valuables. And the police were hobbled by a widely shared reluctance to view "victimless crime," including pornography, vagrancy, prostitution, and even street-level drug dealing, as matters for serious enforcement. Much of what went on in Times Square was treated as the more or less inevitable and more or less tolerable consequence of urban life.

Police officers, says the Reverend Hansen, "would stand on the corner and watch drug deals going on like cigar-store Indians." After a community meeting at which local residents had vented their outrage at the chaos on the streets, Hansen recalls that the precinct commander took him aside and said, "Father, you've just got to learn to live with it." This was the kind of despairing surrender that drives Travis Bickle over the cliff of sanity; Hansen decided on a less violent, but almost equally shocking, course of action. At the time, a kind of citizens' patrol known as the Guardian Angels had been formed. The Angels were teenage boys and girls, mostly from the ghetto, who wore red berets and affected a somewhat paramilitary air; they were widely condemned as vigilantes-in-training. But Hansen and the merchants of the area were desperate. They established a post near St. Luke's and gave the kids free meals and walkie-talkies; Hansen blessed their berets in church. And the Angels essentially walked up and down the street; they were a presence, and very little more.

"At the height of the battle," Hansen recalls, "we probably had twenty or thirty of them on the street at any one time." The Angels, it is generally agreed, eliminated some of the more outrageous behavior on the street—though they could hardly suppress crime itself—and brought a novel sense of calm. Hansen was perfectly happy to live with the charge of encouraging vigilantism. But, of course, the very fact that the beleaguered citizens of West 46th Street had had to turn to a private security force—and a force consisting largely of impoverished teens—was an appalling indictment of the collapse of order in New York City.

In the summer of 1981, *The New York Times* ran one of its periodic articles on 42nd Street, which constituted the paper's backyard; the difference between that moment and 1960, when Milton Bracken had explored the block, was far greater than that between Bracken's 42nd Street and the one the Beats had discovered in 1940. The 42nd Street of 1981 wasn't troubling; it was depraved. The reporter, Josh Barbanel, went to talk with the street people who had, he wrote, "witnessed the final moments of a naked 26-year-old man from Connecticut as he was chased to his death on a subway track in Times Square by a bottle-throwing crowd" nine days earlier. There was, it turned out, a simple explanation for the man's death, and Barbanel heard it from a thirteen-year-old girl hanging out on the street in the middle of the night. "They wanted to see some action," she said. "He was just bugged out, and everybody started going wild on him. They had nothing better to do." A drug dealer, standing a few feet from a police officer, describes the stream of summonses he had received as the cost of doing business. A "squat young man with a crewcut" comes by to announce, "I rob people. I like to rob people." A copiously bleeding man bangs on a theater door, demanding the arrest of a security guard who he says beat him with a nightstick. And the night rolls on, in its lassitude and its lunacy.

OVER THE PREVIOUS three quarters of a century, Times Square had inspired a literature of revelry and celebration, of withering contempt, of arch delectation, of prophetic disgust. And now something quite new appeared: a literature of diagnosis. Times Square had become not only a place, or a state of mind, to be limned, but a disease to be cured—if possible. By the late 1970s, moves were afoot to renovate Times Square, and especially 42nd Street. And in 1978, a group of scholars at the Graduate Center of the City University of New York published a study commissioned by the Ford Foundation and titled *The West 42nd Street Study: The Bright Light Zone*. The study constituted a definitive social anthropology of 42nd Street and the surrounding area—its "social ecology," its markets, its sex and drug business, its hustles and so forth. The *Bright Light* study would soon be followed by yet others.

The Bright Light Zone documented the enormous volume of crimes committed in the area, but its essential subject was not crime but pathology—a pathology that seems to have defeated all attempts at control. Here is a typical excerpt from one researcher's field notes:

> As I returned south on 8th Avenue I saw an older black man urinating on the sidewalk. This same man has been around this corner of 42nd and 8th for years. He is sick and should be hospitalized. His street name is Cadillac. Year after year I've seen him there, drunk, loud, menacing the passers-by. A well-dressed white man appealed to two policemen about the man's conduct. The police said in effect that there was very little they could do—about a sick, drunken man publicly urinating on the west side of 8th Avenue between 42nd and 43rd Streets!

The authors note that Cadillac "circulates in a world of bottle gangs"—groups of alcoholics—"and street violence which destroys the civic culture of West 42nd Street as well as the men themselves."

The *Bright Light* study is generally quite sympathetic to the police, who appear to spend much of their time reviving wasted derelicts who have collapsed into the gutter, or dealing with the crazies who have come to live on the street. At one point a street character with no legs takes a bite out of a cop's hand; handcuffed on the floor of the precinct house, he whacks passersby with his bloody stumps. An exhausted patrolman says to his partner, "This job's like shoveling shit against the tide." The problem is not even crime so much as rampant antisocial behavior; the drunks and the nuts and the bag ladies and the small-time hustlers have created a self-perpetuating street culture that seems beyond the reach of enforcement. One commanding officer says, "If we could go back to the old style of police work, when men on the beat could enforce standards of public decency and order, we could clean up West 42nd Street in no time." But at that time neither the city's judges nor many of its citizens—certainly not elites—would have tolerated such aggressive, and such moralistic, policing; nor was there any willingness to reverse the policy of "deinstitutionalization," which had released thousands of mentally ill people to the streets with little supervision or care.

The Bright Light Zone was a work of cultural anthropology; the authors were at pains to demonstrate that Times Square served the needs, and satisfied the appetites, of many constituencies. "The heterogeneity of people and their life-ways along West 42nd Street is astonishing even to social scientists who are used to the wonderful layering and stacking of Manhattan neighborhoods," the authors write. Far from being the "Ghetto Street" imagined by terrified suburbanites, they noted, 42nd Street was filled with a great throng of tourists, office workers, and fun seekers, and at least at midday was among the most crowded blocks in New York City. The cheap movie theaters and restaurants and arcades were a tremendous draw for perfectly law-abiding young people and families, especially from neighborhoods like Harlem with few movie theaters of their own. Forty-second Street was not beyond help. While only 21 percent of respondents to a survey said "I would enjoy" going to West 42nd Street, and 38 percent said "I would avoid" the area, a sizable majority also said that they would come to the street if "legitimate theater and dance" returned there. In other words, if you could somehow end the cycle of pathology, you might be able to restore something of the old life of 42nd Street.

This in turn raised the question of exactly how that cycle had gotten started in the first place. One of the authors of the study, Stanley Bruder, argued in a discussion of the history of Times Square that the demise of theaters and restaurants, and the rise of penny arcades and shooting galleries and grinders, which "tended to cater to the lowest common denominator," drove away "respectable elements." That is, bad uses attracted bad people, rather than the other way around. And so the opposite must be true as well: "eliminating these businesses through changing the use of the street should cause the undesirable population to leave on its own," Bruder concluded. While several of his colleagues were more inclined to sympathize with the "undesirable population" than with the "respectable elements," William Kornblum, the director of the study project, adopted Bruder's view and made it the central prescriptive device of *Bright Light Zone*. "A check on the vicious circle of demoralization and decay in the 42nd Street area does depend on increased police details and more forceful application of police action," Kornblum wrote. "At the same time, all authorities agree that only the economic redevelopment of the area can significantly alter the present patterns of street traffic and vice."

Here was not only an urban policy but an important act of moral recognition, especially coming from liberal academics: vagrants and hustlers and prostitutes could not be tolerated, or accepted as the price of "authentic" urban life, if the streets were to be made welcoming to "respectable" folk. At the same time, 42nd Street had a role as a low-cost entertainment center that ought not simply be discarded in its wished-for renaissance. And of course, it had a history to be respected, as well. The study raised a question to which there was no obvious answer: how could you eradicate whatever was pathological about 42nd Street and its environs without, at the same time, eliminating everything that made it worth caring about in the first place?

PART TWO

MAKING A NEW
FUN PLACE

SELTZER, NOT ORANGE JUICE

IN LATE DECEMBER 1976, Alexander Parker, real estate magnate, gazed down upon 42nd Street and saw a world made new. A reporter for a business magazine wrote, breathlessly: "Alex Parker stands in the large, high-ceiling board room with floor-to-ceiling arched windows looking out over Times Square. He doesn't see the prostitutes, pimps, molesters, muggers. He says he sees a huge, shining complex where tourists will flock for excitement of another kind in a revitalized Times Square." Parker was a Times Square arriviste, a developer who owned properties in the Garment District, in the West Thirties. The year before, he had purchased 1 Times Square, the old Times Tower, the fountainhead of Times Square, from the Allied Chemical Corporation; and it was from the old boardroom of the *Times* that he had launched his dream of a new 42nd Street. The "huge, shining complex" was a convention center, which would stretch from 40th to 43rd Street and from Seventh to Eighth Avenue. The rendering depicted in the article has the sterile beauty of a thing imagined ex nihilo: a plaza with gardens and fountains and walkways leading to a cluster of rectangular granite slabs, which would presumably house the conventioneers. Parker said that he planned to use "a large wrecking ball . . . to crush the decaying structures" of the old 42nd Street. And in fact not only the prostitutes and muggers, but the street itself, and even the street plan, have been eradicated from the picture. This new 42nd Street bears a strong resemblance to the United Nations Plaza.

Parker's timing wasn't very good. By 1976, the real estate market, and New York City's economy, had collapsed; he never managed to raise the $500 million he said he needed for the convention center. He ultimately sold the oft-sold 1 Times Square, and then disappeared from the history of Times Square and 42nd Street. But the dream, as it were, lived on. By the mid-1970s, 42nd Street was understood to be a dead place. Once it had been the very heart of the greatest city in the world; now, like New York itself, it felt like a relic, a reminder of past glories. Yet 42nd Street could not simply be abandoned, like the polluted terrain of an old factory. At the level of symbolism, the block's predatory environment was disastrous for a city that already had a well-deserved reputation as one of the seamiest and most dangerous places in the country. What's more, it was located in the heart of Manhattan, at the convergence of subway lines and bus lines and at the intersection of major streets. Here was a wasting asset of colossal proportions. The authors of the *Bright Light* study noted that "commercial lenders who have business in midtown Manhattan regard the Times Square area as a prime location for investment," but added: "This mood depends on continuous action on plans to renew the 42nd Street Bright Lights District." It is worth noting the difference between "Times Square" and "42nd Street" in this calculus: while the entire area was degraded, and in need of rejuvenation, it was understood that the distinctive pathologies of 42nd Street were the chief problem to be addressed. In the process of redevelopment, the destinies of 42nd Street and Times Square came to be seen as linked, but nevertheless separate.

And so men like Alexander Parker stood high above 42nd Street and imagined it anew. Forty-second Street's very centrality, its antique associations, made it a thrilling screen on which to project visions of an urban future. And yet what a strange tabula rasa! Here was a teeming block in the midst of a teeming city, a block whose glamorous buildings were very much intact, if terribly degraded. Could such a place actually be called dead? Could it be "rescued," rather than obliterated? And if so, what was to be preserved? The buildings themselves? The "spirit" of the place? Which spirit? The lobster palace society of 1910 or the carny, flea-circus world of 1940? Was the underworld once again to meet the elite? Or was the whole idea of consciously and conscientiously designing a place that for generations had been a monument to the ungovernable appetites of urban man an absurdity, a self-contradiction? Starting in the 1960s, and then increasingly in the seventies and eighties, 42nd Street became a place to be saved, restored, reimagined. The process of redevelopment became a cockpit of competing ideas not only about 42nd Street and Times Square, but about urban life itself.

At the same time, since urban development is a quintessentially political process rather than an aesthetic exercise, these ideas and images were wielded by different individuals and groups with their own interests and their own sources and degrees of power: real estate developers, urban planners, government officials, theater owners, editorialists, urban flaneurs, and, not to put too fine a point upon it, real estate developers. The prize would not necessarily go to the best or most popular idea—Alexander Parker, after all, had no plans to ask anybody whether they wanted a convention center—so the debate over the redevelopment of 42nd Street was also a struggle over who had "the public interest" at heart, and who would be able to impose that vision.

It is quite possible that there were no good answers to the problem of re-creating 42nd Street. There were only answers that would disappoint different people, in different ways.

ALEXANDER PARKER'S BULLDOZER approach was already becoming passé by the mid-1970s, for the excesses of "urban renewal" had convinced even the most pragmatic that cities could not survive the wholesale destruction of their history and texture. Now 42nd Street began to attract reformers who recognized that the block still had a life of its own, and who thus wanted to rejuvenate rather than flatten it. In 1976, just as Parker was wowing the business press with his grandiose plans, an advertising executive and urban gadfly named Fred Papert was establishing the 42nd Street Development Corporation in hopes of revitalizing the western end of the street. Papert was able to draw on funding from major foundations to create a string of small theaters, now known collectively as Theater Row, west of Ninth Avenue. Papert also had the ingenious idea—or at least is among the half dozen or so people who claim to have had the idea—of offering subsidized apartments in a federally funded project on Tenth Avenue to artists and performers. Papert imagined West 42nd

Street as a burgeoning cultural zone. He began to look east, toward the notoriously incorrigible block between Seventh and Eighth Avenues, and he turned for support to his principal patron, the Ford Foundation.

Ford was then, and is now, not only one of the largest foundations in the country but one of the most prestigious institutions in the city, a charter member of New York's cultural elite. The foundation's headquarters, a glittering glass box, was located on the east side of 42nd Street, and the foundation had in no way sought to identify itself with the tawdry block to the west, or for that matter with the world of popular and commercial culture embodied by 42nd Street. But Ford had a large stake in high culture; and, at about the same time as Fred Papert approached the foundation, Roger Kennedy, the Ford official who oversaw arts programs, was looking to buy a theater for the dance companies the foundation subsidized. He had asked Richard Weinstein, an architect, and Donald Elliot, an urban planner, to take a look at the fabled, and long abandoned, New Amsterdam Theatre just west of Seventh Avenue. The two reported back that the block was such a shambles that no one would come to the New Amsterdam, even if it was restored to its original glory. Kennedy gave them a small grant to think about what, if anything, could be done with 42nd Street. This is how the Ford Foundation backed into a peculiar role as the patron and prime mover of 42nd Street redevelopment.

The project began modestly; Weinstein says that the initial goal was to "look for ways to bring commercial development to the block, with the idea that we skim some of the benefits to redevelop the theaters, and in the process get rid of the pornography." But developers told Weinstein and Elliott that their plans wouldn't generate sufficient capital to restore the theaters, so they began thinking in far more ambitious terms. By the time the new group, including Papert, met at the Ford Foundation in February 1978, Weinstein had devised a plan as grandiose as Parker's. "The plan," he explained, according to notes of the meeting,

> includes converting the ten existing second-floor auditoria in the theater buildings into a consumer-oriented exposition center with people moving across 42nd Street by means of pedestrian bridges. The expositions would be sponsored by major corporations for promotional purposes and would create an audio-visual experi-

ence similar in technique to that utilized by the Smithsonian's National Space Museum. The ground floor would be developed for retail and restaurant business designed for the middle-class population (estimated to be between 200,000–300,000 people a day) going through the Port of Authority [*sic*] Terminal.

Thus was born Cityscape, a theme park in the heart of Manhattan. Customers would buy tickets and circulate among the rides and exhibits. Like any theme park, Cityscape was designed as a self-contained world, two city blocks encased in glass and communicating with each other not principally by way of the street but through aerial walkways. Unlike Alexander Parker's pastoralized plaza, Cityscape offered an extremely inventive and even playful rendition of 42nd Street's character, adapting its identity as a rialto of popular entertainment to a new culture and new technology. Weinstein hired the artists and designers who had created the celebrated Czech pavilion at Expo 67 in Montreal, including Milos Forman, as well as the design firm of Chermayeff & Geismar, which was responsible for the American pavilion—the one with Buckminster Fuller's geodesic dome—and the accompanying exhibit at Osaka in 1970. Cityscape was not a preservation project: its premise was that 42nd Street needed to be projected forward rather than backward.

The design firm produced a cutaway aerial view of the project which today has about it a Flash Gordon sense of the fantastical. A monorail runs all around the perimeter on an upper floor—the orientation ride. Then, moving from east to west along the southern side of 42nd Street, the plan shows a theater containing "the world's largest movie screen," utilizing the then novel IMAX technology to offer a bird's-eye view of the city's five boroughs; the restored New Amsterdam Theatre and two other legitimate theaters; a kind of fashion theater in which a narrator, according to Weinstein, explains "the relationship between fashion and the social-cultural-political moment the fashion was created from," while lights pick out mannequins lined up in niches along the walls (after which viewers would be treated to an actual fashion show); and sound stages and studios where visitors could watch commercials or television shows being made. The northern side of the block included the project's two most ingenious inventions: a conical theater in which patrons seated

around a spiraling rim would look straight down at a movie screen showing a balloon's-eye view of the world's great cities, and a Ferris wheel,
"The Slice of Life," in which viewers would appear to rise from the cables
and tunnels far beneath the streets all the way to the rooftops of the highest skyscrapers—"to make people understand the city as a sectional reality," as Weinstein said.

For all its imaginative richness, Cityscape was steeped in self-
contradiction. Here, after all, was a theme park whose theme was "the
city," which is to say that it would function as a simulacrum of urban life
while urban life in all its messy actuality tumbled along the street on the
other side of the walls. Here was a controlled environment designed to il-
lustrate the urban creativity that springs from uncontrol. Underlying the
Cityscape plan was something of that horror of the streets, and of their
culture, which had made Alexander Parker brag about large wrecking
balls. And the figures behind Cityscape, unlike Parker, were not moved by
calculations of self-interest; they were reacting to what was a virtually con-
sensual view of 42nd Street, and perhaps more broadly of the urban street
itself. The *Bright Light* study, which Ford had commissioned, seemed only
to confirm the sense of 42nd Street as irretrievably lost, though the authors
themselves scarcely took this view. "At the time," says Fred Papert, "all you
had to say was 'Forty-second Street' or 'Times Square,' and it evoked a
groan. So part of the appeal was that you were protected or isolated from
the street." Roger Kennedy, especially, did not view the idea of enclosure as
inimical to urban life. Before coming to Ford, he had worked as a banker in
St. Paul and had funded a downtown redevelopment that had connected
buildings with aerial bridges. Just as St. Paul had arctic blasts, so the streets
of New York had obstacles of their own. "If you want to go to dinner or
theater without putting your coat on, that's pretty nice in New York," says
Kennedy. "It's not a bad thing not to have your pants splashed walking past
an ugly puddle. And if someone's going to put their hand in your pocket,
that's an additional reason."

The project required the approval of city officials, who would have
had to condemn the private property along the block and turn it over to
Cityscape. The designers built an elaborate model of the project, and in
late 1978 and early 1979 invited journalists, civic figures, potential investors, and officials from the administration of Mayor Ed Koch to come

to the Ford Foundation's splendid headquarters for a viewing. Both the model and the project itself were generally well-received, save by one all-important figure: Mayor Koch himself. The mayor had apparently taken a visceral dislike to the model. In an interview with Paul Goldberger, the architecture critic of *The New York Times*, Koch said, "New York cannot and should not compete with Disneyland—that's for Florida. People do not come to midtown Manhattan to take a ride on some machine. This is a nice plan and we want to be supportive—but we have to be sure that it is fleshed out in a way appropriate to New York." And then came the killing, very Kochian bon mot: "We've got to make sure that they have seltzer instead of orange juice." It was an unforgettable kiss-off. "The Disneyland image was so powerful," Weinstein says, "that no matter how we advanced the substance of what we were trying to do, it was nevertheless perceived as an urban theme park."

Nor was that all. It had become plain that the cost of buying the condemned property and of building the attraction would greatly exceed the revenues from corporate sponsorships and paying customers. So Cityscape underwent another transformation. What had begun as a modest attempt to revitalize a block had expanded into a theme park; now the theme park expanded yet again, into a giant real estate venture. The organization's financial advisers concluded that Cityscape, now known by the more corporate-sounding title "The City at 42nd Street," would have to include substantial office development and then plug the revenue gap with rental payments. Paul Reichmann, head of the Canadian development firm Olympia & York, agreed to build office towers on three parcels at the crossroads of Seventh Avenue and Broadway; in order to make the deal more attractive, the City at 42nd Street agreed to transfer the unused "air rights" available in the middle of the block to the three parcels, thus allowing the developer to build a much larger structure than zoning regulations would otherwise have permitted. Rockefeller Center, Inc., and Harry Helmsley, one of the city's biggest real estate operators, also agreed to construct a "fashion mart," which would run from 40th Street to 42nd and would take up an additional 2.3 million square feet. Since the attraction itself amounted to slightly over 500,000 square feet (and the restaurants and retail downstairs occupied an approximately equal space), the enormous tail of real estate would now be wagging the rather modest dog of entertainment. The City at 42nd Street was now a blockbuster project that would transform the street almost as drastically as Parker's convention center would have done.

Mayor Koch had never actually pronounced a death sentence on the City at 42nd Street; and as the project grew into a juggernaut involving many of New York's leading foundations, financial institutions, and real estate developers, it seemed that the resurrection of 42nd Street was finally at hand. But it wasn't. In May 1980, the Koch administration finally rejected the plan. At the press conference at which he administered the coup de grâce, Koch dispensed with orange juice and seltzer in order to discuss the city's role in development. "We aren't going to let one group get the inside track," he said, "no matter how good they are." For all its avowals of public-spiritedness, the City at 42nd Street was a private project; in New York, with its tradition of strong government, accepting private control over so symbolically fraught a piece of property would have been an abdication of municipal authority.

And yet the Disneyland factor was never far from Koch's mind. These many years later, the former mayor vividly recalls his trip to the Ford Foundation to see the model. Koch was seventy-seven years old at the time of this recent conversation, perfectly bald, potbellied and suspendered, but he was every bit as vociferous, as theatrically hyperbolic, as he had been as mayor. "Their exhibit included a *Ferris wheel* on Forty-second Street!" he cried—freshly amazed, across the gulf of decades, at the sheer gall. "It was shit, to put it bluntly. I don't pretend to be a city planner, but I know dross from gold. So I said, 'We're not going to do this.' " Unlike the Establishment figures who sponsored the City at 42nd Street, Koch viewed himself, and was widely accepted as, a son of the sidewalks, the First Cabdriver of a garrulous, wisecracking town. He was the steward not only of the city's interest but of its zeitgeist. To him, the Ferris wheel symbolized the intrusion of an alien sensibility. Koch would not, on the other hand, find the corporate identity that was about to descend on 42nd Street out of keeping with the street's turbulent traditions.

MAYOR KOCH'S DECISION to scotch the City at 42nd Street placed his administration under an obligation it could not afford to ignore. The defunct project, whatever its flaws, had given force to the idea that 42nd Street's degraded state was not an inevitable evolutionary outcome but a condition that could be changed; city officials could no longer satisfy themselves with the usual halfhearted efforts to improve police tactics. A new stage arrived in the process of redevelopment: now it would be public actors, rather than private ones, who devised a destiny for 42nd Street. But they would be reluctant actors. The city was only just emerging from a frightening brush with bankruptcy. And the very idea of heroic, large-scale development had been virtually discredited with the demise of Robert Moses, a legendary figure who, as commissioner of the city's parks and head of various development agencies, had destroyed neighborhoods in order to build highways and commercial developments, though he was also very much responsible for the city's system of parks and public beaches. The only major development project the city had promoted in recent years was an underground highway along the Hudson River, known as Westway, which had been locked in bitter debate and litigation since 1972.

In June 1980, only weeks after Koch consigned the City at 42nd Street to the scrap heap, city and state officials signed a memorandum of understanding to work jointly on revitalizing the block. By February of the following year, officials had produced a "discussion document" to be circulated among developers, urban experts, and the press; and in June the group, now constituted as the 42nd Street Development Project, published the General Project Plan, which laid out the scheme's rationale and goals: "The principal object of the project is to eliminate the blight and physical decay that prevails in the Project Area." The city had, of course, been trying to eliminate blight along 42nd Street for years without success; the premise of the new plan, like that of the City at 42nd Street, was that piecemeal efforts at reform or enforcement were bound to disappear into the block's thriving and dysfunctional economy. The project's environmental impact statement (which was not issued until 1984) confirmed the view advanced in the *Bright Light* study: "The continuation of the existing uses in the project area will undoubtedly perpetuate the loitering and criminal activity on 42nd Street. . . . Unless and until this perception of 'turf' is changed through the introduction of new uses and new users, crime and illegal activities associated with loitering will continue."

The elimination of blight was a means—but to what end? After an earlier public relations debacle in which the city had agreed to raze two historic theaters in order to make way for a new hotel in Times Square, theater preservation had become a nonnegotiable issue; and so city and state officials vowed to protect and revitalize the New Amsterdam, the Lyric, the Apollo, and the other great 42nd Street theaters, now being used to show pornographic or Grade Z movies. The city also promised to make improvements to subway stations and other public amenities in a way that would "preserve the unique ambience of Times Square." But most of all, the plan provided for large new office buildings. The General Project Plan foresaw four office towers at the eastern end of the project, which was one more than the City at 42nd Street had proposed. (The plan also adopted from its predecessor the idea of building a merchandise mart, where wholesale goods are sold to retailers, and a hotel, at the western end of the block.) As in that proposal, air rights would be transferred from midblock to permit developers to construct extra-large—indeed, gigantic—towers. Current zoning laws permitted structures on the four parcels to rise as high as 280 to 370 feet; with the additional air rights, they could range from 365 to 705 feet. The tallest of the buildings, at the northeast corner of 42nd and Broadway, would be one of the most massive office buildings constructed in New York in many years. Why were such big buildings necessary? To make everything else possible. Developers would not build in Times Square without large-scale inducements; and without revenues from development, the planning documents explained, it would be impossible to finance improvements or to preserve the theaters. In effect, 42nd Street's unique character had to be annihilated in order to be preserved.

Why would the construction of office buildings make it possible to improve the subways and preserve the theaters? Because it was the developer, not the city, who would pay for the renovation of 42nd Street. The developer who won the right to build the office towers would be expected to pay for improvements to subways and the street, for private property that public authorities would seize in the condemnation process, and to some extent for the preservation of the theaters. Had the city chosen to pay those costs itself—as it had in other projects, such as the recent Battery Park City in lower Manhattan—it could more readily have dictated terms to developers. But the Koch administration made the fateful decision to sacrifice a large measure of public control in exchange for private investment. In doing so, it also surrendered pieces of the sky, and of the urban landscape: intangible assets that seemed, at least to city planners, far easier to part with than money. And so the Koch administration preserved public control of the project by surrendering precious public assets.

Commercial development was not only a means to some other good on 42nd Street, but an end in itself. The city had been trying since the 1960s to shift development westward; by the late 1970s, the west side of midtown retained the low scale it had had for generations, while the east side was choking on office buildings. As Herbert Sturz, who was then the city's planning commissioner, recalls, "You had the AT & T Building and the IBM Building going up on Madison Avenue; you had high-rises in mid-block. It was bringing midtown to a halt. We very much wanted to shift development to the West Side." And so, at virtually the same time that the 42nd Street project was announced, the city also began the process of developing new zoning regulations. The new rules, announced in 1982, eliminated many of the bonuses that had made it possible to build colossi like the Trump Tower on Fifth Avenue, though that by itself would not have accomplished the city's goals; parts of the West Side were also "up-zoned," which is to say that developers would be permitted to construct larger buildings, and would pay far lower taxes on them. The 42nd Street Development Project, like the new zoning rules, was designed to stimulate commercial construction.

So the new project was shaped by the political imperative of inducing private actors to pay for public goods, and by the real estate imperative of fostering the creation of a new business district. Whatever happened to "seltzer"? How, that is, could you "preserve the unique ambience of Times Square"—that precious essence which Mayor Koch had vowed to preserve—if you were erecting a forest of massive high-rises? The answer was that you couldn't, since that ambience was plainly connected to Times Square's scale. The city's second-best answer was to establish design guidelines that would accommodate these conflicting goals as far as possible. Public officials assigned this task to the architectural firm of Cooper & Eckstut, which had created the specifications for the well-regarded Battery Park City development. The highly detailed guidelines required that the buildings in midblock retain their low scale and continue to be festooned with signs and light. But the key requirements applied to the office buildings, which constituted the great threat to Times Square's traditional character. They were to have a highly reflective skin of glass or metal to distinguish themselves from the old masonry structures of 42nd Street; the skin would stop fifteen feet or so above ground level in order to create a sense of pedestrian scale for shops. Lower elevations would feature "prominent signage and dramatic lighting" to keep 42nd Street from looking like just another office district. Storefronts would be 75 to 85 percent glass. The buildings would be sharply set back at the fifth floor to preserve the area's traditional cornice line, and then set back again at intervals, while "diversity and contrast in the use of materials, colors and finishes" would "prevent a monolithic appearance." The Times Tower would be preserved as "a focal point for Times Square." The entire street would be bathed in brilliant white light from 120-foot-high poles.

Most important, the guidelines offered a guarantee of public control. The city was turning over 42nd Street to private owners—or rather, by means of condemnation, transferring it from one set of private owners to another—but doing so only under stringent conditions. The guidelines, in effect, precluded the kind of privatized decision-making represented by the City at 42nd Street. And they stood for the values that the city's unofficial stewards held dear. William Taylor, a prominent urban scholar and essayist, described the Cooper & Eckstut plan as an homage to the city's traditions and "a strong statement for public values" rather than those of the marketplace. Paul Goldberger wrote that the design "emerges out of a strong understanding of the nature of the existing city, with strong architectural ties to what is best in what is already there."

The detailed guidelines meant, at least in theory, that many of the architectural decisions had been made in advance. The city would not be choosing an architect; it would be choosing a developer, who in turn would supply an architect. In September 1981, developers submitted proposals to the 42nd Street Development Project. The following April, planners offered "conditional designations" for the twelve sites. The most important, by far, involved the four parcels set aside for office towers, which went to a developer named George Klein. This was a surprising choice, for Klein had far less experience, and cut a far smaller profile in the world of real estate, than virtually all of his competitors. Heir to the Barton candy fortune, Klein had started building just eight years earlier, in Brooklyn; he had erected only two office buildings in Manhattan. He was an outsider in the intensely clannish world of New York real estate, politically conservative and religiously Orthodox in a liberal, Reform culture. Klein was a circumspect, solemn, and eminently respectable character who had decided to make that respectability his calling card. "The best way to break into this world," he had concluded, "was to get the finest architects and put up the kind of buildings that would attract the best tenant." In his brief career as a developer he had already worked with I. M. Pei, Edward Larrabee Barnes, and Philip Johnson.

Klein was, in his quiet way, a man of very large aspirations, much larger than those of the old-line families whose status he hoped to share. Klein wanted to change the face of the city—for the better, of course. His very first real estate venture had been an urban renewal project which he felt had spurred the revival of downtown Brooklyn. And in the redevelopment of 42nd Street he had been granted, he felt, "the opportunity to do something on a grand scale." Klein would never have accepted the distinction between the real estate dynamic and "public values"; he saw Times Square as a blighted area which, like downtown Brooklyn, could be restored to life through development. "Times Square was a real mess," he recalls. "Children were falling into this den of drugs and crime. It was not a place that was correct for New York to have." Like Alexander Parker, Klein aspired to erase the old 42nd Street and put a new one in its place. What Times Square should be, and could be, he felt, was something like Rockefeller Center—a tasteful home for large corporations and elegant shops. He even dubbed the project "Times Square Center."

Klein offered the architectural commission to Philip Johnson, who he felt had "the prestigious image that was important to attract corporate tenants." At the time, in fact, Johnson had a reputation among corporate clients that very few American architects, if any, have ever enjoyed. The headquarters he had designed for AT&T, half-affectionately known as the Chippendale Building, had become the emblematic postmodern structure and had landed him on the cover of *Time* magazine. And like Klein, Johnson was unambiguous about the virtues of erasure. As a young man in prewar New York, he had loved the Astor Hotel. But the Astor was gone, and now Johnson, like Klein, thought of Times Square as a place to avoid. He thought of it, really, as no place at all; he and his partner, John Burgee, felt that their role was to impart a sense of place to an urban wilderness. Times Square Center would be not merely an array of buildings but, like Rockefeller Center, a place in and of itself, an urban settlement made of office towers.

In late 1983, Johnson and Burgee unveiled their design for a suite of four buildings, varying in height and bulk but identically designed in glass with a sheath or screen of light pink granite. The buildings were topped by glass mansard roofs with iron finials—like the nearby Knickerbocker Building, Johnson pointed out, though they also bore a strong resemblance to a building he had just finished in San Francisco. The complex was a true center not only aesthetically but physically, with individual buildings linked to one another and the subway by underground passageways. Corporate tenants, like theatergoers in the City at 42nd Street plan, could be spared the indignity of the street. And there was no sign of the Times Tower, which for eighty years had been the pivot around which Times Square rotated. Bedizened with signs, the Times Tower had become an embarrassment, a ludicrous street person of a building. As Klein says, "Rockefeller Center had a skating rink with a tree as the center. Here was a building with signs all over it. What statement did that make?" Johnson planned to substitute a fountain with a laser light show. He had, all in all, created precisely the image for Times Square that George Klein had craved.

In recent years Johnson had enjoyed, at worst, an equivocal reputation among architecture critics; the Chippendale Building had been praised as lavishly as it had been mocked. But when the critics saw Times Square Center, they came down on him like a ton of bricks. The *Times*'s Ada Louise Huxtable, a qualified fan in years past, derided the proposal as "enormous pop-up buildings with fancy hats." *The New Yorker*'s Brendan Gill described the structures as "great gray ghosts of buildings, shutting out the sun and turning Times Square into the bottom of a well." Critics in both the popular and the professional media lamented the massiveness, dullness, homogeneity, and overwhelming corporateness of the proposed buildings; only Paul Goldberger suggested that "they could cut a sharp and lively profile on the skyline," though he added that "it is difficult not to be concerned" by their bulk. And the idea of demolishing the Times Tower provoked an additional bout of horror.

What had happened? Had public tastes changed while Philip Johnson was sketching out his granite cliffs? This is the view of Paul Travis, who as vice president of the city's Public Development Corporation played a major role in implementing the project. "Johnson's view," Travis explains, "was that historically Times Square had these sober buildings, like the Paramount Building, along the avenues, and that's what he was trying to create. What he missed was that everyone's view about what Times Square was was beginning to change. We decided which Times Square we wanted to create. And the mythical moment we wanted was V-E Day, with the honky-tonk and the crowds." But it is also true that Johnson and Burgee themselves crystallized this new view of Times Square. Though many New Yorkers had spent years thinking of 42nd Street as George Klein did, as a nightmare to be banished, the idea of four colossal slabs towering over the street reminded them of what that street was, or rather, meant. You could put up anything you wanted on Sixth Avenue, or Third Avenue, and the worst it could be was ugly, because these corporate thoroughfares had no past to violate and no soul to corrupt. Even on Broadway and 45th Street, where a hideous new Marriott Marquis was rising, the imperative of development outweighed matters of aesthetics and preservation. But 42nd Street was different; it was a tangible repository of the vivid, racy culture that had been blotted out by the abstract world of the office tower. The Johnson/Burgee buildings felt like an act of profanation, and a terrible challenge.

The Johnson/Burgee plan not only contradicted a collective sense of Times Square but also flagrantly ignored the guidelines. The buildings rose straight up from the ground, with no setbacks at the fifth-floor level to provide an illusion of low scale; they included neither signs nor lights, save for formal lanterns to play across their own grandiose surfaces; and their skin consisted principally of granite, rather than metal or glass. The guidelines were meant to be binding, but Klein understood that they were, in fact, negotiable. Richard Kahan, then head of the Urban Development Corporation, a state body that had the lead role in the redevelopment process, recalls, "George Klein came to me and said, 'What am I supposed to do with these guidelines?' And I said, 'You know exactly what you'll do. As soon as I'm gone, you and Herb Sturz will throw them in the garbage.' " Though self-serving, this explanation seems to be more or less true. Klein argued that setbacks would create upper floors too small to rent to the kind of corporate tenants the project was designed to attract; and the city officials who were managing the project accepted his claim. They also agreed to waive the requirements for signage and lighting, which Klein insisted prospective tenants would consider vulgar.

Of course, it was the guidelines that had reassured architecture critics and civic groups that the project would be carried out according to public values rather than the dictates of the marketplace. But it was now plain that if public authorities had to choose between the real estate imperative of fostering orderly growth by shifting development to the West Side, and the civic imperative of creating a Times Square with which New Yorkers could identify, growth would trump aesthetics and culture. At the press conference where the Johnson/Burgee plans were unveiled, a reporter asked Mayor Koch why the buildings so blatantly violated the guidelines his own administration had established, and he snapped, "I, for one, have never felt it necessary to explain why we improve something." What was there to explain? The buildings *were* the answer. As Vincent Tese, who succeeded Kahan as head of the UDC, later put it, "The buildings may be big and ugly, but the numbers work."

As the plan moved closer to approval by the Board of Estimate, a body that consisted of the presidents of the five boroughs and three other leading officials and that governed all land-use decisions, journalists, academics, urban experts, and lovers of the city began to leap to the defense of this embattled piece of turf. Was the Deuce really so very blighted that it needed so drastic an overhaul? Was it dead, or just somewhat ill? *New York Times* reporter Martin Gottlieb wandered around the block and found no shortage of families, most of them black or Hispanic, enjoying themselves at inexpensive restaurants and movies. "If you come here looking for trouble, most likely you'll find it," said one young man. "But if you look for a good time, you'll find that, too." Gottlieb quoted William Kornblum, the City University professor who had headed the *Bright Light* study as saying, "People go there for the same reason they did when we were kids. You come in from another borough or from uptown looking for some fun. You grab a burger and you go to a movie." This was, of course, the same street where, according to *The Times,* bored teenagers had chased a man to his death on the subway tracks a few years earlier; but now it was seen in a different light.

To the critics, the 42nd Street plan was an urban nightmare they thought had long since been put to rest—"a back-from-the-dead example of the thoroughly discredited bulldozer urban renewal of the 1960s," in the words of the architecture critic Ada Louise Huxtable. Thomas Bender, an urban historian at New York University, wrote in *The Times* that Philip Johnson's "gargantuan office towers" would turn 42nd Street into the equivalent of downtown Washington—"and everyone knows what kind of frightening urban space that becomes after 5 o'clock." Brendan Gill, a writer of suave and lapidary essays on architecture at *The New Yorker,* the president of the Landmarks Conservancy, and one of the city's great boulevardiers, fought the project at every turn, arguing at a UDC hearing that the "four million square feet of conventionally dreary office space" would kill Times Square, not revitalize it. Martin Gottlieb of the *Times* raised a series of disturbing questions: "Can a buoyant street life be designed without seeming contrived and lifeless? . . . Would the sense of place of Times Square be ruined by the demolition of the curved Rialto Building at 43rd Street and Broadway, which houses Nathan's, or of 1 Times Square Plaza?" The answer to the first question was no, and to the second, yes.

The critics did not, on the other hand, have a convincing answer to the question of how one could eliminate the predatory street culture of 42nd Street without making the large-scale changes that would alter the character of the place beyond recognition. Some of them, like Gill, seemed perfectly happy to accept the predatory street life as the price to be paid for preserving 42nd Street's roguish charms, whatever they were. There was a much more plausible argument for smaller buildings, or for less grimly uniform ones, than there was for no office buildings at all.

But it scarcely mattered. This was a public process, but not a plebiscitary one. And the plan had too much political momentum to be stopped in its tracks; both Mayor Koch and the new governor, Mario Cuomo, were committed to it, as was much of the city's corporate and media elite. *The New York Times,* which considered 42nd Street its front yard and which had become increasingly disturbed over the years about the deterioration of the neighborhood, strongly backed the project, even going so far as to accept the proposed demolition of the Times Tower. The Board of Estimate hearings, in late October and early November 1984, were an elaborate formality. Public officials praised the project, while local politicians, community board members, scholars, and gadflies grandiloquently denounced it. The Board of Estimate heard one and all, and then voted unanimously to approve the project.

The argument over 42nd Street redevelopment, like virtually all issues involving planning, was largely a debate among elites. And it was the pro-growth elite, not the preservationist elite, that held the balance of power. But there could be changes at the margin. Neither George Klein nor Philip Johnson wanted to put up buildings the public hated, and the outcry forced them back to the drawing board. Johnson, in particular, seems to have had immediate second thoughts. He told an interviewer in 1994 that he had "never liked the big towers." Asked why, then, he had designed them, he said, "Because I wanted a reminiscent thing that would look like the Pierre Hotel. I thought it would look natural. You have to have a top on these things. I was totally post-modern at the time, and I wanted to get that going." This offhanded self-dismissal is vintage Johnson; he is a profoundly ironic character who has long protected himself from his own absurd cultural authority with a bulletproof irreverence. In a recent conversation, Johnson, age ninety-five, raised an amused eyebrow at pictures of his design and murmured, "I must have been out of my mind."

Back at the drawing board once again, Johnson produced a new set of buildings—sleeker, more abstract, and less referential. The towers were now made almost wholly of glass, as the guidelines foresaw, and they no longer formed a wholly matched set; but they still lacked setbacks as well as signage. In a final design, executed in 1989, John Burgee, by then separated from Johnson, produced far gaudier buildings, with busy surfaces and with extensive electronic signage incorporated into the structure; these came closest to satisfying critics' wishes, though the setbacks that had been so integral to the guidelines were now a mere memory. None of these designs, in any case, were destined to be executed.

It turned out that in the new, post-Moses world of planning, the political process had become vulnerable to outsiders in all sorts of ways. Opponents had learned that even if you couldn't outvote the party of growth, you could peck it to death through a combination of bad publicity and litigation. And the pecking process over 42nd Street began right away. Indeed, the first lawsuit came even before the project was approved; and then came the deluge—forty-seven suits in all. This was an astounding number even by New York standards. And though they alleged violations of free speech or due process rights, or of antitrust or eminent domain statutes, all but two of them, according to one tabulation, were filed by those with vested interests, principally developers who hadn't been awarded—or hadn't even sought—a piece of the action, or property owners who hoped to force public officials to pay them more in exchange for their property. These included such families as the Milsteins and the Dursts, who had been playing the game of real estate for generations, and who understood very well how to get things done, or blocked, in New York.

The biggest potential loser in the development process was the Brandt family, which operated a near monopoly of the movie theater mini-district on and around 42nd Street. Running eighteen hours a day, the fourteen theaters in the project area controlled by the Brandts and a partner generated enormous amounts of revenue even if most of their seats were empty at the average showing. The Brandts also owned two office buildings on Broadway between 42nd and 43rd Streets, and another on 43rd between Seventh and Eighth. If it was an empire of sleaze, it was an empire nonetheless, and the Brandts were not about to surrender it without a fight. The Brandts had bid for the rights to develop the five theaters that were to be restored to use as private legitimate theaters, but the real game always had to do with compensation. "They were using the development designation as a carrot to try to get us to agree to the low values," says Robert Brandt, who directed the family's real estate operations. "The numbers they were putting on the table for our properties were grossly inadequate." The Brandts fought back in letters to the editor and op-ed articles; they hired a prominent social scientist to trumpet the evils of urban renewal; and they ended with a fusillade of litigation.

The implacable opposition of the Brandts and other powerful real estate forces demonstrates why it was so difficult to use urban renewal laws to revitalize Times Square: the state was seizing property with great current economic value and even greater potential value. If the state had to pay what the owners considered fair value, the project would never happen. But the battle also proved why forceful state action was necessary. The businesses that catered to Times Square's population did very well; they had no more incentive to enter a more respectable line of work that would draw different customers than opium farmers have to grow wheat. As long as 42nd Street was dominated by porno theaters and sex shops and liquor stores, good restaurants and retailers weren't about to lease space there. Current uses would continue drawing current users. "The perception of turf," as the environmental-impact statement put it, could only be changed by force majeure: the urban renewal laws.

The lawsuits dragged on for years, just as the complainants had hoped. And while Klein might have been able to build in the mid- to late eighties, when the real estate market was strong, by 1990, when the last lawsuit was dismissed, the market had gone into a tailspin. The banks and white-shoe law firms that Klein had carefully cultivated as anchor tenants had long since given up, and the entire project went into the deep freeze. Litigation offered a force majeure of its own. The aesthetic and intellectual critique of the project had hit home, but produced only modest changes, whereas the lawsuits had been shaky, even frivolous; yet the suits had succeeded where criticism had failed.

SAVING BILLBOARD HELL

T HE REDEVELOPMENT OF 42ND STREET, whatever its flaws, was an act of urban planning, a conscious re-creation of a bounded urban space almost from the ground up; but the rest of Times Square, seedy but not pathological, was for many years permitted to develop, or not, according to the fluctuations of the marketplace. No large structure had gone up along the great spillways of Broadway and Seventh Avenue since the 1930s. But the real estate boom of the sixties, which had filled the East Side of midtown Manhattan with big buildings, had made the West Side, with its traditionally low scale, look increasingly appealing as a development site. In 1966, the Astor Hotel, a remnant of Times Square's age of opulence that occupied the block immediately to the north of the Paramount, was closed, and then demolished, to make way for a fifty-four-story building to be designated 1 Astor Plaza, a fabricated address designed to link a new and thoroughly unloved building to the past represented by the building it had replaced. But 1515 Broadway, as the building was universally known, remained a solitary, and largely empty, foray into Times Square for many years.

A developer named Peter Sharp had been patiently assembling parcels on the block immediately to the north of the Astor throughout the 1960s. By 1970, Sharp was ready to commission a design. He turned to Robert Venturi, the provocative architect who wrote *Complexity and Contradiction in Architecture*. Venturi proposed something radically different from 1 Astor Plaza: rather than replace the hodgepodge of buildings with a tower, he proposed to wrap the entire assemblage in huge signs. Venturi described his thinking in a subsequent book, *Learning from Las Vegas* (written with Steven Izenour and Denise Scott Brown). "Times Square is not dramatic space," he wrote, "but dramatic decoration. It is two-dimensional, decorated by symbols, lights and movement." Thus he concluded that "a decorated shed" would be a more apt homage to its traditions than "megastructural bridges, balconies and spaces." Venturi was the first architect to propose a new idiom faithful to Times Square's helter-skelter, mongrelized past; but since he had done so with an almost perverse indifference to the site's economic value, the developer rejected the idea.

Sharp was, on the other hand, dazzled by the work of John Portman, the architect-developer who had built the Peachtree Center in Atlanta, and who was becoming known for his glass hotels with soaring interior spaces. Portman was one of the iconic figures of the age of urban renewal, for he built immense structures which spanned, or simply abolished, the traditional street grid; many of them turned a great, blank concrete wall to the street. Portman was a very busy man; he was then working on the Renaissance Center, in Detroit, and Embarcadero Center, in San Francisco. He proposed to build a two-thousand-room hotel where Venturi had hoped to raise a decorated shed. The plan envisioned two great concrete slabs rising fifty-six stories connected by five-story-high bridges like the rungs of a great ladder.

As the planning went forward, it became plain that two cherished and irreplaceable theaters—the Morosco and the Helen Hayes—would have to be destroyed, as would several less important theaters. City and state officials tried to persuade Portman to take an alternative site farther north on Broadway, or to cantilever the hotel above the theaters; but he refused. By 1980, theater groups had begun to mobilize to stop the project. A group of prominent actors, including Jason Robards, Lauren Bacall, and James Earl Jones, tried to dramatize the impending disaster through performances at the two theaters and with public protests. The debate over the Portman project turned out to be a kind of dry run for the 42nd Street renovation, for here, too, the preservationists took arms against the forces of development. The threatened destruction of the theaters had placed Times Square in an entirely new light, as an endangered neighborhood harboring beloved cultural artifacts. Robards, with a theatrical flair for the apocalyptic, described the Portman project as "the end of everything." When the city refused to budge, opponents turned to the courts, and lawsuits went all the way to the Supreme Court before failing. The Morosco and the Helen Hayes were demolished on March 23, 1982.

The Marriott Marquis rapidly became the most hated building in Times Square, indeed, one of the most hated buildings in New York. When the hotel opened, in 1985, Paul Goldberger described it as "an upended concrete bunker," "a sealed environment," and "a hulking, joyless presence." While Robert Venturi proposed to celebrate Times Square as it was, or had been, John Portman designed his building to keep the street at bay. "People are still hung up on the goddamn corny image of what's in Times Square," Portman was quoted as saying. "There's not one great thing about it." The Marriott Marquis, like so many of Portman's other projects, ostentatiously turns its giant concrete back on the street. The lobby is on the eighth floor, a remote perch that no casual pedestrian is likely to reach; the floors below are low, gloomy, red-carpeted spaces pierced by thick concrete pillars. Even when, after riding up many an elevator, you reach the lobby, a great overhang still blocks the view; only by walking out to the bar can you look up and see the vast atrium that is the building's central architectural feature.

The Marriott Marquis came to pass not only because protest failed and public officials took Portman's side, but because at the time questions of design, as well as the loss of cherished theaters, seemed niggling compared to the imperative of building. As the editors of *Architectural Forum* noted in 1973, "Any Portman in a storm (especially that of Times Square) will do just fine." Prominent figures on Broadway and in the preservation world supported the project. A *New York Times* editorial observed that "lovers of Broadway should concentrate on what they can gain, not on what they can stop." And indeed, the Marquis has been one of the most successful hotels in the Marriott chain, bringing tens of thousands of modestly heeled tourists to a secure, exciting environment in the middle of tumultuous Times Square. As the architect Hugh Hardy wryly notes, "The Marriott Marquis is just about the grossest building ever, but you walk in there and there's forty-three cheerleaders coming out of the elevator. It's some sort of Middle American refuge where people feel comfortable."

The fight over the Marriott Marquis implied a choice between a dreadful building that quickened the pulse of Times Square while laying siege to its traditions, and an aesthetically and culturally satisfying one that served no development objective and so could not be built. It implied, in other words, that Times Square would have to be destroyed in order to be saved, just as the General Project Plan implied that 42nd Street would have to be destroyed in order to be saved. That's no choice at all; and over the next few years, a struggle would be waged to save Times Square in a way that made it worth saving.

NEW YORK CITY DOES not have much of an unfettered market in real estate, or any other commodity. And so it would be a mistake to say that "the market" was transforming Times Square. A combination of state and local incentives had made the Marriott Marquis worth building. The 1982 zoning rules, which conferred tax breaks on new development and permitted extra density in the area, made building in Times Square far more attractive than it ever had been before. What's more, the rules included a sunset provision: builders had to break ground by May 1988 in order to qualify for the benefits. So a race quickly developed to build along Broadway and Seventh Avenue. By 1984, when the Board of Estimate approved the 42nd Street Development Project, thus making Times Square Center an apparent fait accompli, a few buildings had already begun to rise at the edge of the zoning area, and it was plain that there would be many more to come. Philip Johnson's colossal suite of gray flannel towers offered an image—a nightmarish image, to many of New York's urbanists—of how the new Times Square was to be colonized. And so, in the mid-eighties, as the 42nd Street Development Project began to recede into a mist of litigation, the question of Times Square came to the fore.

The widely shared sense of urgency about conditions on 42nd Street, and the prestige both of George Klein and of Philip Johnson, had combined to sway or at least neutralize elite opinion on the redevelopment project. But this would not be so in Times Square. Lawyers and architects and editorial writers still went to plays and restaurants there; the words "Times Square" conjured up much warmer associations than the words

"42nd Street." "Times Square was a place you went to celebrate," says Hugh Hardy, who had grown up watching musicals from the balcony of practically every theater in Times Square and could still bang out a show tune on the piano. "And here you had the developer talking about turning Times Square into Rockefeller Center." Klein's decision to demolish the Times Tower seemed like the worst sort of proof of his earnestness. Hardy was a leading member of the Municipal Art Society, the most venerable of New York's civic groups and a bastion of preservationist sentiment—the very same elite body that had tried to abolish signs in Times Square back in the day of O. J. Gude. The group had endorsed the Johnson plan, if tepidly; but now it recognized that the northward march of corporate towers could annihilate something precious in the life of the city.

The MAS formed a committee to study the problem, and its members quickly realized that Times Square was not, in fact, 42nd Street—that the movie theaters up and down Broadway sold more tickets for first-run films than the rest of the city's theaters combined, that the hotels and the restaurants were full of life. The obvious campaign for the MAS was to call for the preservation of theaters, and in this it had the passionate support of a theater community still outraged over the destruction of the Hayes and Morosco. But that would not be enough. The question arose, as it had on 42nd Street, as to what exactly it was, beyond or perhaps besides physical structures, that needed to be preserved; and the answer Hardy and others came up with was that it was the scale of Times Square, the raffish atmosphere, and above all, in a great historical irony, the lights and signs. These were the tangible elements that produced the intangible phenomenon that went by the name "Times Square." Hardy told the group's board that the committee's goal was "to counter the argument that you have to abolish Times Square in order to clean it up." The group would accept neither preservationist absolutism nor annihilating gentrification.

The Municipal Art Society now began a crafty and relentless public relations campaign. In March 1984, the MAS staged a competition to design a replacement for the Times Tower—an event that proved architects were a great deal fonder of that misbegotten building, and thus of the degraded urban texture surrounding it, than were George Klein and Philip

Johnson. And then it went to work dramatizing the idea that bright lights were indispensable in Times Square. On a Saturday evening in the fall of 1984, when the debate over 42nd Street was about to come to a head, the group arranged to have all the lights in Times Square turned off at 7:30, when the place would be jammed with theatergoers. The one sign that remained blared, "HEY, MR. MAYOR! IT'S DARK OUT HERE! HELP KEEP THE BRIGHT LIGHTS IN TIMES SQUARE!" This cheeky scare tactic garnered tremendous publicity.

In 1985, the society commissioned a design firm to build a model of what Times Square would look like if every available parcel were built out to the maximum height and density permitted by the zoning rules. The model, which could be easily manipulated to demonstrate various hypothetical outcomes, became the centerpiece of a short film narrated by Jason Robards. This may have been the most effective gimmick of all, in part because it was not merely a gimmick. The film described Times Square, in rather oddly pastoral terms, as "a tremendous, well-proportioned outdoor room," a neighborhood whose character was defined by its low scale. The new zoning law, it warned, would permit the addition of sixteen million square feet of space. The model, shot from above, showed the tiny slit of light that would reach the street level were the zoning law to be fully exploited. "Instead of a bowl of light," Robards admonished, "we would be offered canyon walls." The theaters would remain, but only as "curiosities of a bygone era."

The MAS had adroitly raised the stakes so that Times Square itself seemed to hang in the balance. And they succeeded in altering the consciousness of New Yorkers—or at least those few New Yorkers who actually played a role in the planning process. After seeing the MAS film, Paul Goldberger, who only a few years earlier had found something good to say about the George Klein project for 42nd Street and even about the Marriott Marquis, wrote that "the light, the energy, the sense of contained chaos that have long characterized Times Square are essentially incompatible with high-rise office buildings, or with stark and harsh modern hotel towers like the Marriott." The MAS simulation, Goldberger wrote, proved that the effect of unchecked construction on Times Square would be "devastating."

The MAS and its allies on the local community board, and among architects and signage professionals and others, understood that the 1982 zoning law could not be abolished; development would have to be shaped rather than blocked. So the actual purpose of the relentless publicity campaign was to get the city to reopen the planning guidelines for Times Square in order to prevent developers from putting up the same glass slabs they would have built on Sixth Avenue. The developers themselves opposed this movement to a man (and virtually all of them were men). Among them, it was a matter beyond debate that the law firms and investment banks and even entertainment companies who were their most prized tenants do not like buildings with signs. Scarcely any of them currently occupied such buildings. Signs violated the modernist taboo against ornamentation; even the eclectic buildings being designed by Philip Johnson and the other postmodernists had an unblemished façade. More to the point, signs were tacky. As David Solomon, a developer who was counting on Morgan Stanley to occupy the new tower he was building on Broadway at 47th Street, put it, "Investment bankers and lawyers don't want to work in an environment of flashing lights. They want trees and clean streets . . . museums and sidewalk cafes." In short, they wanted Fifth Avenue, or perhaps the Faubourg St. Honoré—just as the MAS itself had three-quarters of a century earlier.

But the destruction of the theaters and the decision to approve the George Klein plan had mobilized community, civic, and theater groups as they had not been mobilized before. The public relations campaign had changed the balance of opinion; and in late 1984, the New York City Planning Commission agreed to reopen the design guidelines. Perhaps more important, the commission retained as consultants several experts who were committed to a very different vision of Times Square, and of New York City, than were the city's chief developers. In order to advise it on issues of signage and lighting the city hired Paul Marantz, a specialist in theatrical lighting and a lifelong devotee of Times Square. Marantz considered the very idea of planning antithetical to Times Square, and said so when city officials first approached him. "My feeling was that it should happen as a force of nature, not as the result of some fiat," Marantz says. But planning officials persuaded him that the Times Square he loved would cease to exist if nature had its way. His job, he was told, was just "to start the engine."

Marantz and his colleagues at Jules Fisher and Paul Marantz, Inc., set about trying to understand the Times Square–ness of Times Square—what it was in the juxtaposition of light and signs and buildings and sight lines that gave Times Square its inimitable look. They spent hours wandering around the denuded Times Square of the mid-eighties, poring over old photographs, and studying the design of the neon precincts of Tokyo, Hong Kong, London. "We decided it had a lot to do with scale," Marantz says; "what was on the first floor, what was on the second floor." The Times Square look was, in effect, vertically tiered: regulations would have to distinguish among retail or marquee-type signs at the ground level, larger signs above, and then "super-signs" at the roofline or the setback. This was in effect Marantz's recognition that the chaotic energy he loved about Times Square could be provoked, or at least ignited, "by fiat." Marantz also made a list of the different types of signs in Times Square—billboards, neon, Plexiglas sheets over lightbulbs—and proposed that every new building wear a collage of such signs.

It was plain that not just signs but light would have to be mandated. If signs gave Times Square its look of gorgeous disarray, its epic higgledy-piggledy, then electricity was what made the place magnificent. When you thought of Times Square, you thought first of a riot of light. But how much light was enough? And how could you possibly quantify that amount? Marantz wanted lighted signs at least as brilliant as the few, mostly Japanese ones, that remained in Times Square. "It's very hard to stand on the street and measure the actual impact of a sign," Marantz says. "You could measure the amount of light coming from the sign, but not the impact that one sign makes on the viewer." That was what Marantz wanted to measure: the sign's actual effect. He drilled a hole in the back of a 35-millimeter camera, mounted a light meter on the back, pointed it toward a sign, and took readings. In this way, Marantz invented a new unit, christened the LUTS: "light unit Times Square." His team compiled a book of LUTS readings from current signs.

The new zoning rules, eight pages of extraordinarily specific and demanding requirements, were approved by the City Planning Commission in 1986 and finalized after a tumultuous, late-night session of the city's

Board of Estimate in February 1987. The regulations required new buildings along Seventh Avenue and Broadway to be sharply set back after sixty
feet—a stricter version of the principle the city had set for 42nd Street in
1981, and that it had permitted George Klein to flout. And Marantz and
Fisher's proposed guidelines were adopted in the form of minimum
LUTS readings, to be measured by the contraption Marantz and his team
had devised. The guidelines required, as well, minimum numbers, sizes,
and types of signs, as well as minimal levels of illumination. A block-long
building would thus have to provide at least 16,800 square feet of lighted
signage, or about as much as already existed on Times Square's brightest
blocks.

Here was something absolutely new in New York history: until this
time, zoning rules had been used to prohibit, or sharply limit, lighting
and signage, never to require it. Fifth Avenue couldn't have lighted signs,
and Times Square could; but now Times Square would become a kind of
protected neon enclave. Here was preservationism designed to protect
precisely the phenomenon that had, in years past, constituted the preservationists' greatest target.

FORTY-SECOND STREET HAD to be drastically transformed, for the
street had swallowed up all the piecemeal solutions that had been tried before. The rest of Times Square, for all its seediness, was a functioning entertainment district. And so whatever was lost of Times Square in the
process of development did not have to be sacrificed for the good of the
neighborhood. Indeed, the angriest critics of the new Times Square felt
that the very act of "developing" such a place was a profanation, a blow
against urbanness itself. Writing in *The New Yorker* in 1991, Brendan Gill
described Times Square as the heart of a new urban Disneyland. In place
of "a gaudy, tawdry medley of theatres, restaurants, rehearsal halls, hotels," and so on, Gill wrote, public officials and private developers had fostered "a cold-blooded corporate simulacrum of an amusement park,
designed to contain millions of square feet of offices filled with tens of
thousands of office drones."

The Municipal Art Society's simulation had persuaded Paul Goldberger that Times Square's spirit of "contained chaos" would evaporate

amid the office towers. This might or might not prove to be true, but there could be no question that development had eliminated Times Square's defining sense of scale. In *The Experience of Place*, published in 1990, the journalist Tony Hiss, who had worked closely with the MAS and contributed the image of the bowl of light, evoked the last moments of Times Square as a place of human scale. Standing in the afternoon sunlight, he wrote, "I took a good look at the low buildings along Broadway and realized that from the center of the Square, these small buildings seemed to be much farther away than just across the street. At this point, one part of what I was experiencing began to make better sense to me: Although Times Square isn't as big or as open or as carefully planned an open space as, say, the Grand Army Plaza in Brooklyn, it used to have an unusual feeling of welcoming spaciousness that wasn't to be found at the Brooklyn plaza or at any other New York intersection. It gave you the sense of being protected, because it gave the sense that there was room enough here for all."

And so something irretrievable, something precious, was lost when the floodgates of development were opened in Times Square. Gill, in fact, prophesied that the resulting horror would become so manifest that it would undermine the very idea of the skyscraper—a prospect he heartily welcomed. That, of course, hasn't happened. And it would be terrible if it had, for no truly modern city can accept the retrograde notion that office buildings, and the white-collar economy which they make possible, are inherently philistine. The argument may work in Florence, but not in New York. Does this require the remorseless destruction of the old? Perhaps it does. But that's what cities do: they build the new right on top of the old.

DISNEY EX MACHINA

Throughout the 1980s, the 42nd Street Development Project had appeared to consist of a cluster of office towers dragging a tail of theaters and stores, and a giant wholesale mart glimmering in the remote distance. By the end of the decade, though, the office towers were locked in the doldrums of a sinking real estate market, the mart had become a tar baby from which one developer after another had extricated himself, and the planned hotel across the street was barely a hypothesis. The only noticeable effect of this immense public venture was on 42nd Street itself. In 1990, the lawsuits that had held up the development having finally been settled, the Urban Development Corporation formally condemned the eastern two-thirds of the block, which included all the theaters and most of the proposed retail space. Soon the storefronts were emptying out and the street was turning into a wasteland of shuttered shops. There were afternoons when it looked as if you could drive a golf ball down 42nd Street without hitting anyone, though porn continued to thrive at the uncondemned Eighth Avenue end. Here was a wholly unexpected situation: while the office towers languished, the condemnation process had taken a wrecking ball to 42nd Street's perverse ecology.

The block had finally become the tabula rasa developers always wished it to be; the question was whether anyone would come along to write a new script. The premise of the 42nd Street Development Project had always been that everything had to happen at once; in fact, George Klein had originally bid for the entire package in order to protect himself from a situation in which he was trying to attract corporate tenants at one end of the street while the wrong sort of people streamed out of *Ginger's Wet Dream* at the other. But now the street was being held captive to the towers.

It was the condemnation process, oddly enough, that freed public officials to see the street anew. The 42nd Street DP now owned much of the block, and thus had to take responsibility for it. "The best thing that happened is when we took over the street," says Rebecca Robertson, a former New York City planning official who became the DP's executive director at the time of the condemnation. Robertson spent a good part of 1990 talking to the sex shops' owners, and the theater owners, and the lighting and costume suppliers and rehearsal studio managers who worked in the buildings upstairs. She came to realize that 42nd Street was not simply a case history of urban pathology, as it seemed to George Klein or Philip Johnson, but a great mecca of entertainment in serious disrepair. She saw, or felt she saw, the vanished traces of Hubert's and Nathan's and the penny arcades. "If you spent time on the street," Robertson says, "it spoke to you. Much of it was in ruins, but there's something more powerful about ruins than any reality."

The city-state plan had envisioned that the theaters on the block would be restored to operation as legitimate theaters, which of course they had not been for more than half a century; two, the Victory and the Liberty, were to open as nonprofit venues, while the others were to be self-supporting. Exactly where the audience for these new theaters would come from was hardly clear. And it was obvious to Robertson, and to everyone else in the theater world, that, with the exception of the New Amsterdam, the 42nd Street theaters were too small to turn a profit. Robertson concluded that the public planners had cynically dangled the prospect of theater preservation before the public in order to win approval for commercial development. But preservationism itself seemed like a specious response to 42nd Street's crude, commercial, hectoring soul. "If they had more respect for what the street had been," Robertson says, "they never would have fashioned a plan like that." Her vision for 42nd Street was not so very different from Hugh Hardy's for Times Square: flashing lights, big signs, popular entertainment. The new Times Square zoning rules offered a forward-looking program designed to preserve the area's essential character—though they, too, conceded the inevitability of overscale office towers.

Robertson's ambition was to fashion a populist alternative to the backward-looking and in any case unachievable elitism of the original plan. And she had arrived at her job at what turned out to be an oddly propitious moment to forge a new 42nd Street. It was becoming fashionable to embrace the heady chaos and cheap thrills of Times Square, as it had not been a decade earlier, when Cityscape would have enclosed 42nd Street in glass. Pop culture, which is to say commercial culture, was lapping at the ramparts of high culture. The controversial "High and Low" exhibition at the Museum of Modern Art, held in 1990, questioned the hierarchical distinction between high and low art. Herbert Muschamp, who replaced Paul Goldberger as *The New York Times*'s architecture critic in 1992, brought a very new voice to the newspaper of record. In an article in the summer of 1992, Muschamp described Times Square as a pop icon where "the Popular and the Cultural converge, where crowds cross paths with icons: pop songs, pop drinks, chorus lines, headlines, hemlines, posters, cartoons, paperbacks, magazine covers, billboards, blue jeans, lipsticks, double features."

Goldberger had, after some hesitation, taken the traditional preservationist view that tall buildings violated the historic scale of Times Square; but Muschamp embraced the office tower as the perfect symbol for a new Times Square devoted to the production of pop culture: "Why not," he deadpanned, "an intersection where Sony, Disney, ABC and Spike Lee Enterprises square off against one another from King Kong towers?" Muschamp elicited suggestions for a new Times Square from four architects and designers, who proposed among other things a twenty-four-hour glass-walled health club where pedestrians could gape at hard and curving bodies, or a twenty-four-hour "News Café" set in the Times Tower in which passersby would be invited to "tell us your dream" by means of a video monitor connected to a screen mounted atop the building.

Here was a new, frankly celebratory urban aesthetic, reveling in the goofy contradictions of pop culture and, perhaps even more important, prepared to accept the giant corporations that pumped it out. The phrase "a corporate Times Square" was no longer an automatic term of opprobrium; what mattered was the difference between a vital and a moribund corporate Times Square. A new atmosphere had arrived; Rebecca Robertson was one of the few public officials who got it. "The idea of populism had changed," she says. "You couldn't bring back the carny populism of the thirties"—Hubert's and Lindy's and shooting galleries. "What populism means now is corporate culture, whether you like it or not. Our idea of populism was whatever it is people would choose for entertainment in their spare time; it required that we be nonjudgmental." Once you choose to be nonjudgmental in matters of taste, you will eventually find common ground with the equally nonjudgmental purveyors of mass culture.

From a pragmatic point of view, the immediate question was how to uncouple the fate of 42nd Street from that of the office towers. Robertson and other officials reached an agreement with George Klein to develop an interim plan that would allow a new 42nd Street to rise even as the developer waited for the market to return. The idea had the virtue of mollifying the developer, and the development community in general, for whatever went up could always be dismantled when the time came. Robertson asked the architect Robert Stern to draw up the interim plan; he had the insight, or good fortune, to ask the designer Tibor Kalman to coauthor the plan. They made, to put it mildly, an odd pair. Stern was in many ways a backward-looking figure, a historian of architecture who was sometimes derided for designing charming homes that simulated a genteel past for the benefit of the newly rich—the Ralph Lauren of architecture. Kalman, on the other hand, was arguably the most brilliantly inventive and free-spirited designer of his generation—a prankster and a provocateur, a sixties radical and eighties entrepreneur who managed to alchemize his sense of the absurd into a thriving practice. Kalman's designs featured self-referential jokes, incongruous objects, fractured lettering, and scrambled logic; he famously designed a watch face with the numbers out of sequence. The twenty-four-hour News Café and its dreamcast had also been his idea. Kalman (who died, aged fifty, in 1999) loved disorder as much as Stern loved order. The two men argued constantly. "He was always afraid I would turn it into mainstream Disneyland," says Stern, "and I was afraid he would turn it into something in outer space."

Stern did, in fact, sit on the board of Disney and had designed a house for its chairman, Michael Eisner. But he was also a former student of Robert Venturi's at Yale, and he had absorbed Venturi's reaction against the high modern aesthetic into his own form of postmodernism, more playful than Johnson's. He was, as well, a New York kid who had fond memories of the era of carny populism in Times Square. Stern would resist what he called "the Rockefeller Center impulse." Though he shared none of Kalman's subversive impulses, Stern, like Robertson, felt that you could use pop culture and kitsch to trace a path back to the old 42nd Street without losing yourself in nostalgia.

The interim plan, evocatively called *42nd Street Now!* and released in September 1993, was a Kalmanesque manifesto as much as it was a planning document. Probably it was the first document of any kind in the history of Times Square redevelopment that excited urbanists more than it did real estate developers. Stern and Kalman evoked the "thrillingly unpredictable daily drama" of the block's street life in its age of glory, as well as its shameless commercialism: "42nd Street celebrated, as perhaps no other street or neighborhood did, the individual entrepreneur, whose brash confidence and on-the-money commercial instincts went such a long way towards defining the city's energy and outlook, at once wildly optimistic and coolly bottom line." The idea that there need be no contradiction between the drama of the streets and the ring of the cash register, between "authenticity" and the marketplace, was itself something of a revelation, at least in the debate over the future of 42nd Street. Indeed, the document pointedly, if hyperbolically, observed that "top quality office buildings have always been part of the 42nd Street Project Area, and will continue to be a major part of the long-term redevelopment." Even office towers need not be incompatible with a vibrant street life. (And by this time, the original Johnson/Burgee design was history.)

A brief on behalf of a theory about a place, *42nd Street Now!* was more a rhetorical document than a planning one. "The new 42nd Street will be an enhanced version of itself," Stern and Kalman wrote, "not a gentrified theme park or festival market." But there was a problem. How can a plan foster a spirit whose essence is spontaneity? How can you intentionally recreate a thing never created by intention in the first place? Martin Gottlieb of the *Times* had asked the same question ten years earlier, without offering an answer. Stern and Kalman argued that the answer lay in 42nd Street's peculiar archaeology. "New had been heaped on old," they wrote, "so that the street now has a richly layered, collaged look almost unique in the world's great entertainment places." Forty-second Street was "a collage awaiting yet another layer." They proposed to add, not subtract; and what they would add, essentially, was a gaudy layer of lights and signs and shiny new outer surfaces. They could not specify how these would be added without destroying the spontaneity they hoped to spark; indeed, *42nd Street Now!* presented itself as "an unplan"—a very Kalmanesque word—whose goal was to provoke wild diversity by prohibiting "any uniform or coordinated system."

Stern and Kalman's premise was that if you gave 42nd Street a new skin to wriggle into, the old spirit would eventually return on its own. The plan included three "conceptual drawings" of 42nd Street sites decked out in glowing signage, but these are only suggestions (though the northeast corner of 42nd and Eighth now looks very much as Kalman and Stern imagined it). Stripped to its essentials, *42nd Street Now!* was a mildly redacted version of the 1987 Times Square guidelines. The plan mandated minimal levels of signage and lighting up and down the street, transparent façades, long hours of operation, sidewalk amenities, and the like. Like the earlier guidelines, it largely left the question of usage—of what would actually happen on the street—up to the tenants themselves.

It was a bold idea, though the language may have been more brilliant than the idea. Absent the polemics, the design itself was just a little bit . . . Disneyesque. The conceptual drawing for the eastern end of 42nd Street, with a huge globe plastered with TV screens and a giant can of Diet Coke launched halfway out of a billboard and a wrapped gift box on a rooftop, looked like a delirious version of Disneyland. There was no Ferris wheel, but one wouldn't have been out of place. Wasn't this, then, old orange juice in new cartons? The answer was "Not quite." The City at 42nd Street had offered a semisealed and altogether controlled environment, an unspontaneous monument to urban spontaneity. The *42nd Street Now!* plan offered a design matrix, a set of materials and dimensions and aesthetic principles from which infinite possibilities could spring. And the plan was oriented to the street—to the pedestrian—rather than to the interior; it embraced the daily drama. Nevertheless, the new willingness to explore pop culture, with whatever level of irony or camp, meant that "Disneyesque" was not the epithet it had been in 1980. The Technicolor world of the urban theme park no longer inspired the horror it had before.

A public that had long since given up hope for the block greeted *42nd Street Now!* excitedly. (Muschamp called it a "wonderful plan," which would "encourage the dormant genius of the place to shine.") But the Cooper & Eckstut guidelines had been admirable, too, and they had been brushed aside when they proved inconvenient (though the design principles for Times Square had been strictly applied). George Klein was just as eager as Rebecca Robertson to see glimmers of life on 42nd Street, and Prudential Insurance, which was financing the office development, had agreed to pay $20 million to bring the interim plan to life. But the plan applied to Klein's five sites as well as to the rest of the block; and Klein was still dreaming of Rockefeller Center. "If you're tearing an area down because of tawdriness," he asks plaintively, "why are you putting the tawdriness back in?" Klein argued, correctly, that the welter of signs and the flashing lights were native to Times Square, but not to 42nd Street; Stern and Kalman had, at the very least, stretched a point. But Klein was in a much weaker position than he had been in 1984: Prudential had already paid out well over $200 million for condemnation and improvements. "We had so much money in this already that we really didn't have much of a choice," as he says. And Robertson would not back down. So this time, when the real estate dynamic came up against public values—or at least against a publicly determined sense of the common good—it was the latter that won.

Now a stunning new script was ready for 42nd Street; but it was still only a script, until someone actually decided to move in. Since the street would be about popular entertainment, it plainly needed one of those giant entertainment companies Herbert Muschamp had fantasized about. And this led to a crowning irony. The single brand name that could do the most for 42nd Street was plainly Disney. But Disney was not only a nonurban but a fundamentally antiurban entertainer; the supremely orchestrated environment of a Disneyland was utterly incompatible with the accidental nature of urban life, not to mention the thrillingly unpredictable daily drama of 42nd Street. But by 1992, Michael Eisner, the chairman of the company, was thinking about creating live stage plays from Disney's hit movies, starting with the new *Beauty and the Beast*. And Eisner was himself a New Yorker and a theater buff who rarely missed a Broadway play.

Both public and private officials in New York had been urging Eisner to look at Broadway as the flagship for his new theater effort. Eisner had consistently declined, unwilling to bring Mickey Mouse into such close proximity with massage parlors and head shops. In March 1993, Eisner paid a visit to New York and went to see the blueprints for his new house in Robert Stern's office. Stern showed him the twenty-five-foot-long foam core model for *42nd Street Now!* and suggested that the new 42nd Street would be perfectly compatible with the new Disney. They talked about the New Amsterdam Theatre, the home of Ziegfeld and the fabled rooftop theater, as well as the site that had launched the Ford Foundation's ill-fated dalliance with 42nd Street; and the following day, Eisner, his wife and children, Stern, and Rebecca Robertson took a tour that has since become the stuff of legend in the little world of Times Square redevelopment—boots plowing through deep water, pigeon droppings, crumbling masonry, the dim outlines of the art nouveau splendor. Eisner immediately said that he would be interested in taking over the theater, though he made no further commitment.

Disney went through some odd contortions as it began to seriously contemplate the alien idea of an urban environment. The company at first thought of closing off the entire block to produce a Disneyland in midtown Manhattan, or of converting the entire street to a unified Disney attraction. Eisner could have asked for almost anything and the city would have complied, for such was Disney's reputation that 42nd Street was likely to fill up simply on the strength of its commitment; fortunately, the company recognized that it would be better off inhabiting the new environment being established on the street than throwing up a shell around itself. In the end, Disney insisted that the city pay virtually the entire $34 million cost of repairing the theater; and though this was the exact opposite of the strategy the city had pursued with the overall project, where the developer had borne all the costs, the city capitulated. At the end of 1994, with the negotiations almost at a close, Disney suddenly added a number of other conditions, two foremost among them: that the city find two "nationally recognized and reputable companies who are actively engaged in the entertainment business" to lease sizable amounts of space on the block, and that it clear all twenty or so sex shops from the area. The city reached agreements with Madame Tussaud's Wax Museum, which had seen a deal for the Times Tower and an adjacent office site fall through, and with AMC Entertainment, which agreed to operate a multiplex near the Eighth Avenue end of the street; the new mayor, Rudolph Giuliani, eagerly promised to rout the pornographers. The deal was signed on December 31, 1994; and so the new 42nd Street was born at last.

IT HAD BEEN AN article of faith among New York City planning officials for a good quarter of a century that the city's future lay in the steady proliferation of office towers, and that those vertical factories of revenue would make it possible for New York to continue to produce the charming and noble artifacts of culture that gave the city its special character. Supposedly, the most precious asset theaters had was the air rights they could sell to developers. That was the central thrust of the 42nd Street Development Project: trade the air rights to developers, who would in turn pay for public amenities and the restoration of theaters. What an irony, then, that it was a theater that sparked the new life of the street, and that the kitschy exuberance of *42nd Street Now!* was what gave the block a marketable new identity. And all this while the four office towers, supposedly the salvation of this derelict block, slumbered on. The project had taken so long that a new world, in which popular culture was as powerful, and as fully globalized, a product as cars or steel, had dawned meanwhile. In this postindustrial world, Times Square had natural advantages that scarcely anyone had noticed before.

George Klein, who had hung on for so long, could hang on no longer. By the mid-nineties, Prudential had laid out over $300 million in condemnation costs and public improvements. And the company, which had financed such colossal projects as the Prudential Center in Boston and Embarcadero Center in San Francisco, decided that it wanted out of the real estate business. By 1992, Klein was looking for new partners to buy out Prudential. "We tried desperately," Klein says. "We went to every investment bank in the city." There were no takers. Prudential began actively looking for buyers in 1995; it wasn't hard by then, because the market had turned up once again. Douglas Durst, who had been one of the chief litigants in earlier years, and who had quietly subsidized other opponents of the development, now purchased the right to develop the biggest and most desirable parcel, the one at the northeast corner of 42nd Street and Broadway known as 4 Times Square. The Rudin family, one of the city's ancient real estate clans, and Boston Properties, owned by the publisher Mort Zuckerman, bought the three other parcels. Prudential escaped with a small profit.

Only George Klein was left a loser. Klein virtually stopped building after the debacle of 42nd Street. He was hoping to work with Prince Charles, that arbiter of conservative architectural tastes, to rebuild the district of London, next to St. Paul's Cathedral, that was destroyed in the Blitz—but this project, too, fell through when the market sagged. An undemonstrative man, Klein is stoical in the aftermath of defeat. "It was," he says, with a small smile, "an interesting lesson to learn." Klein feels that the real hero of 42nd Street is not Rebecca Robertson or Robert Stern, but Prudential, for—while the developers for the mart and the theaters and the hotel decamped—the company stuck with the project, patiently laying out the money that made the revival of the street possible. "I think developers have some civic responsibility," says Klein. "It isn't just squeeze the last nickel." He makes it clear that he is referring to figures like the Milsteins and the Dursts, who used litigation to block the project. He has, he feels, nothing to be embarrassed about. "I don't think anyone ever said that we didn't keep our word or have integrity or do our best," he says. "We could differ about what 'best' means architecturally." One cannot dispute this judgment.

INSOFAR AS THE 42ND Street Development Project worked, it did so by failing. Public officials accepted a bid to build four enormous office towers in the heart of Manhattan before the developer had even chosen an architect, much less showed a model; and when the architect ignored the guidelines they had laid down to ensure that the buildings conformed to the civic ideals they had in mind, the guidelines were quietly discarded.

Only public pressure forced a change in design. And then litigation, against which city and state officials were powerless, prevented the new design from being implemented. The collapse of the real estate market killed the office towers altogether. And the developers who had agreed to build the merchandise mart and the hotel, and to restore the theaters, slunk away one by one; one of them, a former Koch administration figure named Michael Lazar, who had won the bid to restore the five theaters on the north side of the block although he had no prior theatrical experience, was indicted, and later convicted and jailed, for accepting kickbacks while in office. These failures turned the street into the sort of blank slate that made the *42nd Street Now!* plan possible.

Could it have been otherwise? Let's imagine two alternative scenarios, which may be thought of more or less as the marketplace and statist scenarios. Both free market conservatives, who consider New York's development process far too intrusive, and some real estate officials argue that the city would have been much better off had it simply waited for 42nd Street to become attractive to private development. Had the city done nothing at all to 42nd Street save make it as clean and safe as possible, the argument goes, development would have inevitably shifted westward as costs became prohibitive east of Fifth. Forty-second Street would have had its office towers just as Seventh Avenue and Broadway did. They would have been less dense, and perhaps there would have been fewer of them; whatever revenue the city lost would be made up for by the fact that the owners would be paying their full share in taxes. Likewise, the new global entertainment companies would have flocked to 42nd Street and Times Square—at least, assuming the kind of vigorous anticrime campaign Mayor Giuliani waged starting in 1994—for the same reason that European designers converge on Madison Avenue: the address confirms their status as world players. That city planners could not imagine such an outcome in 1981 only shows the limits of planning.

No one will ever know what would have happened had the 42nd Street Development Project never existed. But the essential problem with the laissez-faire theory is that 42nd Street already *was* a self-sustaining marketplace in the early 1980s—a market for pornographic and action movies, for drugs and alcohol and sex and con games. Absent outside intervention, the perverse ecology of the street would have remained—

which is to say that the street could not have been cleaned up without the use of the state's condemnation powers. And the pattern of fragmented ownership would also have precluded much new investment: there were 240 owners in the project area as of 1981. The real estate heir Douglas Durst insists that a patient assembler—like the Durst family—could have slowly amassed property until they were ready to build, but the Dursts themselves have been assembling parcels for thirty years on 42nd Street immediately to the east of Seventh Avenue without finding the opportunity to build—and this without the perverse ecology of Times Square. What's more, developers eager to build office space on the Deuce would have had a tough time persuading tenants to relocate to a street whose sidewalks were crowded with hustlers and vagrants.

What about the opposite scenario—a *more* obtrusive, more intellectually serious, and better-heeled state? Look at the city of Paris, which in recent decades has rebuilt its highway system, expanded its periphery, and built such extraordinary monuments as the Pompidou Center. This last, in fact, was a part of a much larger project to level and rebuild the ancient quarter known as the Marais—a project as large as the 42nd Street redevelopment, and occurring at much the same time. In *Post-Industrial Cities*, H. V. Savitch compares the two projects, as well as the renovation of Covent Garden, in London. Paris, as Savitch points out, is the great pride of France and of the French people; it would be unthinkable to leave so profound a matter as the expansion or preservation of an ancient Parisian neighborhood to the marketplace. The French government bore much of the $1 billion cost of the redevelopment of the Marais, and the plan was fashioned by the Prefect of Paris, an *haut fonctionnaire* operating at the highest reaches of the bureaucracy and insulated from virtually all outside influence—a modern version of Baron Haussman, who dynamited ancient Paris and created the modern city in the middle of the nineteenth century. The public had virtually no role in the reconstruction of the Marais: the great market area of Les Halles was leveled without so much as a hearing. And private developers had little more say than the public. In New York, by contrast, as Savitch writes, development is a matter of "political entrepreneurship" in which various contending forces struggle to assemble a coalition of the self-interested. It's no coincidence that Paris feels like a supremely planned city, and New York like a supremely unplanned one. Paris is shaped according to a set of beliefs about its nature; in New York, Savitch writes, "The momentum for growth is so strong that little is sacred when it comes to matters of architectural preservation."

If New York were more like Paris, then the redevelopment of 42nd Street would have been guided more by a sense of the street's place in New York's history and culture, and less by the wish to expand commercial space westward. Planning would be a far more serious occupation than it is now. And city government would not have surrendered its municipal obligations to the private sector by counting on developers to pay for public amenities. Presumably, if Americans loved their great cities as the French do, New York would not have been permitted to suffer through its fiscal crisis in the first place.

Of course, it's impossible to imagine New Yorkers sitting still nowadays as an ancient neighborhood is demolished. After all, New York City once had an omnipotent *haut fonctionnaire* of its own; his name was Robert Moses. And Moses's very name is now synonymous with the discredited vision of bulldozer development. Much of the messy and time-consuming panoply of the 42nd Street development process—the hearings, the guidelines, the environmental impact statement—is a reaction to that autocratic form of development. New Yorkers have decided, in effect, that they would rather risk getting nothing built at all than to have a vision of the city simply imposed on them. And the process does not inevitably lead either to paralysis or to mediocrity: it was another city-state entity that chose the acclaimed architect Daniel Libeskind to design a new complex on the site of the World Trade Center in 2003.

The competition over the rebuilding of the World Trade Center offers a model for urban planning that does not submit to the whim either of the developer or of the government functionary, and that allows the public will to express itself without descending into chaos. Of course, the city-state body overseeing the development process at the World Trade Center site agreed to stage a worldwide architectural competition only after an impassioned public rejected the unimaginative choices that were initially offered. That was an unprecedented moment in the history of urban development; the rebuilding of 42nd Street took place under more normal conditions of public disengagement. And in the early 1980s architects had nothing like the kind of prestige they have today; the idea that an architect's vision might transform a neighborhood, or even an entire city, was something quite foreign. In New York, architecture has, until very recently, functioned almost entirely as the handmaiden of development.

And so perhaps it is vain to wish that Mayor Koch and Governor Cuomo had invited the half-dozen greatest architects in the world to reimagine 42nd Street, as Mayor Michael Bloomberg and Governor George Pataki ultimately did in the case of the World Trade Center. It wasn't in the cards. And yet it would have been one of the most thrilling and illuminating architectural competitions ever staged. Great architects love great cities. Who among them wouldn't have viewed the opportunity to reinvent the greatest urban space in the greatest city in the world as the achievement of a lifetime? Who would have sneered at "the goddamn corny image of what's in Times Square," or fantasized about giant wrecking balls crushing decaying structures? It's true that the horror of urban life so widespread a quarter century ago might have made the prospect of erasure appealing, as it was to Philip Johnson. But others might have designed a 42nd Street Futurama, like the architects of Cityscape; or a 42nd Street of the decorated shed in the manner of Robert Venturi; or something else nobody ever thought of. What 42nd Street needed, as Robert Stern and Tibor Kalman understood, was not an architectural straitjacket, but a master plan—a plan that could pay homage to all that the street and Times Square had been, while launching it into an unknowable future.

It's too late for regrets, or even for blame. One can only imagine what might have been and take comfort in the fact that the public seems more aroused on matters of architecture and design than it has ever been before. Perhaps the next time, whenever the next time is, the process will work because it worked, and not because it failed.

PART THREE

CORPORATE FUN

A MIRROR OF AMERICA

T AKE THE SUBWAY to the Times Square station. It only costs two dollars, you can get there from practically anywhere, and it's been working perfectly well, more or less, for one hundred years. Emerging onto the corner of 42nd Street and Broadway, you will be much impressed by the sheer scale of the neighborhood. Four immense glass office buildings tower above you. None is particularly distinguished as architecture, though the lights and signs they wear make them more playful than their kin on Sixth or Third Avenue. The Reuters Building, on the northwest corner of 42nd and Broadway, even has a bit of V-shaped deco-style trim running around the corner, a wan recollection of the Rialto Building, which once occupied the same spot. The principal tenants of the office towers are law firms, investment firms, and media and entertainment firms, which is to say that they are not much different from office towers elsewhere in midtown Manhattan. The biggest of the towers, at the northeast corner of Broadway and 42nd, houses Condé Nast, publisher of such glamorous magazines as *The New Yorker, Vanity Fair,* and *Vogue.* Times Square is no longer interesting enough, or chic enough, to be an important subject for these magazines, as it was seventy-five years ago; it is, on the other hand, a far more suitable setting for their corporate headquarters than it ever was before.

Now you may turn back toward Eighth Avenue. Immediately to the west of the office zone is the culture zone, which is also the preservation zone—the lovingly restored New Amsterdam Theatre to the south and the New Victory Theater to the north, as well as the Ford Center, where the play *42nd Street* has long been entrenched, and an entirely new building, known as the Duke, which houses studio space as well as the Roundabout Theatre, a highly respected nonprofit theater company. The Duke is a nine-story building that at night lights up with multicolored horizontal neon strips; it is the only aesthetically pleasing new structure on 42nd Street. The street also has a museum. On the south side, where Peepland and, before that, Hubert's Museum once stood, is Madame Tussaud's Wax Museum, an institution that traffics in immaculately reproduced copies.

The remaining two-thirds of the block, where once the all-night cafeterias reigned, and the penny arcades and the shooting galleries and the novelty shops and the hot dog stands, is now a Global Retail, Fast Food, and Entertainment Concept Zone. Moving east to west along the southern blockfront, you would find (as of the middle of 2003) the world's largest McDonald's; a food court where the visitor can choose among Applebee's, California Pizza Kitchen, Chili's, Cinnabon, and yet others; an HMV music store; and New York's largest multiplex, the AMC 25. Crossing the street and reversing course to the east, you would first encounter Chevys, a bait-shack-themed restaurant that sells thirteen kinds of margarita, including the Midori and the Lava Lamp, and then a Japanese fast-food place, a Yankees merchandise store, and the Sanrio store, purveyor of the Hello Kitty line. In the middle of the block are the Broadway City arcade and the B.B. King Blues Club, both owned by actual New Yorkers, making this the Indigenous Institutions Microzone.

Richard Simon, owner of the arcade and heir to its traditions, is in fact the last unimpeachably authentic son of the soil left on 42nd Street. Simon is a middle-aged, balding gentleman, slightly querulous, with the classic New York sense of preulcerous aggrievement. "I'm the only legitimate New York entrepreneur who's not sending the money to the home office in Peoria," he says. "I'm the quintessential New York guy." (It takes a quintessential New York guy to imagine that the home office is in Peoria.) The Broadway City arcade is a lineal descendant of the Broadway Arcade, established in the late fifties by Simon's father, Albert, on Broadway between 51st and 52nd Streets. The old arcade had pool and Ping-Pong tables downstairs, and upstairs pinball, a magic shop, costumes, homemade candy and home-roasted nuts, and of course arcade games—a juicy slice of Times Square, Late Golden Era.

Simon, the son, fondly recalls that far-off time when things were where they were supposed to be and what they were supposed to be: when Lindy's, Damon Runyon's old haunt, sat right there on 49th Street. When your dad took you to lunch there you ate chopped steak and creamed spinach, and never thought to ask for anything else. Simon's office, in a quiet warren behind a door at the otherwise insanely noisy arcade, is a shrine to his hero of heroes, Mickey Mantle, the blond god of the fifties, and to the slightly ratty pizzazz of his father's era. In the time even before the Broadway Arcade, Albert sold coin-operated arcade games from an office on Tenth Avenue between 42nd and 43rd Streets. Mayor Fiorello La Guardia banned pinball as part of his campaign against vice, and Richard has a photo of goons smashing his father's stock. More authentic than that, you don't get.

The Broadway City arcade is generally a nice place, which can't be said of all arcades. The Playland, which flourished for years along the west side of Broadway between 42nd and 43rd, was an ominous dive where both fake driver's licenses and male hustlers were readily available. I never set foot in Playland, though at one point in my life I walked past it daily. On the other hand, I often go to the Broadway City arcade with my son, Alex, who is always up for a few rounds of virtual boxing (bob, weave, kayo the reigning heavyweight champ). It's a clean, inviting, and safe place—except late at night, when it isn't. But you wouldn't mistake it for the old Broadway Arcade. A sculpture of old-fashioned construction workers eating their lunch on a plank is suspended from the ceiling—a retro touch designed, Simon says, to convey the old-time "warmth and character" that he remembers so well. Of course the very act of evoking that atmosphere italicizes it, makes it a marketing decision rather than an aspect of the place's character. Perhaps the simple fact that the Broadway City arcade is new, and that it is (mostly) safe and clean, and that it is located in the middle of the new, safe, clean, bright 42nd Street, opens up an immense gulf between it and its progenitor. Simon could serve home-roasted nuts, and it might not matter.

To which one might well say: So what? Simon himself says, "I wanted to be part of the resurgence of Times Square, and especially Forty-second

Street." And he plainly is (though he complains that the rent is stratospheric, the local businessmen don't patronize his "corporate space," and he is besieged by the "Eighth Avenue crowd"—that is, black kids). Forty-second Street had become the kind of place where many New Yorkers, and certainly many tourists, wouldn't set foot in an arcade. Now, on the new 42nd Street, they do. As in so much of modern life, material progress offers itself as compensation for spiritual loss.

IT IS PERFECTLY OBVIOUS that 42nd Street could not have become once again any of its past selves—not, at least, without unintentional self-parody. Neither could it have become the enclosed gallery of futuristic entertainments imagined by the authors of the City at 42nd Street plan. But did it have to be this? Did it have to be Chevys and Applebee's and Hello Kitty? In *42nd Street Now!*, Stern and Kalman had promised that 42nd Street would become "an enhanced version of itself," not a "gentrified theme park or festival market." The possibility that it might become a honky-tonk theme park seems not to have occurred to them. New Yorkers tend to view the block as a deracinated fragment of global monoculture grafted into the city's street plan—a place with none of the characteristics of locality. Couldn't it have been more . . . *real*? The *Bright Light* study had suggested all sorts of exotic entertainment activities for the block, including a "sports exhibition center" where amateur athletes could compete in pickup basketball games, skateboard slalom, karate, and so on; a roller disco; a jazz cabaret; and a gallery of "futuristic electronic amusements." (Actually, that sounds like the Broadway City arcade.) What's wrong with that?

The answer is that roller disco doesn't pay the rent. The 42nd Street Development Project was designed to make the block attractive to private developers, who would lease most of the space on the street. Public officials would establish design guidelines, but the marketplace would decide who would occupy the space. And the marketplace was going to supply the lowest common denominator. Bruce Ratner, a former city official who had become a major real estate force in Brooklyn, ultimately purchased the lease on the south side of the street, while John Tishman, a member of one of the city's great real estate clans, took over the north.

Both men believed that immense crowds would flock to the new 42nd Street; that these tourists and office workers and passersby constituted a tremendous new market; and therefore that they could charge tenants stratospheric rents. And the kind of tenants who pay $1 million a year for a modest storefront are not normally adventurous.

Ratner says when he sought tenants in 1997, he received proposals from the Hard Rock Café, the Rainforest Café, the Moulin Rouge night-club, Cirque de Soleil, Fred & Busters game rooms, Universal Walk, the ESPN Zone, and so on. It was, he says, "the era of entertainment concepts." None of these chains had even existed twenty years earlier, when the CUNY researchers had suggested their charmingly homemade entertainments. In the interim, Disney and Warner Bros. and Viacom had transformed the very nature of entertainment, while the Gap and Barnes & Noble and HMV had similarly transformed the nature of retailing. "Popular culture," that localized, handcrafted thing, had become "mass culture," an extrusion from mighty corporate ovens. These entertainment and retailing leviathans roamed the globe in search of sites suitable to their brand. To see how mass culture has changed the places where it is situated, you need only think of Las Vegas. As recently as the 1970s, Las Vegas had consisted of the eccentric and largely family-owned casinos that so fascinated the authors of *Learning from Las Vegas;* by the nineties it had turned into a giant Monopoly board of entertainment concepts. So with 42nd Street.

The idea that the city is the home of intense particularity, of the un-trammeled individual—the idea at the heart of so much of Balzac and Dickens and Dostoevsky, and then of Dreiser and Howells—has given way, in recent years, to a new and alarming idea of the city as the site for a deracinated, universalizing popular culture: the city as Las Vegas. The architect and theorist Rem Koolhaas calls it "the generic city"—"the city without history," "the city liberated . . . from the straitjacket of identity." (Koolhaas *likes*—or straight-facedly claims to like—the generic city.) Another architecture critic and urban theorist, Michael Sorkin, writes, "The new city replaces the anomaly and delight of [the old] with a universal particular, a generic urbanism inflected only by appliqué. Here, locality is efficiently acknowledged by the inclusion of the croque-monsieur at the McDonald's on the Boule Miche or the Cajun Martini at the airport lounge in New Orleans (and you're welcome to keep the glass)." In other words, authenticity has been reduced from a touchstone of value to a marketing concept, a salable commodity the up-to-date city traffics in.

Along 42nd Street, locality is acknowledged by the sculpture of the workingman in the Broadway City arcade, and of course by the lights and signs that line the street. The most common epithet that critics, and for that matter contemptuous New Yorkers, apply to 42nd Street is "Disneyesque." In fact, the very first sentence of a recent critique of the redevelopment process reads, "The cheerful face of Mickey Mouse now greets visitors to Times Square from atop a Disney superstore." Used as an epithet, the word "Disney" conjures up the image of a meticulously engineered, and thus secondhand, and thus spurious, form of fun. It must be noted, in all fairness, that if anyone has Disneyfied 42nd Street in this sense, it's not Disney, which has meticulously re-created the archaic splendors of the New Amsterdam Theatre and has used it to present *The Lion King,* an exercise in avant-garde puppetry that has confounded the company's critics with its insistent modernity and its unmistakable stamp of individual authorship. But the street may be Disneyesque nevertheless. The author of the critique, Alexander J. Reichl, goes on to predict: "From the towers to the superstores to the orgy of lighted advertisements, Forty-second Street and Times Square will epitomize the corporate dominance of publc space."

And yet . . . somehow, 42nd Street doesn't feel like a simulacrum, or like a "site" of global entertainment culture—at least, not only like that. Take that subway once again to the IRT station, but this time at night. Now the generic street is suddenly alive. When you stand in front of the station and sight down the block, 42nd Street looks like the inside of one of Richard Simon's arcade games, glowing red and blue and green. The buildings, with their inane products and cardboard food, seem to subside behind the wildly flashing signs, just as Stern and Kalman hoped they would. The sense of arid calculation subsides as well beneath the great tides of humanity eddying up and down the block. On a warm summer's night, 42nd Street is a kind of fiesta, a commercial carnival. Teenagers, mostly black, loiter in front of the subway station on the northern side of the street. An impromptu audience, gathered in a semicircle, watches a spray painter make moons and pyramids and skyscrapers on his little square of oaktag. A pedicab cycles past with a passenger, charging a hundred times the going rate in Calcutta, and then a great white limo slides by like a submarine before it plunges beneath the waves. The doors open up at the Ford Center, and the audience for *42nd Street* spills out for intermission, forming little knots that block the sidewalk as they chat blithely about that last tap number.

Further along, another crowd waits for the late show at B.B. King's, and a line of less patient teenagers wait to be patted down before gaining entrance to the Broadway City arcade, the bright white lights running around its jukebox façade. Three cops on horseback keep watch on the entrance. Sketch artists sit in folding chairs, waiting for customers for their portraits and caricatures. More cops; more swirls of tourists; more teenage boys, leaning against the wall, staring out at the passing show, enjoying a night out for the price of a subway token. It's as if an electric current that was carrying the life of the great city all around had been strung just beneath the sidewalks. The street, which felt vapid and almost too wide in the daytime, isn't big enough now, and you wonder how 42nd Street can contain the kids, the tourists, the cops, the vendors, the traffic, the noise, the lights, and the sense of possible violence that sometimes lies just below the surface.

It is, in short, the barely contained energies of that crowd, and the noise and the blur of the traffic, and the huckstering along the sidewalk, that save 42nd Street from the Disneyesque. The life of the place is on the streets. As I walked westward one Saturday night in late October 2001, I joined a big crowd watching a spray painter at work. The painter was a wiry young man with a red cap pulled low over his eyes, the bill expertly rolled. Another spray painter, farther down the street, stood idly by his wares, but here the crowd was two or three deep. When they finally moved away, I stayed to talk. The painter's name was Ayhan Colak; he had come to Times Square from Istanbul three years earlier. Ayhan said that he always attracted a crowd because he understood something about his setting. "It's very hard in New York," he said; "there's so much competition. But here I am on Forty-second Street; everybody is performing, and I give a performance, too." And he did. Ayhan was swift, nervous, intent; as he moved rapidly with his spray cans over the surface of his cardboard canvas, he bristled with some of that manic energy you see in footage of

Jackson Pollock, though it is probably fair to say that his work did not quite aspire to the same level of art, or for that matter to any level of art.

Ayhan had, in fact, never studied art at all; he was a street performer. But he was a virtuoso street performer. He wielded his paint cans like a master chef: sometimes he upended the can and popped the nozzle a few times against the canvas to produce a wedge of paint, or, by angling the can a little lower, a thick stream of paint. His tools also included a piece of crumpled newspaper, a pot lid, a chisel, and a palette knife. Ayhan had a limited repertoire; his big seller—and everyone else's—was a painting of the pyramids of Giza superimposed on an imaginary Manhattan skyline, with the earth, the moon, and maybe Saturn suspended above in a black sky—a kind of spiritualized fantasy designed to lift the viewer above the neon bath of 42nd Street. The performance was free, and the work itself was available for $20. On this particular evening, the crowd burst into applause when Ayhan straightened up. A customer stepped forward to pay; one of the customer's friends, overwhelmed in the face of genius, timidly asked Ayhan if he had anything else left in his portfolio.

I was on 42nd Street again two weeks later, on a chilly Sunday afternoon, and there was Ayhan once again surrounded by a crowd, which included three Hasidic men, a sailor, and a young woman from New Jersey named Michelle who had bought four of Ayhan's works. I asked Michelle whether she had asked for a special bulk price, and she looked at me reprovingly: "You can't tell an artist what to do." They made, we agreed, perfect Christmas gifts.

Yet even Ayhan is not exactly "authentic," at least not if authenticity requires indigenousness. Street culture has become almost as globalized as retail culture. Ayhan, who speaks Russian, Bulgarian, and German in addition to Turkish and English, traveled a circuit that includes Tokyo and Houston, and he learned his art from a Mexican guy he met in San Francisco; another spray painter I met learned in Paris, and also worked in Miami, where, he said, he was expected to paint fish rather than office towers. You can buy the same caricatures and the same Chinese calligraphy that you find on 42nd Street on the Ponte Vecchio in Florence, and probably in Kathmandu as well. The street population is globally mobile and transitory; few people return to the block year after year. And so even the vendors and artists do not "belong" to 42nd Street much more than the shops do. By the time you read this, Ayhan will have been replaced by someone else. Does it matter? Indigenousness is an anachronism in a global city like New York. Creativity and spontaneity should be enough.

One of the few aspects of the street's culture invented and practiced by natives is break dancing, which is featured in the Times Square subway station and up and down Broadway and Seventh Avenue, wherever a large enough parcel of sidewalk makes performance possible. With their one-handed handstands and standing somersaults and dizzying head spins, the break-dancers are arguably the most talented performers in Times Square. And, like Ayhan, the dance crews understand the need for theatricality in the world's epicenter of the theatrical. One afternoon I encountered Rasheem, who comes down from Harlem with a crew of younger kids, on the traffic island between 44th and 45th Streets. He had recruited four volunteers from the crowd, who would, when so instructed, line up side by side and bend over at the waist; a crew member anchored the group. Rasheem strutted around the gathering crowd, explaining that he was going to jump over "all six"—well, actually five—and land on the other side. "First, I want everyone to hold up a ticket," he cried. "Everyone know what a ticket look like?" Rasheem held up a dollar bill. Then he cranked up the rap music from his boom box, went to the far end of the island, and commenced to flex and twist. "Everybody outta the way!" he shouted. "I don't got no insurance." Another crew member went around with a bucket; Rasheem wasn't going anywhere until the audience had deposited major tickets. This turned out to be a very long process. Finally, Rasheem began to trot, picked up speed like a broad jumper until he hit his mark just in front of the first person, launched himself into a somersault, and landed clean on the other side. It was the human equivalent of Evel Knievel on his motorcycle. Rasheem later admitted to me that though he had never landed on a volunteer, he did occasionally hit a crew member. Such mishaps, he added, were the fault of an uninspiring audience.

It is not all that easy to make money on 42nd Street. Many of the vendors I came to know had made more money, and lived a distinctly better life, back home, wherever home was, than in Times Square. Many of them talked about leaving, and some of them did abruptly disappear. There were simply too many of them, even given the great size of the crowd. And the trade was tightly controlled. Vendors who deal in artwork enjoy First Amendment protection, but they can be regulated with regard to time, place, and manner of expression. The city prohibits vendors from setting up shop on 42nd Street before seven P.M., in order to give the rush-hour crowd time to dissipate, and then forces them to close up around eleven, as the theater crowd is pouring out onto the street. One night I watched the cops order everyone to close up shop at ten-thirty. I asked an officer what the hurry was, and he said, "The captain says it's 'exigent circumstances.'" This was apparently the technical term for dangerous overcrowding. "We don't want someone to walk out into the street and get hurt." By eleven, the vendors had vanished, save for a lone sketch artist, squatting, a pad propped on his thigh, while he drew a picture of a little boy whose mother looked on patiently.

Most vendors fail, but few fail tragically. Virtually all of 42nd Street's sidewalk merchants are young male immigrants, and most of them have the immigrant resilience that has been one of New York City's defining characteristics for the last century. One slightly chilly evening in the spring of 2002 I met Ivan Ivanoff, the pride of Veliko Tirnovo, in Bulgaria. Ivan was pale, with a blocky face and a determined set to his jaw. He was a man of many professions. He said that when he had first come to New York, he had joined a break-dancing crew, which he had quit in disgust over the group's spotty work ethic and his low-man-on-the-totem-pole share of the take. I asked whether he had learned to break-dance in Bulgaria. "I have been break-dancing for, like, seventeen years," he said proudly. Ivan was thirty, and as a teenager he was, he said, "one of the most successful break-dancers in Bulgaria." He and his friends had learned from American movies and music videos. "We would have break-dancing battles, between different crews," Ivan explained. "But the problem is, there is no profit in break-dancing in Bulgaria. People do not pay money to see it. Also, nobody dances on the street in Bulgaria." Ivan opened up a pizzeria, and then a second and a third. "Then I realize," he said, "is good business, but is local business. I want to do national business." So Ivan started a factory to produce women's clothes. "I put in all the money from the pizzeria; and I lose everything." There had been, apparently, a drastic softening in the Bulgarian economy. And so he had left Bulgaria with his girlfriend, in search of opportunity.

Ivan had now taken up spray painting, and he said he was earning $100 on good days, which this manifestly was not: nobody came by to disturb our conversation. But Ivan was not discouraged. "I have many ideas for what I will do," he announced. Idea number one was transferring photos onto T-shirts. Ivan had already spent $5,000 to buy a top-quality digital camera, a transfer press, and a printer. But even that wasn't the big idea. "I want to go back into the food business," Ivan said, almost conspiratorially. This idea was so powerful that he couldn't take the risk of revealing it. "It's a very good product," he allowed. "The product is new. It will cost only two or three dollars." He was still refining the concept, but he promised that it did not involve Bulgarian cuisine.

The "street culture" of the new 42nd Street consists of pavement dwellers like Ayhan and Ivan, and the middle-aged Chinese ladies who glumly peddle their photographs of the Flatiron Building and the World Trade Center, and the great tides of pedestrians passing this way and that, and also the visitors who roost long enough to be described as loiterers. And that population consists largely of black teenagers. This is a peculiar irony, for critics of 42nd Street redevelopment described it at the time, and have continued to describe it, as a gentrification process designed to erase the street's minority population in order to lure back white professionals. If you ask kids, they will tell you that 42nd Street is a good place to pick up girls, that you can hang out for free as long as you don't mind being moved around by cops, that you can see a movie at the AMC 25 and then have a cheap meal at Applebee's—just what William Kornblum, the principal author of the *Bright Light* study, said that kids had been doing back in the 1970s. The Broadway City arcade attracts a heavily minority, and of course young, clientele. And 42nd Street tends to become less white later at night; sometime around eleven P.M., the movie theaters shift from a largely white to a largely nonwhite audience.

The arcades, and the kids who hang out near them, have had the effect of restoring a soupçon of the old 42nd Street sense of menace—perhaps just enough to satisfy critics who fear wholesale embourgeoisement. One Saturday night I waited in line to be admitted to Bar Code, an arcade on Broadway and 45th that closed up in early 2003. A sign prominently posted in the window announced that no one wearing "colors," "do-rags," "skullies," sports jerseys, or "velour suits" would be admitted. In front of me were four high-school-age boys from Sussex County, apparently a rather pastoral zone of New Jersey. A tall, skinny kid with his cap on backward asked what "colors" were, and I explained that the word referred to gang insignia. He blanched. He worried that his high school football sweatshirt would fall afoul of the rules.

I had never heard of banning sports jerseys, and when I got to the front of the line I asked the security official. "Let's say you come in wearing a Giants jersey, and the other guy, he's wearing Jets," he explained. "That's enough to start a fight." Velour suits? They were banning sweat suits, and so they had to prohibit the far more expensive designer track suits to prevent an aggrieved kid from saying, "How come me and not him?" Once inside, we were forced to empty our pockets, and then each of us was very briskly patted down, our shoes squeezed, a metal wand waved over us, before we were allowed to pass upstairs to the arcade itself. Bar Code seemed to have reached a DEFCON 4 level of antigang alert: once I finally got inside, it was so quiet and modestly populated that you had to wonder if the place was scaring away its own clientele. Perhaps that's why it closed.

The Broadway City arcade had a much less rigorous security system, and was a much more wild and woolly place late at night. For all his distaste for the "Eighth Avenue crowd," Richard Simon understood perfectly well that they were his clientele, and he had opened up a dance space on the second floor for the late-night weekend crowd. At 2:40 one morning, as rap music shook the walls, a mêlée broke out between two groups of black teenagers from the same neighborhood in Queens; there had been "a look across the dance floor," a detective later said. Weapons, undetected at the door, were suddenly brandished; eight people were shot and two stabbed (none fatally) before the police were able to rush in and quell the violence. Here was a sudden and terrifying reminder of 42nd Street as it once had been. The overwhelming irony of the event was that the violence had issued from the street's most "authentic," least Disneyesque, spot. This was more authenticity than even the most single-minded opponent of development could have wished. It also constituted an implicit argument for the virtues of embourgeoisement, of regulation, even, perhaps, for the corporate dominance of public space. You never heard about gang violence at Applebee's.

—

BRUCE RATNER, THE DEVELOPER responsible for Madame Tussaud's and Applebee's, is all too familiar with the complaint that New Yorkers—at least New Yorkers in his class—make about 42nd Street. And so he was at first inclined to be defensive when I asked him about all the mass-produced dreck on the block. But the more he thought about it, the less inclined he was to be apologetic. Ratner is not a native New Yorker with a New Yorker's possessiveness over the city's past; his father had started the family real estate business in Cleveland, and he remembers visiting the city as a boy. "Look at it in 1960," Ratner said, sitting in his office in the renovated business district of Brooklyn. "It would have had arcades. I remember the arcades; I remember the movie theaters. Now there are arcades with electronic games in them; twenty-five years from now, people will remember that." Ratner began to pick up speed as he warmed to his topic and perhaps saw his way clear to his own position in the new 42nd Street. "Applebee's and Chevys—they're what America is today. I'm not saying that's good or bad, any more than Bond Clothes was." Bond, on Broadway and 44th, was Times Square's biggest retailer in the forties and fifties. "That's what it has been for seventy years. I would argue it's more of a mirror of America. In 1900 it was a mirror of that genteel way that America was: it was ruled by a small group of people who went to see plays and stuff like that. For the last seventy years, it's been for the average person. It's a reflection of America."

Ratner's implicit point was that 42nd Street was being true to its own past precisely by virtue of being dominated by McDonald's and the ESPN Zone. Forty-second Street was the home of popular entertainment, and in our own time mass culture is produced by giant companies. The elite can afford the local and the particular; ordinary folks consume less expensive, franchised products. And so a "corporate" 42nd Street was a democratic 42nd Street. Ratner's aides were now chuckling with some embarrassment at the boss's swelling oratory, but he plunged on, the bit between his teeth. "It's always been a place to go out for the lower-middle-income New Yorker. You go out on a Saturday night, and it's basically people of low-middle-income means, from the boroughs, from New Jersey, from Long Island, out for a date. If you think about all the great streets in the world, it's about seeing people from that culture. And it does that. And you know what? Maybe at the end of the day, that's what a successful street is. Should it be Applebee's or should it be someplace else? Who knows? It's a great place."

Is 42nd Street a great place because it's a mirror of America? If that's so, then the average shopping mall is a great place, too. When 42nd Street really was great, it stood for something larger than itself—glamour, excess, sex appeal, decadence. The one thing 42nd Street stands for now is the power of global marketing—and perhaps "the corporate dominance of public space." Forty-second Street is not a great place anymore; on the other hand, it hasn't been one for a very long time. Throughout the sixties, seventies, and eighties, 42nd Street mattered only as a case history in urban decline. Perhaps what one should say of this new 42nd Street is simply that it *worked:* it drew people to the heart of the city. People wanted to stand on the sidewalk and watch Ayhan paint; they wanted to hang out in front of the subway and even, alas, at Applebee's. Perhaps that was enough.

YOUNG HAMMERSTEIN
MEETS DARTH NADER:
A DIALOGUE OF THE
DEAF IN FIVE ACTS

ACT I

IN THE MID-1970S, Show World, the biggest and easily the most professional of the Times Square sex shops, opened on the northwest corner of 42nd Street and Eighth Avenue, in a spot previously occupied by a Chemical Bank. A vivid contemporary description of its operation comes from Josh Alan Friedman, the Damon Runyon of Times Square's pornographic subculture:

> The scene is a crowded weekday lunch hour at a modern Times Square sex emporium in the late 1970s. . . . There are twenty occupied booths, each with a glowing red bulb that indicates a quarter has been inserted, giving the viewer his thirty seconds. Cocks of every age, race and size are being drawn out in the booths. Some will spurt onto the walls, some into Kleenex, some will even discharge into fifty-cent French tickler condoms from the store's vending machine. These will be discarded on the floor. . . . Roving quarter-cashiers double as barkers, trying to perpetuate some cosmic momentum of flowing cash. "C'mon fellas, keep those quar-

ters comin', take a booth or clear the aisle, get your change here for live sexy girls, four for a quarter." Every ten minutes, one of the four sexy girls is replaced. A hidden female emcee announces each new entry, guaranteeing they'll love her. "Foxy Bertha joining the sexy girls now, big daddy, all for a quarter, love to love you, come in your pants, yeah, right now!"

That was Show World in its heyday—the very model of the Times Square "scumatorium," to use one of Friedman's most evocative terms. The owner, Richard Basciano, an ex-boxer, was "The King of Porn," as *New York Newsday* dubbed him, the owner of sex shops up and down 42nd Street and Eighth Avenue—eleven in all, it was said, employing more than four hundred people (thirty in "management," wrote Friedman, plus "endless girls, quarter cashiers, mop-ups"). As an immensely profitable cash business, pornography was enormously attractive to organized crime, and Basciano's chief partner was Robert DiBernardo, a member of the Gambino crime family. In 1986, DiBernardo was murdered on orders from John Gotti, the Gambino capo, and Basciano took over his share of the properties. Basciano himself was never connected either with the murder or with any other criminal activities associated with the mob (though he was convicted of mail fraud unrelated to his sex business). He was, by most accounts, a gentlemanly figure who ran his porn empire according to up-to-date principles, investing in the latest technology for his video peeps and his coin-operated machines. As the owner of the nine-story building on 42nd Street, another building on 43rd, and others elsewhere in Times Square, he was, whatever his associations, many orders of wealth, and perhaps also of respectability, above his fellow pornographers. He was also a mysterious figure. Basciano never gave interviews, not even to Josh Alan Friedman, the most sympathetic auditor a sex entrepreneur was likely to find.

The war against vice, which had been going on in Times Square virtually since there had been vice, had picked up again around the time of Friedman's account, when the Mayor's Office of Midtown Enforcement began closing down massage parlors, which fell under laws forbidding prostitution. And during a brief moment of abandon when the sex parlors took down the peep windows and let the customers and the girls touch one another, some of Show World's competitors had also been closed down as brothels. But the windows went back up and the sex shops remained beyond the reach of the law for the same reason that the porno movies did: they were deemed forms of expression, protected by the First Amendment. In fact, the number of sex shops in New York rose from 131 to 177 between 1984 and 1993. Times Square alone had forty-seven "adult" stores, even though many of those on 42nd Street had been closed down by the process of condemnation. Indeed, Richard Basciano received $11.3 million as compensation for three of his stores that lay within the catchment area of the 42nd Street Development Project.

If good uses were to drive out bad ones, as the public officials in charge of Times Square hoped, then it was the pornographic movies and sex shops, above all, that had to go. But a combination of Supreme Court decisions protecting obscene material and New Yorkers' own impulse to defend freedom of expression at virtually any cost had thwarted earlier attempts to expel the sex industry from Times Square. Nevertheless, when the Times Square Business Improvement District (BID) was established in 1992, local property owners concluded that they would have to take on the porn industry in order to stimulate change in the area. Gretchen Dykstra, the BID's executive director, says that she approached Norman Siegel, then the head of the New York Civil Liberties Union, who, she says, "hated the whole idea" of targeting the sex industry, but explained that she could succeed only by proving that the stores had a harmful effect on property values and local conditions, and then seeking to regulate them through zoning. So in 1994 the BID produced a report showing—though far from conclusively—that "adult use establishments" had baneful "secondary effects" on Times Square.

By this time, Rudolph Giuliani had become mayor of New York. Giuliani was not even remotely troubled by the thought of limiting access to sex shops; what's more, he had promised Michael Eisner, the chairman of Disney, that he would eliminate pornography and suppress crime in the area around 42nd Street. At the same time, the mayor understood that he could not simply ban sex shops altogether. Both he and the BID favored "dispersal zoning," which limits certain uses to a city's periphery. Giuliani wanted to remove all sex establishments to manufacturing areas in the city's outer boroughs, but members of the City Council representing those districts bridled at the prospect of their becoming a pornographic dumping ground. In March 1995, the mayor and the City Council agreed to a compromise that would permit the stores to remain in designated commercial areas, including Seventh Avenue and Broadway from 48th to 55th Streets, and Eighth from 38th to 41st. All stores with "a substantial portion of their stock in trade or materials characterized by an emphasis on specific anatomical areas or sexual activities" would be subject to stringent regulations: they would be prohibited from operating within five hundred feet of residences, schools, churches, or one another. Gretchen Dykstra triumphantly declared that the number of sex shops in Times Square would drop from forty-seven to five or six.

The new ordinance was part of Giuliani's larger effort to redraw the boundaries between collective goods and individual rights; and it ran into some of the same resistance that his campaigns against predatory and antisocial street behavior had. Gay and lesbian activists complained that the law would eliminate harmless sex-toy boutiques in Greenwich Village. Norman Siegel described it as "a sign of the times and of a repressive new climate toward sexual expression that is totally contrary to New York's rich cultural history." Through its chief lawyer, Herald Price Fahringer, the sex industry disputed the secondary effects study. Nevertheless, in late October the law was passed by the city's community boards, then once again by the City Council, and it went into effect the following year.

The authors of the legislation had clarified the term "substantial portion" by declaring that any store more than 40 percent of whose stock consisted of adult articles would fall within the new rules. One of the city's more high-profile pornographers observed at the time that he could evade the rule with ease. "A lot of fetish movies don't have sex in them," he noted. "And if I have to put violent and horror movies in, I'll do that too." It was a prescient comment. Though many sex shops closed up rather than attempt compliance, others filled their shelves with kung fu movies. And when an inspector from the city's Department of Buildings tried to shutter a store, the owner would turn to Fahringer, the silver-haired and silver-voiced chief attorney for the adult entertainment industry. Fahringer was, he says, "27 for 27" on such cases; he claims that the net effect of the "60–40 rule" on Times Square was zero. Eighth Avenue remained a hive of sex shops, as well as a happy hunting ground for drug dealers and pimps. Nevertheless, pornography was eliminated from 42nd Street; in the central areas of Times Square, nothing remained of the old carnality save for a high-class strip joint on 47th Street called Lace. The new law cleaned up Times Square without making it squeaky-clean. "What's Times Square without sex?" as Gretchen Dykstra asks. "It's the concentration that hurt Times Square, not the sex. A few porn shops never hurt anybody."

ACT II

RICHARD BASCIANO COULD easily have filled 60 percent of his selling area with Bruce Lee movies, but he was a man with a broader vision. Basciano spent, according to Fahringer, over $100,000 reconfiguring the upstairs rooms where he had shown live sex acts into theatrical stages; and then he began to look around for a producer to provide legitimate theater. Basciano found that well-established theater companies did not want to relocate above New York's most notorious sex parlor; unhoused avant-garde troupes were not so choosy. A group called Collapsible Giraffe began putting on plays in 1998. In the summer of 1999, Aaron Beall, a promoter of what is loosely known as Off-Off Broadway, stumbled into Show World with his girlfriend while three or possibly four sheets to the wind. Already in an impressionable state, Beall was overwhelmed by Show World's surreal décor—leering clown, carousel figures, coffin—"the circus of death," as Beall calls it. He had, he decided, found his new home. By October, Beall's Todo Con Nada theater had replaced Collapsible Giraffe.

I first met Aaron Beall in December 2001. He was sitting in Show World's black box theater, wearing a scarf and a red nightcap. He was a young man with a middle-aged man's shapeless tummy, octagonal granny glasses, and a beatific smile—something in between a dime-store Santa and a Jewish leprechaun. Aaron was one of those people who require no encouragement whatsoever to tell his story. "I opened up my first theater in 1989, at 167 Ludlow Street on the Lower East Side," he said, sitting in the darkness of GoGo 1, Show World's principal theater. "We kept opening up more and more theaters on Ludlow Street—the House of Candles, the Piano Store, the Pink Pony, the Lower East Side Tenement Museum." The theaters were typically named after whatever it was the storefront had done in its previous life. "My basic method of producing plays was, I would sit by the phone and people would call up and say, 'Can I do a show?' And I would say yes. We were the epicenter for nineties theater on the Lower East Side. In twelve years we did twenty-five hundred shows."

I assumed that I had misunderstood and asked, "You mean twenty-five hundred performances?"

Aaron corrected me. "No, individual productions. We had shows at seven, ten, and midnight—three shows a night, and sometimes we did four showlets at midnight. We put on a total of ten thousand performances, with fifteen thousand performers. It was like an explosion of activity." Aaron and his mates also started up the International Fringe Festival, which mushroomed into the largest theater festival in the United States.

And then Aaron learned a lesson about the relationship between culture and real estate. "We were," he said, "brought in by a couple of landlords to gentrify the neighborhood." By the nineties, thanks to people like Aaron, the Lower East Side, which had already evolved from a shtetl to a Hispanic and Asian slum, metamorphosed into Bohemia; and Todo Con Nada—"Everything with Nothing," a jokey reference to Aaron's willingness to soldier on with very little outside support—was evicted from one theater after another as the buildings were converted to co-operative apartments. Aaron had also lost control of the Fringe Festival to more mainstream and well-heeled players. "I was experiencing the lessons of capitalism," he said with a shrug. Aaron accepted the verdict; he did not buy the idea that the avant-garde had to fail the test of the marketplace in order to prove its legitimacy as art. Quite the contrary: Aaron saw himself as the impresario of a burgeoning counterculture he called Alternative Broadway. What's more, Aaron wasn't quite the mooncalf he appeared to be. He had, it's true, spent his formative years living with his mother and little sister in an abandoned chapel in a hippie commune in Mexico, but his mother had also thrown him into a Mexican parochial school where, Aaron said, "I learned everything about machismo." One thing Aaron had plainly learned was how to dust himself off after getting beaten up. And so, when he lost the Fringe Festival, he founded a rival, albeit much more modest, event: Pure Pop, "the fringe of the fringe."

Then Aaron and his girlfriend stumbled into Show World, and Nada Show World was born. Aaron loved the place—not the way Richie Basciano did, but not exactly ironically, either. Aaron, thirty-seven, was of the generation that grew up watching *The Gong Show* and *The Rocky Horror Picture Show,* and whose artists, like Jeff Koons, practiced a deadpan appropriation of schlocky household objects. "My generation thinks of cheesy as fabulous," as Aaron put it. Aaron came along too late to see the scumatorium in full flower, and perhaps he might have felt differently if he had; but as it was, he identified with Richie Basciano, whom he saw as an entrepreneur who had brought a marginal activity into the mainstream, and succeeded by mainstream standards. Aaron talked about Basciano as he walked me through the Big Top Cabaret and the former Peep Room—"the sanctum sanctorum," Aaron said, semi-mock-reverently—and then upstairs to the dance studios, which Basciano rented out. "He was the Ziegfeld of his day," Aaron said. "He created an industry; he was the person who really put it together, maximized the floorspace. Ultimately, Richie Basciano is a master builder." Aaron, too, saw himself as a master builder, a Hammerstein of Alternative Broadway. Hadn't he built the Ludlow street scene, and the Fringe Festival, and Pure Pop? He had dreamed of hooking up with a modern equivalent of the nineteenth-century impresario—Ted Turner or Time Warner. Instead, he got Richie Basciano.

Aaron had been much influenced by the theater of spoof, camp, and pastiche associated with the late Charles Ludlam, founder of the Ridiculous Theatrical Company. He described Ludlam's *Vampire Lesbians of Sodom* as the "defining play of the 1980s," which might come as news to devotees of Tom Stoppard, David Mamet, or Terence McNally. Like Ludlam, Aaron was deeply versed in classic drama, and loved the idea of running old plays through a kitschy modern sensibility. He had invented something he called Super-Theatrics, based on the insight that "you could deejay or sample any style of theater onto any text." One of his first productions at Show World was *Pervy Verse,* which he described as "a retelling of *The Bacchae* in fetish gear." He put on a production of *Waiting for Godot,* as well as all twelve of Anton Chekhov's early comedies, which Chekhov had called vaudevilles. He staged a "Ridicu-fest" to honor Ludlam's work. Nada Show World's first hit was *God of Vengeance,* a 1910 Yiddish play by Sholem Asch that takes place in a brothel. The play had attracted a supremely odd combination of blue-haired ladies and Hasidic Jews; the latter invariably arrived without their identifying hat or overcoat, for *God of Vengeance* was a notorious play that had been banned for blasphemy. Besides that, it was being staged above New York's most famous sex shop. This was the kind of incongruity Aaron lived for: he and Times Square were a match made in heaven.

Over the next few months, I periodically dropped in on Aaron and his expanding empire. Getting there was always half the fun. Show World had a kind of nonadult foyer or antechamber with animal sculptures propped on pedestals; a sign near the front door said, "No Live Girls." (Aaron had also staged a "No Live Girls" festival.) It was extremely discreet by Eighth Avenue standards. Straight ahead, beyond a pair of saloon doors, were the peeps; downstairs was the big sex supermarket, with videos and every kind of dildo known to man, and more booths. You could walk upstairs from the foyer, or you could go around the corner to a separate entrance, where the risers on the staircase read "Talk to the Stars," "Nude (25 cents) Shows," "Fantasy Booth," "Live Nude Girls," etc. Upstairs were GoGos 1 and 2, the Big Top, and various lounges—all painted black, with red trim and diamond-shaped mirrors. It felt like an all-new, jazzed-up Ludlow Street setting: the House of Sex.

Aaron felt that Richie Basciano intuitively understood him because they were both dreamers. Aaron had been nurturing the same dream since the early nineties: to unify the scattered energies of Alternative Broadway and to fully realize the cultural and economic power of the fringe—under his own tutelage, of course. He had been tinkering for years with a document that laid out his vision. Now he had relocated that vision from the Lower East Side to 42nd Street and Eighth Avenue. In June 2001, he had prepared a new draft of his grand plan and sent it to Basciano. Aaron's ulterior motive was to save his skin: rumors were flying around that Basciano was preparing to sell his real estate for some astronomical sum—$300 million, says Aaron, whose sense of money is extremely approximate—and Aaron was trying to make a case that his patron could make more money by staying. Aaron was, in effect, laying out another version of the argument that Rebecca Robertson and others had been making for almost a decade: that culture was what would drive economic development on 42nd Street and in Times Square. But Aaron was making a case for a different branch of the culture—more demanding, more ambitious, more homemade, more "real." He was proposing, he wrote, "a true alternative to the 'new' Times Square that recaptures the spirit of the 'old' Times Square." Aaron would offer authentic entertainment, rather than the synthetic product being peddled on the new 42nd Street.

Todo Con Nada @ Show World @ the Times Square Theater and Entertainment Center Plan 2002 is one of the truly odd documents of the Times Square redevelopment process. The plan is suffused with a sense of breathless anticipation, of a "historic collaboration" between business and the arts and a giant windfall for both. Show World would become a "scene," a "neighborhood," the new center of Bohemia; it would be the home of an all-new arts complex that would attract a minimum of 250,000 visitors a year, and a maximum of two million, which Aaron figured as one-quarter of the total annual attendance of Off-Broadway, though he appears to have confused this figure with the total attendance of Broadway. The implicit theory was "Build it, and they will come." Aaron proposed ten new ventures, meant to work synergistically with one another and with the more traditional attraction downstairs. The big moneymaker was *No Live Girls,* a nonpornographic video peep show using forty-one booths that had just been packed up at Basciano's defunct Peepland, on 42nd Street. Aaron's ingenious inspiration was to offer 128 channels of video material and to charge a quarter for ninety seconds, just like they did downstairs. And *No Live Girls* wouldn't need a mop.

Aaron also proposed a late-night club, a gift shop—"think museum gift shop"—an art gallery, and the Show World Bar and Restaurant, where a spruced-up version of Show World's "original décor" would provide "that 1970s *feel.*" In a hardheaded touch, Aaron suggested that Todo Con Nada's plays and festivals be scheduled only when the four theaters could not be rented. At the same time, Aaron's surreal sense of numbers led him to calculate that, at optimum capacity, the new Show World Center would have a potential annual revenue of $47,123,100. It was a beautiful vision, a vision that promised to transform Times Square, Show World, and Aaron Beall, in that order. Todo Con Nada would receive 10 percent of gross rentals, 12 percent of gross receipts from the bar/restaurants, and 25 percent of the proceeds from the sale of art.

By the spring of 2002, Aaron saw the new Show World Center beginning to emerge. The art gallery was up and running, he was outfitting the Big Top Cabaret with video monitors, and Basciano had built new offices up on the third floor. One afternoon, Aaron took me up to his office, a big, empty room with a table and a few books. A workman stopped by to ask, "What time would you like me to start up every morning?" Aaron shook his head in amazement; it was some kind of miracle. Aaron accepted miracles with the same good humor, almost the same fatalism, he brought to fiascos; it was precisely the fact that anything could happen that Aaron relished about his peculiar corner of show business. It was hard to imagine that Richie Basciano could take Aaron's blueprint seriously, but Aaron believed in himself too much to wonder that someone else would, too. "When I look back someday and see what I've accomplished over fifty years," he said—on this particular day his thinning, straggly hair was covered by an incongruously rakish black beret— "I could have had no better apprenticeship than with Richie."

ACT III

ONE AFTERNOON IN THE first week of May 2002, I walked up to the third floor to see Aaron and noticed, in an adjacent cubbyhole, an entirely unlikely figure, a man of about fifty dressed in a white shirt and tie, a pen clipped to his pocket, his silver hair combed straight back. Aaron said, "Would you like to meet our general manager?"—and just like that, the silver-haired man walked in. His name was Marc Barbanell. Marc began talking in a strangely indirect fashion about how Richard Basciano—not "Richie," as Aaron called him—had organized and amplified and modernized and so forth the "concept" downstairs. I noticed he never used the word "sex" in connection with the concept. He talked about a "longtime association" with Richard, though in a "private, personal capacity." Now, he said, he had been asked to join "the corporate side of the organization." He was, himself, a "corporate" person. He proved this point by using elaborate metaphors about pulling the trigger, and not going beyond the water's edge, and so on. "You could say that I'm the vehicle," he said, and now for the first time he looked at Aaron—he was the vehicle to ensure that the enterprise succeeded in regard to dollars and cents. That didn't necessarily sound like a positive development. And in fact, when it came to the bottom line, Marc wasn't the least bit ambivalent. "I am under serious profit pressure from Richard," he announced. He talked about thirty-day, sixty-day, ninety-day "time frames."

There may have been some setting in which Marc Barbanell wouldn't have seemed out of place—a scene from George S. Kaufman's hallucinatory *Beggar on Horseback,* for example—but at Todo Con Nada Show World he stood out like a unicorn, or like a unicorn in a suit. I immediately followed Marc back to his cubbyhole, where I found that he had busied himself with paperwork. He had a beeper clipped to his pocket. I asked Marc whether he thought I might be able to talk to Mr. Basciano. This provoked another monologue: this is an organization that plays close to the vest, that operates according to certain principles, that is not interested in celebrity . . . Marc said that the organization received "requests" from a wide variety of sources—"Air Force One—"

"Air Force One?"

"Yes; Richard's response was that he was not interested." In what? Marc wouldn't say. The cryptic drone resumed: "We will make a determination as to whether this opportunity fits with our organizational goals . . ." I finally excused myself and backed out the door. I went over to Aaron's office and gave him a skeptical waggle of the eyebrows. Aaron said, "Marc is a corporate person." He appeared not to be joking, which I took to be a bad sign.

The next time I saw Marc, in early June, he explained that he had agreed to talk to me, though Richard would not. He said that he, Marc, had just booked a new play, *Hopscotch*—"a real uppity play, attracts a nice, clean, uppity crowd, kind of a midweek, clean-cut dating crowd." This didn't sound very much like the audience for *Pervy Verse,* not to mention for nonpornographic video booths. Then I noticed that Aaron's door was locked. "He went out," Marc said brusquely. "I ruffled his feathers. He's having trouble accepting what's going on here. I told him, 'Aaron, Marc is here: We're going to make some money.' " Apparently, Aaron had drastically misread the tea leaves: he had run through his patron's stock of patience, as well as his bankroll. Marc was heading out for a meeting, and as we walked together down the ratty staircase to the second floor, he recalled his last exchange with the young Hammerstein. "I said to him, 'Aaron, you've had two years. When are you going to start making money?' And he goes, 'We've got a new play coming in, we've got this thing and that thing.' 'Aaron, it's a fucking loser. It's a quarter of a million dollars so far, and no end in sight. I mean, it's getting embarrassing.' " Marc had suddenly stopped talking in metaphors, which perhaps was also a bad sign. The name "Todo Con Nada," he said, had already been removed from the marquee. In future, Marc said, "Aaron will have control over nothing." He would be a promoter; he was free to promote, and Marc was free to buy or not buy.

Workmen were climbing all over the second floor, creating a very new kind of Show World. As we walked by, Marc pointed to a gray-haired figure standing with two workmen. "That's Richard," he said. I asked if I could at least say hello. Marc shook his head. "Best not," he said.

I came by the following week for my interview with Marc and found him administering a dressing-down to Aaron. The latter was standing in the doorway in a red T-shirt and sky-blue sneakers, looking like a character from a Robert Crumb comic book. Aaron's most recent production had bombed, and Marc, who was seated behind the desk in his tiny office—Aaron standing, Marc sitting—was delivering a lesson in accounting. "It doesn't do any good to come to me and say, 'Marc, I made eight grand last night' if you lost twelve grand the night before. We're still down four G's, you get what I'm saying?" Marc was making imaginary entries on an imaginary ledger book. Marc talked about Frank, the accountant, and "the long finger of ET"—Frank's probing finger, apparently. He spoke with the inch-thick patience one uses when addressing a refractory child. The child in question stood with his shoulders slumped, taking the blow, saying nothing. Aaron always seemed to know when not to be a smart-ass. He also knew when to take a punch—Mexican parochial school had taught him that. But he was still, in Marc's ledger book, a loser.

Marc's office was a bit cozy for an interview, unless one was sitting and the other standing, so he suggested we adjourn to the theater lobby. We walked down the fire stairs, threaded our way through the workmen, and sat in a blood-red banquette. An article on Show World's transformation had just appeared, and it had used words like "smut." Marc was fairly quivering with outrage; he seemed to be scrutinizing me with grim suspicion. He talked about Richard's "integrity," his "sincerity," his "legitimacy," even his "godliness." It wasn't just Richard but the "facility" that was misunderstood. "It's kind of like looking in retrospect to you in junior high school," Marc said. "When you dated a girl, what was your real assertion of why you dated the girl?" Marc gave me a waggish look; it was one of those questions that, at least inside Show World, answered itself. "Now you're older, you want to marry her. So when you're young at heart, years ago, back in the days of Show World, we had another image, and another assertion. Now we're older, now we're wiser, now we're up-to-date in the evolution of the city." The new Show World was the marrying kind. The irony was that Aaron wanted to exploit the dark cachet of pornography, but Marc was thinking of the uppity, good-time feel of dinner theater. Aaron seemed to believe in Show World a lot more deeply than Richie Basciano did.

Marc was a little defensive on the whole cultural-positioning front. "I want to make it clear that we're *very* sensitive to the arts," he said. They would be putting on shows in GoGo 1 and GoGo 2, including whatever downtown kind of shows Aaron could demonstrate would actually turn a profit. There would be fashion shows and maybe "an environmental thing that needs glitz and mirrors and strobe lighting." The Big Top Cabaret would become a classy lounge–cum–sports bar. "If you're coming here as a businessman," Marc explained, "you want to see sports, you get a free cocktail, which is a beautiful cocktail glass full of scallops and shrimps and cocktail sauce which will be free to you upon two drinks." Marc, too, dreamed of turning Show World into a scene; but it wasn't quite the scene Aaron had in mind. "If Times Square Entertainment Center becomes a stigma," Marc explained—he used the word "stigma" as if it meant its exact opposite—"if it's the meeting place for theater, all the photographers are here, all the show people are here, all the people in the know are here, why would I want to remain from the sixties image in the lobby, when I know that the people that are visiting the peep shows are visiting them on a regular basis, basically it is what it is what it is what it is?" This was Marc's way of expressing the idea that perhaps someday Show World could dispense with pornography altogether. It was Josh Alan Friedman's worst nightmare.

ACT IV

THE FOLLOWING WEEK I met Aaron for lunch at Joe Franklin's Memory Lane Restaurant. Aaron had a fedora perched on the back of his head like an old press agent. He was not, I discovered, any kind of a vegan: he had a filet mignon and two glasses of red wine. Marc had suspended Aaron's entire theatrical schedule while construction continued, but Aaron was serene and upbeat, as always. Marc appealed to his sense of irony. "He's an amazing English stylist," Aaron said. "He goes, 'Hey look, guy, I'm no Darth Nader from *Star World.*'" But Aaron also insisted that he and Marc "have a nice synergy together." They were both "salespeople." Aaron still believed that the *No Live Girls* booths, the art gallery, and much of the theatrical schedule were going to happen. But he also conceded, "I exist within the bubble"—within, that is, a transitional moment in the history of Times Square, in which the marketplace had not yet definitively dealt some in and others out. Aaron might well turn out to be too outré for the new Times Square. But, of course, that was the larger pattern of his life: create a new thing, and then watch it be appropriated and subsumed. There would always be the next venue. "I wanted," he said, "to leave a template of ideas that, even if I was a failure, they could be picked up at a later date."

Aaron had, it turned out, misread the tea leaves once again. The next time we spoke, in mid-July, Aaron said that Marc had booted him, and Todo Con Nada, out of Show World. Aaron was welcome to book either of the GoGo rooms, but with rentals set at $600 and $1,000 a night, Marc had, Aaron said, "priced out the world of alternative Broadway." I mentioned that that seemed to be pretty much the idea, and Aaron said, "Well, the philosophy at Show World has always been, 'Accentuate the negative.'" It was a rare moment of bitterness. But no matter. Aaron had already moved his operation to an old Broadway curtain factory on 45th Street between Ninth and Tenth Avenues. The place was saturated in

Times Square lore: it overlooked the park where the notorious "Capeman murders" of 1959, which Paul Simon had dramatized in a play, had taken place. Todo Con Nada Times Square would be opening soon with a few solo shows. Aaron would be mounting productions in abandoned storefronts, as he had on Ludlow Street. He wasn't defeated in the least; if he had to move the locus of Alternative Broadway to a new site, then so be it. Big things were in the offing. Aaron was working with a collaborator on a new production, titled *Icarus and Aria*. It would be, he said, *"Romeo and Juliet* meets *Any Given Sunday* meets *Traffic*—in verse."

ACT V

BY EARLY 2003, the renovation of the Times Square Entertainment Center was complete, and Marc Barbanell was eager to show off his new $2 million baby. Marc was still occupying his teeny-tiny windowless cubicle, though he had doffed the shirt and tie in favor of a black turtleneck. It was snowing heavily the afternoon I visited, but Marc took me out to the Eighth Avenue sidewalk to make a point. Here, just north of the Show World entrance, was the $75,000 LED sign announcing the new cabaret space, Le Club at Show World. Show World here, Le Club at Show World there—two separate entrances, two separate places. "It's got a different *address,*" Mark explained, as if that said it all. "One is 673, the other is 669. Show World is a different place. It's just like I have a Duane Reade next door." We went back upstairs to the cabaret, which was state-of-the-art everything, from the six giant drop-down screens to the "intelligent lighting" system ($328,000), the sound system ($220,000), the cappuccino machine ($6,000), the "ventless cooker" ($10,000), and the plasma screens in the bar providing "total video continuity" (no price given). It was a dream. "We've got smoke, we've got lights, we've got dancing, we've got movement," Marc said. "This place *rocks.*"

The walkie-talkie buzzed. It was Richie Basciano. Marc seemed flustered. "I'm giving a gentleman a tour of the facility," he said. Apparently he hadn't cleared my visit with top management. Richie's disembodied voice was urbane and measured; he didn't probe. They agreed to meet later in the day, and nothing further was said of the Man Who Is Show

World. But it was Basciano, of course, who had agreed to throw what he hoped was good money after bad. After Marc had noticed that professional dancers could get a sluggish dance crowd up on its feet, he had put together the Le Club Dancers—"real dancers, not go-go trash." They were drop-dead gorgeous, they had their own special outfit of sequins and bustiers, and they were trained by a professional choreographer. "Think of the Playboy Bunnies," Marc said, "but without the Playboy."

Marc had done his best to transform the interior into an Eighth Avenue version of a Playboy Club. The walls were red and black with bands of mirror tile, in homage to the Show World tradition, and the tables, the chairs, the VIP banquettes, and pretty much everything else was red and black as well. The foyer had been turned into a photo gallery, with big blowups of Frank Sinatra, Marilyn Monroe, and Audrey Hepburn, as well as the Statue of Liberty and the Flatiron Building. The bigger of the two theater spaces, where Aaron had staged *God of Vengeance,* was now a dance space, while the smaller GoGo 2—now "Theater 2"—featured improv and stand-up comedy. Thanks to advanced soundproofing technology, Marc could have one deejay playing salsa in one space, another playing reggae in the second, and a third playing hip-hop. Marc referred to this in his own private lexicon as "the tripaletic effect."

But the more Marc talked about the plasma screens and the fully automated micros, the more I could sense the desperate frailty of the whole enterprise. The facility was trapped between identities. "I keep trying to tell people it's not Show World anymore," Marc said plaintively. "It's Le Club *at* Show World. We're keeping that name because it still has the stigma of Show World. But it's mostly a negative, I promise you. You say 'Show World,' and people think 'nude girls, live acts.' That's long gone. It's *decades* old." The name was driving away the upscale crowd—Asian girls, in particular, didn't want to have anything to do with the place—and attracting the wrong kind of attention. *Law & Order* wanted to shoot a murder scene on the premises; *Sex and the City* wanted a sex scene. Marc wasn't interested. "No sex, no murder, nothing negative." But where was the positive going to come from? Marc admitted that he was hurting; the promoters he booked in weren't making the bar minimums he charged, and he was being forced to shift to a different pricing mechanism. The economy was killing everyone.

Maybe this bid for respectability would crash, and Show World would end with racks full of kung fu videos like everyone else. But I was rooting for Marc. It was obvious, in retrospect, that Todo Con Nada at Show World had been foredoomed. Richie Basciano did not aspire to be alternative anything; neither, for that matter, did Times Square. And this particular rear entry to Times Square, here on Eighth Avenue, was not about making weird stuff broadly acceptable; it was about making dirty stuff broadly acceptable. Aaron Beall had been a false start; Marc Barbanell was the right man to negotiate the treacherous passage to respectability—from Show World to Le Club. Someday, many years from now, with the old Times Square only a picturesque memory, Richie Basciano's grandchildren might come to think of him just as Aaron did: as the Florenz Ziegfeld of Eighth Avenue. And who, after all, remembered Ziegfeld's invisible fish?

DEFINING DEVIANCY UP

IN SEPTEMBER 1993, Rudy Giuliani, a former federal prosecutor then taking his second run at the mayoralty of New York, gave a speech in which he said that residents of the city had come to feel consumed by "a sense of dread"—about the ubiquity of the homeless and the mentally ill, about garbage-strewn streets, about crime both petty and grave. And he vowed to act in the face of these numberless incivilities. He would, he promised, not only crack down on serious crime but imprison panhandlers and "squeegee operators" who try to extort or intimidate passersby into giving them money. David Dinkins, the incumbent mayor, snorted that "killers and rapists are a city's real public enemies—not squeegee pests and homeless mothers." (Giuliani had not proposed incarcerating homeless mothers.) Elite opinion took Dinkins's side, but ordinary New Yorkers—middle-class whites, of course, but many minority voters as well—plainly warmed to Giuliani's message. The challenger narrowly won the election, and then was reelected in a landslide four years later.

Giuliani was speaking out of intense personal conviction, but he was also drawing on a growing body of opinion about the consequences of urban disorder. A few months earlier, Daniel Patrick Moynihan, a U.S. senator from New York and a distinguished social theorist, had said that a city in the throes of social disintegration had accepted a defeatist strategy of "defining deviancy down." Moynihan described a place in which the forces of social control seemed to have surrendered to the forces of disorder. Giuliani cited this resonant expression in his speech, and mentioned instances of it that few could deny. He also drew on the "broken windows" theory, advanced by the criminologists George L. Kelling and James Q. Wilson, who had argued that "serious street crime flourishes in areas in which disorderly behavior goes unchecked. The unchecked panhandler is, in effect, the first broken window." Giuliani vowed to reverse the process by arresting the window breakers.

As mayor, he did just that. Crime had begun to drop after Dinkins obtained the funds to increase the police force to unprecedented levels. But under Giuliani and his first police commissioner, William Bratton, it dropped much further, to levels not seen in thirty to forty years. What was more, Giuliani found ways of characterizing infuriating forms of disorderly behavior, such as soaping up the windshield of helpless motorists, as criminal behavior, and he enforced laws against low-level crimes that had previously been ignored, like public drinking. He moved decisively against pornography. And in those parts of the city where offensive behavior and "quality-of-life" incidents were as pervasive a problem as serious crime—in places like Times Square—the new policy produced immediate effects.

Gretchen Dykstra, executive director of the Times Square BID, says that the BID had tried and failed to wipe out the three-card monte games that flourished all over the area, blocking the sidewalks and preying on tourists unwise enough to trust their luck. But Chief Bratton ordered police officers to arrest violators, and by 1996, the scam had virtually disappeared from the streets. Police officers had almost stopped making arrests for street-level drug sales after a series of corruption scandals; Giuliani and Bratton reversed the policy. "It was a more aggressive style of policing," says Detective Adam D'Amico, the veteran of Times Square. "It used to be, if we stopped someone for a quality-of-life offense, like urinating on the street or drinking beer, we'd give them a summons and they'd go their own way. Now we would bring them into the station house and ask them to produce ID, and then make a phone call to verify the ID. If they didn't have ID, or couldn't prove it, they could spend a night in jail. We found out that a lot of people were using fake ID. Or maybe there was a warrant out for a much more serious crime."

Giuliani believed that he was waging a battle not only against the forces of social disorder but against an ideology that legitimized that disorder, and that had paralyzed New Yorkers from acting in their own interests. And some adherents of that position now concede, grudgingly or not, that he was right. Gretchen Dykstra, a self-described ex–sixties lefty, succinctly describes the attitude of the *bienpensant* classes when she says, "There was a tendency to romanticize the gutter." But it is not enough to say that the critics of the cleanup of Times Square refused to recognize that the "street culture" of the area was predatory, or that it drove "decent" citizens away; it was, rather, that they bridled at the very language of decency and at the idea that some citizens were more decent than others. The argument over social control was really a debate about who it was that urban spaces like Times Square belonged to—who deserved to be considered its "authentic" dwellers and users.

There is a history, stretching back at least to the time of Baudelaire, the bard of mid-nineteenth-century Parisian life, of cherishing the city as the great bulwark against overweening bourgeois propriety, and as home to a culture of deviance and eccentricity. In "On the Heroism of Modern Life," Baudelaire writes, "The spectacle of fashionable life and the thousands of floating existences—criminals and kept women—that drift about in the underworlds of a great city . . . all prove to us that we need only open our eyes to recognize our heroism." "Fashionable life and the thousands of floating existences"—that is Times Square to a T. What is the poetry of Times Square but one long celebration of the human impulse to subvert propriety—from the glittering underworld of Damon Runyon and Texas Guinan to the penny-ante chiseling of Liebling's Hymie Katz, and from Allen Ginsberg's "atomic disease" to the country-boy hustling of Joe Buck and even the sexual Olympics that Josh Alan Friedman narrates? In the Times Square mythos, it is the lawman and his accomplice, the bluenose, who play the heavies. And so it is all too easy to see Rudy Giuliani's campaign against public disorder as only the latest feverish effort to stem the force of illicit appetite, beginning with Anthony Comstock's war against prostitution, continuing with Fiorello La Guardia's against burlesque and, later, the legal assault on pornography; now this. Perhaps the city would be better served by an honest reprobate like Jimmy Walker.

But the analogy is false. By the 1970s and eighties, the Runyonesque, or Baudelairean, characters of another day had exited Times Square and other old urban spaces. The frankly predatory or just plain pitiful figures who came in their stead—the drug dealers and the hustlers, the homeless and the mentally ill—inherited the old mantle of antibourgeois legitimacy. Indeed, in a new twist, their very marginality came to be seen as proof of the failure of bourgeois society; and the impulse to clean up degraded places came to be interpreted as the wish to erase the manifest signs of that failure. As one author wrote in disgust at the rehabilitation of Union Square Park, a few intersections below Times Square, "The same stroke that restored the park's green statues to gleaming bronze splendor attempted to wipe away the history of homelessness and poverty." Homelessness and poverty were the park's—and the city's—reality; the cleanup was thus a kind of Potemkin fraud.

The habit of mistaking predatory for assertively individualistic behavior—of romanticizing the gutter—is a trope of modern Times Square literature. One scholar, Laurence Senelick, has argued that the difference between the gaudy, bawdy, sporty 42nd Street of days of glory and the supposedly perverse one of our own day has been wildly overdrawn; in fact, the forces of bourgeois propriety have warred throughout the last century against those who wished to test the boundaries of the acceptable. "It is easy to foment outrage about juvenile prostitution," Senelick wrote in 1990. "Having sex with one's own children has been a feature of family life since Lot and his daughters, and the mass selling of juveniles for sexual purposes was common in the Eastern Hemisphere from ancient times until very recently." It was the moral crusade that outraged him, not the sexual exploitation.

The whole argument over "gentrification," as it applied to Times Square and other neighborhoods, turned on the question of who was an authentic citizen and who an outsider. In 1988, when the New York Police Department rousted the punk activists and homeless people who had taken over Tompkins Square Park, the squatters' slogan was "Die, yuppie scum." The squatters had much of the city's liberal establishment, and virtually all of its urban thinkers, on their side. The park was described as "the site of the first major antigentrification effort" and as the precursor to large-scale urban warfare. Yet when it reopened several years later, its actual users were the working-class mothers, and their children, who lived in their neighborhood and who had been driven away by the homeless and their ideological allies. It was as if urban life consisted only of the marginal and the rich, whereas the truth is that it is the middle class, not the rich, who most need a clean, well-ordered civic life, for the rich have private retreats of their own.

Why have critics on the left insisted so single-mindedly on the higher authenticity of the socially marginal? One such critic, Sharon Zukin, speculates that an entire generation of intellectuals, themselves working-class "ethnics," experienced a profound sense of loss as the yeasty urban neighborhoods of their birth were abandoned or obliterated by urban renewal. "Wrapped up in the layers of territorial and tribal dispossession," she writes, "were a political identification with other 'dispossessed' groups—the poor and the blacks—and a disillusionment . . . with the promise of modernity." That deep identification makes any form of "progress" suspect, if that progress makes a formerly neglected area appealing to the white—or nonwhite—middle class. Indeed, Zukin concedes that "many groups claim they support revitalization," but adds that apparent consensus masks deep conflict.

The problem with this way of thinking is not that public urban spaces belong to the middle class rather than the poor, but rather that they are a collective good to be rendered habitable and pleasant for everyone. There is no "authentic class": Times Square, Union Square, Tompkins Square, and other such places belong to all New Yorkers, the poor and the marginal as much as the well-to-do. Giuliani's argument was that only by suppressing behavior that drives New Yorkers away from these places can this collective good be secured; but since that behavior tends to come more from the socially marginal than from the middle class, it is the former more than the latter who will be the target of the kind of enforcement actions he launched. Critics insist on describing this process as the displacement of the poor by the rich—"champagne flutes instead of malt liquor forties, and chorus lines instead of police lineups," as one puts it felicitously—and yet it is the teenagers who hang out on 42nd Street today who benefit from the new doctrines of social control as much as the tourists from Ohio.

Giuliani's passion for order blinded him to the Baudelairean delights of the urban street; given his druthers, he might have dispensed altogether with such irritants as the First Amendment. But this is scarcely the only imaginable alternative to an equally single-minded defense of antisocial behavior; nor, of course, would any fair observer describe it as the tenor of today's Times Square. For a theory of the democratic, individualistic middle course, one need only think of a figure like William Whyte, the social theorist who minutely studied the walking, sitting, and talking habits of people in urban places. Whyte spent much of his career trying to encourage what he called "amiable disorder" by advising on the design of parks, sidewalks, atriums, and other public places. He insisted on the crucial distinction between "oddballs" and "freaks" on the one hand, who constitute "a benevolent presence on the street," and genuinely danger-ous people, whom he did not hesitate to call "undesirables." Whyte made the case for what one might call the bourgeois city—not because he championed the middle class, but because he cared about such bourgeois values as comfort, neighborliness, and charm. And the Times Square of today, though it lacks much in neighborliness, is surely a place of amiable disorder.

TIMES SQUARE STILL HAS a street culture both of suffering souls and of predatory ones; but it is, effectively, subterranean, and only occa-sionally impinges on the life above. There are at least fifty homeless peo-ple on an average warm day in and around Times Square, but a casual pedestrian barely notices them. A few of the regulars, like "Heavy," a shambling mass of a man who rarely speaks, never bathes, and drags be-hind him a battered train of carts filled high with garbage, are almost im-possible to miss. But most of the homeless men in Times Square live quietly on the cross streets and do as little as possible to draw attention to themselves, save when they've had too much to drink. And even most of the drinkers are quiet. A handsome, fine-boned black man named Mark Harris spends most of his day sitting in the lee of a building on 50th Street, just west of Eighth Avenue. He is forty-nine, he says; his goatee has begun to go silver. He has a rhythm guitar, except when he gets fuddled and leaves it somewhere; if you ask, he will plug it into his mini-amp and play a tune like "I Am a Blues Man." In his younger days, Harris says, he was a studio musician with the Drifters, Richie Havens, Baby Washing-ton. Now he claims that he has a few albums ready to go; his producers are "in the hospital." This appears to be a fantasy. Harris says, "A lot of my friends, they're telling me if I slow down on the alcohol, it'll help me with my music." He says this with a rueful smile and a slightly vacant expression; there is no reason to doubt him on this score.

Homeless people like Harris—or even like Heavy—fall well within the permissible boundaries of social control in Times Square: they are not disturbing anyone, and they have a right to their spot of pavement. People who work with the homeless, and the homeless themselves, say that there will always be a vagrant population in Times Square, because the crowds of tourists make for top-drawer panhandling, and simply because the buses and subways seem to disgorge a certain number of helpless or disoriented or addicted people onto the streets of Times Square every year. "Outreach" organizations do their best to help them; but even the most mentally stable among the homeless—like Mark Harris—are rarely willing to trade the fellowship of the streets for "three hots and a cot." The homeless have thus become a Times Square fixture, harmful almost only to themselves and to one another. They lead the "floating existences" of which Baudelaire spoke. It would be heartless to say that they are part of Times Square's "local color," any more than the gang-bangers in the arcades are; but the truth is that they constitute the substratum of the local pageant and a kind of guarantee of amiable disorder.

The other branch of the Times Square street subculture is overtly criminal—the "underworld," in all senses of that term. Even the heightened degree of social control has been unable to eradicate drug dealing and prostitution from the area, and above all from the tawdry blocks of Eighth Avenue immediately above and below 42nd Street, though the substitution of "good uses" for bad on Eighth Avenue—hotels, restaurants, the new headquarters of *The New York Times*—is likely to reduce crime there, as it has on 42nd Street. Yet even this rampant activity has been contained, for Eighth Avenue is not in the least ominous even quite late at night, and visitors are even less likely to notice drug deals than they are the homeless. And on 42nd Street, where at least a dozen police officers are posted many nights, you are unlikely to notice either. There may be trouble inside the Broadway City arcade, but it rarely spills out into the street.

Certainly the instruments of control are, if not powerful, then at least numerous. The area is patrolled not only by the New York Police Department but by security officers from the Times Square BID. The BID, a private body made up of local property-holders that performs what are normally thought of as public functions, both cleans up and patrols (and offers services for the homeless) in an area stretching from 40th to 53rd Street, and east of Broadway to west of Eighth Avenue. At any one time, the BID fields as many as thirty-two officers on both fixed and walking posts throughout the area. They wear uniforms, with big-brimmed Smokey the Bear hats. (One officer said that she had been offered $500 for her hat.) But they do not carry weapons and they are not empowered to make arrests; their job is to serve as "the eyes and ears" of the police, and mostly to be a comforting and friendly sight to tourists, who constantly stop them to ask directions, or just to pose for a picture.

One Friday evening in the early summer, I took a tour of Times Square with Eric Rivera, a veteran security officer with the BID and a genuine connoisseur of street crime. Rivera was a fireplug, self-confident and voluble and fond of action: he had enlisted in the Marines as a kid, and though he alluded vaguely to some youthful misconduct, he would be joining the police department the following week. At about ten-thirty that night, Rivera brought me to the Burger King at the southwest corner of 40th Street and Eighth Avenue. We stood across the street, our backs to the Port Authority Bus Terminal, and Rivera said, "This is one place I would never tell anyone I know to go to. You got more gun-related incidents here than anywhere. Look at all those people hanging out in front; they're selling guns, drugs, girls, you name it. It all comes in through the Lincoln Tunnel." A knot of men stood on the sidewalk, dark silhouettes against the lighted storefront. A police van was parked in front of the restaurant, and an officer was moving from one loiterer to another. "She's telling them they've got five minutes before they have to move along," Rivera explained. "But they'll be back."

As we walked north along Eighth Avenue, Rivera, gesturing around the bus terminal, said, "You got the low-level prostitutes here, the fifty-dollar hookers; they'll turn tricks for a rock of cocaine if they're hard up. Then you go all the way up to the four-hundred-dollar hookers who hang out at the bar of the Sheraton on Fifty-third." Without turning around, Rivera said, "The guy in the black-and-white shirt behind us, he's selling crack. This guy right in front of us here is a pimp. From Fortieth to Forty-eighth, we call it the coke and hooker stroll. They'll just go up and down all night, looking for action." The stroll was on the west side of the avenue, which was still chock-a-block with sex shops and strip clubs. We crossed over to the east side between 43rd and 44th and stood among the parked cars, looking back across the street. Rivera picked out his marks like an expert duck hunter peering from the blinds. "See that guy in the red jersey? Certifiable pimp; they call him Little Joe. And there's Soapman." This was Rivera's own nickname for a dealer who sold crack that turned out to be soap flakes, leaving the unwary buyer sending bubbles up from his pipe. But all the dickering and the dealing vanished into the torrent of the avenue's racing life. "You can walk around here, and it's like nothing's going on," Rivera said. "The buyer drops a five-dollar bill on the ground, the seller covers it with his shoe. A third guy comes and drops the rock or the gel cap on the ground. The seller hands the money to a kid, who vanishes. And it all happens in a second."

Rivera pointed out the subway landing where a gang leader had gotten his throat slashed in the midst of a chain snatching, and then the path he had staggered down until he had bled to death in front of Chevys. But I had gotten the same tour way back in October. It had been a long time between murders. In fact, Rivera said, even chain-snatching and petty thievery were rare. Violent crime was almost unheard-of. Bob Esposito, the BID's chief of security and a former police officer who put in many years in Times Square, says, "The kind of call I get now is, 'The musician's too loud,' or, 'I don't like what the Black Israelites are saying.'" Rivera said that when he was in junior high, twenty years ago, he used to cut school and watch dirty movies on 42nd Street. "In those days," he said, "you could never go to Eighth Avenue unless you had a weapon, or you came with twenty of your guys." Now, forget it. Rivera was hoping, once he became a cop, to be assigned to the most crime-infested neighborhood around. He had just about had it with Times Square; it was too tame.

16

ASK NOT FOR WHOM THE ANIMATRONIC *T. REX* ROARS

O N NOVEMBER 15, 2001, a big, excited crowd gathered at the northeast corner of Broadway and 44th Street. This was the exact same spot where Times Square's very first crowd had gathered, slightly over a century before, to witness the opening of Hammerstein's Olympia. Since that time, the Olympia had given way to an early movie theater that had in turn been converted back into a legitimate theater; the whole structure had been torn down to make way for a modern movie emporium, which in turn had been joined to the Bond's Clothing store and to the International Casino, one of Times Square's biggest and flashiest nightclubs; the entire complex had slid into disrepair, and the whole structure had been demolished once again. Civilizations had risen and fallen, and risen and fallen again, on this one rich archaeological site. And now a new culture, and a new epoch, had come: this crowd had gathered for the opening of the Toys "R" Us flagship store, the biggest, flashiest retail establishment in the history of Times Square. Oscar Hammerstein had hailed the Olympia as "the grandest amusement temple in the world." And the press managers for Toys "R" Us surely were exercising no more hyperbole than Hammerstein had when they called the store "the Toy Center of the universe."

Earlier that day, dozens of attractive young people wearing lime-green T-shirts that said "Xbox" on them had fanned out across Times Square; they were handing out cards that would entitle the bearer to stand in line at midnight and buy the new $299 Microsoft video game machine. Bill Gates himself had agreed to come to the store and sell the first Xbox in the world. And so here, at midnight, were five thousand people calmly and casually snaked around the building. The crowd flooded into the store, bought their games, and happily dispersed. It was a far more professionally managed opening than the Olympia's had been. But the sale of the video games was, in a way, a pretext for a yet larger event. Over fifty media crews from all over the world came to cover this mind-boggling convergence of global brand names. Afterward, Microsoft's marketing team calculated that the event created one hundred million "impressions" worldwide.

This beguiling accident of location, in which an early-twenty-first-century temple of entertainment is built atop the ruins of a late-nineteenth-century one, leads one to measure the course of history through comparison. The Toys "R" Us flagship store is an exciting, energetic, crowd-pleasing place, as the old Olympia was; and it is monumental, and prodigious, as the Olympia was. It, too, is a "theatrical" place, though of course its theatricality is a means to the end of getting people to buy things. The one was for grown-ups, the other is for kids. The Olympia was also a hopeless folly, while Toys "R" Us is wonderfully efficient, as befits the flagship institution of a $13 billion global enterprise. But perhaps the most striking difference is an evanescent one: Toys "R" Us is not only a store or a company, but a "brand"; and it exists in a world of brands, of which "Times Square" is very much one.

THE CORPORATE OFFICE of Toys "R" Us is situated in an office park just off an exit ramp in suburban New Jersey, about forty-five minutes from the Toy Center of the Universe. The headquarters is a bright, sunny, boxy glass building with toys and stuffed animals on landings and in open spaces. It feels like a pleasant place to work. On the top floor is the office of John Eyler, the company's chairman and CEO. Eyler is a blond, square-jawed corporate executive with an earnest, straightforward manner and a basso profundo voice. He is a native of Washington State, a graduate of the Harvard Business School, a career retailer. Before he ran Toys "R" Us, he was CEO of F.A.O. Schwarz, which was the biggest toy retailer in the world in the day when the toy industry consisted largely of small family-owned stores. Toys "R" Us was part of the new world that had eclipsed F.A.O. Schwarz. It was a publicly owned firm that sold inexpensive toys in giant supermarkets, a ubiquitous presence in suburban shopping malls, with 1,500 stores around the globe. But Toys "R" Us had, in turn, been eclipsed by Wal-Mart, which also sold toys as commodities, but sold them even cheaper. Toys "R" Us hired Eyler in 2000 with the hope of regaining the market share it had lost.

Eyler recognized that Toys "R" Us could not compete with Wal-Mart on price and instead needed to forge a new and distinctive identity, more service-oriented, more fun, more dramatic. Eyler and his team retrained salespeople, changed the layout of stores, forged exclusive relationships with prestigious suppliers like Steven Spielberg (himself a powerful brand name in the world of toys). But Eyler understood that he had to not only change Toys "R" Us but find a platform from which to proclaim those changes. Toys "R" Us needed a flagship store. "A flagship store," Eyler said, when I visited him one very pleasant afternoon, "is important to serve as a tangible symbol of change, to be the ultimate example of what the strategy is when the strategy is fully articulated." Eyler felt that the flagship store had to be in New York, since New York was where the media, the big buyers, the finance industry, and the nation's largest toy fair were located. And Times Square was the obvious location. Eyler said, "We chose Times Square because it has evolved into the highest-energy location in the city. Times Square is increasingly becoming the crossroads of the world. It has become a family-friendly place, and we felt that we were a continuation of that trend." Eyler understood that he could re-brand the company by associating with the brand that was the new Times Square: exciting, energetic, urbane, yet clean and family-friendly. And the effect was reciprocal, for he was, as he said, reinforcing the Times Square brand by virtue of joining it.

Eyler hired Joanne Newbold, a store designer who had created the F.A.O. branch stores during his tenure, to design the interior of the new store. And he told her: "I want to create new traditions for kids in New

York City." The new store would feel magical to children, as F.A.O. Schwarz does; it would also be designed so as to transport an unprecedented volume of customers efficiently through the vast space and toward the various selling areas. Newbold created an interior radically different from the bland, bright supermarkets Toys "R" Us had built all over the world: a vast, open cube, an almost raw space with theatrical lighting hung from catwalks, bright colors, a glass elevator rising through the middle. The glass façade of the store is covered with square canvas panels, 155 in all, each of which carries eight images; the panels can be rotated like a shade, so that Toys "R" Us is effectively covered by an ever-changing billboard. The panels can also be rendered transparent so that pedestrians can look straight into the store. And what they see, from the outside, is the centerpiece of the store, of the company, and of the Toy Universe itself: a sixty-foot-high Ferris wheel that rises from the basement toward the upper reaches of the store, its giant red neon spokes flashing clockwise as the ride sedately rolls through the store, providing children and their parents an eagle eye of the store's merchandise. It is also, at $2.50 a head, just about the cheapest form of entertainment in Times Square.

Newbold gave me a tour of the store several weeks after the opening. It quickly became plain that she is not only a highly professional store designer but a student of retail engineering. As we stood at the head of the escalator looking down toward the basement, with people pouring past us onto the main floor, she said, "Originally we thought we would use a merry-go-round or something like that. Then we thought, What a great way to make people look up, look down. As you cycle up, you can look around and see what's on the floor." The Ferris wheel was also a marketing device of its own. The names on the cars—*Toy Story,* Pokémon, Nickelodeon, and so on—represented not just familiar toys but "branding partners." Each one was a brand of its own, sharing in the new Toys "R" Us brand and adding their luster to it, as Microsoft had done. Toys "R" Us charged each firm $250,000 for the "naming rights" (though the actual proceeds from the ride go to charity).

Newbold explained that a ride originating in the basement had an additional advantage. "Besides coming in and saying, 'Oh, wow!,' in order to board the Ferris wheel you have to go down to the lowest level, which traditionally in New York is very hard to get people down to." We took the escalator down to the lower level and walked along a path to the edge of the "R Zone," the electronics area that is any toy store's highest-volume selling space. Everything in the R Zone was zapping, bonking, and blinking all at once. Newbold had to raise her voice. "If you're interested in electronics," she cried enthusiastically, "you're going to get sucked right in!" It was the Christmas season, and the crowd in the store was swelling; the sound system boomed out "I Saw Mommy Kissing Santa Claus," and then "Feliz Navidad." A magician at a station was demonstrating card tricks. Images were flashing across video screens. The Ferris wheel, with its great red neon spokes, was rolling. Noise, lights, crowds, motion—everything was happening at once. It all felt like 42nd Street under glass.

And yet at the same time the store had been ingeniously engineered so as to channel the feverish energies it released. The selling floors are organized in a "racetrack" format so that, Newbold said, "you get pulled from one department to another by seeing something ahead of you." Every other Toys "R" Us store has an armada of shopping carts parked near the front entrance, but shopping carts would take up too much room in this dense urban setting; instead, shoppers get big shoulder bags. This could pose a problem of its own, but the store specializes in what Newbold calls "affordable portables." Newbold obviously had given a good deal of thought to the problem of traffic management in what was destined to be the busiest toy store in the world. As we stood looking into the R Zone, she said, "We only have eight Play Station positions, so it won't become an arcade. What we tried to do was have the *perception* of interactivity without real interaction. Knowing that the traffic would be as dense as it is, we didn't want people pushing buttons on things, and starting things and stopping them, because they would break in a day, and people would come the next day and they wouldn't work. That would be negative." For all its theatricality, the store continuously instructs shoppers that it is, after all, a store.

We rode an escalator back upstairs and continued on to the second floor. This is the store's most dazzling retail area. Immediately to the right of the escalator were twenty-foot-high versions of the Empire State Building and the Chrysler Building made of Lego. Beyond them was the pièce de résistance—an animatronic *Tyrannosaurus rex* that emitted a mighty roar, just scary enough to give little kids a mild fright and make them come back for more. The roar cycle can be adjusted, so that on busy days the dinosaur can roar faster to keep the kids moving along. The *T. rex* marked the selling area for Steven Spielberg's *Jurassic Park* toys, with which the company has an exclusive relation. Next came the silver space-ship of *E.T.*, along with an animatronic version of the lovable alien. Then there was a Candyland that looked like the board game come to life, at least if you were four. Continuing on to the other side of the floor, we came to the Fisher-Price area, which, in a nice touch, had a little tableau of Times Square itself, looking very calm and sensible, with its little plastic people waiting at traffic lights. And then there was a giant Monopoly board, and a giant train set, and at the back of the floor an entire house for Barbie, with its very own elevator. Newbold explained that the displays had been designed so as to be understood from the Ferris wheel. "These are like instant visuals for kids. They don't have to read a sign; they don't have to read a graphic. It's just like, 'I see that dinosaur; when we get off, I've got to go over there.' " The whole store was semiotics for the prelit-erate.

Within weeks of its opening, the new Toys "R" Us store became one of the great tourist destinations of Times Square. It was a familiar name, whether you came from Decatur or Beijing, in an unfamiliar setting; and of course the kids loved it. It wasn't unusual for the store to attract 100,000 visitors in a day, or to do $1 million worth of business—thirty truckloads' worth of toys, as Elliott Wahle, the store manager, proudly pointed out to me, with each truck having to maneuver its way into Times Square, pull into the cramped loading dock, and then make a rapid exit. Vast crowds surged through the store even during the fallow season after Christmas. Wahle said that he was often asked whether it bothered him that so many people came to the new store to gawk rather than buy. "And the answer," he said, "is, 'Not in the least.' This is a $13 billion business focused on a name. And the visit reinforces our brand in the minds of every single one of those visitors." Wahle described the store as "the single greatest execution of the retail-tainment idea." The store could lose money and still be an immense success, because it would make shoppers more inclined to go to the Toys "R" Us back home.

———

BUILDINGS, AND BUSINESS VENTURES, in Times Square have risen and fallen over the decades like so many stage sets; one of the few persistent elements in this rootless and transitory realm has been the dynastic real estate families, who never sell anything if they don't have to, and thus pass their property intact from one generation to the next. The Moss family, which owns the parcel on 44th Street that Toys "R" Us leased, has had a presence in Times Square since the heyday of Oscar Hammerstein. B. S. Moss, the family patriarch, started building nickelodeons in Times Square in 1905; his peers were the Jewish entertainment moguls who went west and founded Hollywood. (It was his brother Paul who closed down burlesque as Mayor La Guardia's license commissioner.) B.S. opened vaudeville theaters, which he ultimately folded into the Keith-Albee syndicate. Then he expanded into movie theaters. He bought the parcel on 44th Street when the Olympia came down, and in 1936, he and a partner opened up the New Criterion, a thoroughly modern movie house that they called "The Theatre of Tomorrow." Engineers in a "tone-control booth" controlled "the slightest variations or modulation in sound volume," while a "four-unit cooling system" maintained a constant, pleasant temperature. The New Criterion, the flagship of the B. S. Moss empire, was a self-conscious symbol of an elegant, streamlined modernity. Many of the blockbuster movies of the next three decades opened there, including *The Ten Commandments, Lawrence of Arabia,* and *Funny Girl.*

At the same time, B.S.'s brother Joe, along with a group of investors, built the International Casino on the northern corner of the old Olympia site. The International was the last word in refinement, luxe, and swank. Here is how a reporter described the opening, in September 1937: "Hollywood on Broadway—a glittering gallimaufry of chromium and glass, crystal fountains, sliding doors, revolving stages, staircases which descend from heaven (when they work), a stainless steel escalator and a three-story spiral bar, where you can drink your way up and fall your way down, or vice versa, as befits your mood." *Life* magazine did one of its "*Life* Goes to a Party" series about the International soon after it opened, and the author noted, with what seems admirable candor for a family magazine, that "most people go to the International Casino to see a hundred-odd youngish girls in various states of undress." The article's opening photo spread shows a glistening chrome escalator with a tuxedoed headwaiter standing at the top, and then half a dozen beauties in two-piece bathing suits balancing spinning plates on long rods. Inside, *Life* offered pictures of bathing beauties descending from the ceiling in an elaborate trapezelike contraption and another riding bareback on a revolving stuffed horse.

And then, of course, this swanky, sexy, air-conditioned culture crumbled away just as surely as Hammerstein's opulent Gilded Age culture had done before it. The Bond's Clothing store booted out the nightclub in the forties, and in the sixties the New Criterion became just another movie theater (though it never stooped to porno). Times Square embarked on its long, slow slide into irrelevance and decay. B.S. and Joe Moss's son sold the parcel in 1968, and then *his* son, Charles, bought it back ten years later. By that time, the block was a huddle of tacky variety stores. The parcel seemed about as valuable as it had when Oscar Hammerstein bought it in 1893. And then, suddenly, by the mid-eighties, with the building boom provoked by the new zoning laws, property along Broadway was worth a very great deal. Moss held out for a long time. He didn't want another office building to go up where the New Criterion and the International Casino had stood—although it is also true that many of his proposed deals fell through. And when he finally agreed to lease the property to Toys "R" Us, he felt that he had found a tenant worthy of his family's history.

Had he? Not exactly. All those other Times Squares, the Times Square of the Olympia and the New Criterion and the International, catered to a cosmopolitan taste, a taste for elegance and nocturnal drama, the drama of grand settings and fine clothing and unpredictable experience. They were for grown-ups seeking a grown-up fantasy. And it is that grown-up sense of fantasy, the fantasy of the spiral bar and the umpteen tiers of box seats rising into the upper air, that has vanished from the spanking-new Times Square. There is fantasy aplenty, at Madame Tussaud's and the ESPN Zone and the Hershey's candy store; but not for grown-ups. The drama of open-ended experience still lives on the streets; but indoors, fun has been ingeniously, minutely, engineered. Here is the difference between popular culture and mass culture. For a global entertainment firm like Toys "R" Us, Times Square is now a "site," a branding opportunity, a marketing strategy. It has, amid these vast calculations, been reduced in size and stature. And its particularity has been diminished as well: Toys "R" Us's very presence makes Times Square more like the other places where Toys "R" Us is present. The Ferris wheel is site-specific "appliqué," to use Michael Sarkin's language.

How can you not feel ambivalent about the Toys "R" Us flagship store? To repudiate it is to repudiate mass culture itself, with all its vitality and its electric fantasies and its relentless wish to entertain. To embrace it is to embrace mass culture, with its numbing sensationalism, its two-dimensionality, its gigantism. That Ferris wheel is probably the biggest, and cheapest, attraction in Times Square, but it's also a reminder of a Ferris wheel that never got built—the one at the heart of the City at 42nd Street project, stillborn in 1980. This was the plan that Mayor Ed Koch dismissed by saying, "People do not come to midtown Manhattan to take a ride on some machine." The Ferris wheel, to an echt New Yorker like Koch, was strictly Disneyland. And that ride, which bore so heavy a symbolic burden, was an educational device designed to evoke the verticality of the city, its infinitely stratified texture. This one is a marketing device intended to spread out a giant store's wares from basement to ceiling.

You don't have to be a dogmatic critic of corporate culture to find the Toys "R" Us store at least faintly sinister; you just have to feel the bombardment of the cheerful booming music and the video monitors and the elevators in the Barbie house and the giant, looming Monopoly board, all of it a minutely orchestrated simulation of the spontaneous life of the place whose brand identity it is so ingeniously exploiting. An adult of only moderately melodramatic sensibility might contemplate the store with the apocalyptic alarm that the new generation of urban critics brings to shopping malls and planned communities. On one particularly insanely crowded day, I saw a friend who had come to buy a Lego for his nephew; he clutched at me like a drowning man in the wild eddy of the crowd and shouted, "It's hell!" before lurching onward to a cash register.

But of course, the store wasn't for him; it was for kids. Children are now in the picture in a way they were not before; the functional unit of popular entertainment is no longer "the grown-up," but "the family." Times Square, even more than Las Vegas, has surrendered to the hegemony of the family. I saw Toys "R" Us through Alex's eyes. He and I generally treated it as an amusement park, though the experience sometimes included the purchase of a game for Alex's GameCube system (which the supremely efficient Toys "R" Us had in stock at Christmastime when every other toy store was out). Once we made the mistake of coming on the Saturday afternoon before Easter, which a salesperson informed us was the second busiest day of the year. We wandered through the pulsing—but not shoving—crowd, pulled ever forward from one sales area to the next, little recking that the "racetrack format" was working its magic on us.

I noticed that about half the customers were black or Hispanic; this was, after all, an inexpensive store with free entertainment, and thus a fulfillment of those democratic traditions to which Bruce Ratner had raised a metaphorical glass. We came to a crowd gathered around a table; it was the display for Rumble Robots, little battery-operated fighting machines. Teams of green bots and red bots were squaring off against each other, with kids clutching controllers on either side. The bout was managed by two cool young guys in black hooded capes—the Rumble Masters. Alex would not leave. Finally he took over a controller for a green bot. And the Rumble Master shouted, "Three . . . two . . . one . . . Rummmble!" It was an eleven-year-old peak experience.

We came back again two weeks later—and the Rumble Robots were gone, as were all the permanent-looking fixtures in the department. Here was capitalism in the raw: all that is solid melts into air. Now an entirely new set of fixtures had been installed to display Sega electronic games. The sales assistant at the display was Deryck Clarke, a thirty-nine-year-old black hipster who plays the French horn in Broadway musicals. He wore a ribbon that said, "I speak German." Clarke was a New Yorker, and he said, "When I was in school I used to come down here with my homies to play the arcades. I was the Donkey Kong wizard." Now he had a five-year-old son. I asked him if he regretted the demise of the Times Square he knew as a teenager. "Not really," he said. "It was sort of menacing. At this stage in my life, I want a place that I can take my family."

17

PLAYS "R" US

I N T H E E A R L Y S U M M E R of 2001, I went with my wife and parents
to see August Wilson's play *King Hedley II,* at the Virginia Theatre on West
52nd Street. The play was set in 1985—Ronald Reagan's America—and
the action took place in the scraggly backyard of a street of row houses in
a barely-getting-along urban neighborhood. A half-demolished brick wall
at the back of the stage formed an enclosure separating the world of the
characters, black people who were no longer young and no longer hopeful, from the prosperous, front-yard world familiar to the audience. No
one was going anywhere; and the ironically named King Hedley and his
neighbors delivered furious monologues about the cruelty of life in Reagan's morning-in-America world, while also not failing to ensure their
own inevitable failure, and even destruction. Wilson was also, of course,
revealing to his audience the backyard world of embitterment and self-
immolation from which they would normally be shielded. Wilson's in-
cantatory language apparently hit its mark: At the intermission, my father
turned to me and said, "They all seem very angry."

Aristotle hypothesized that the theater arts permit the viewer to experience the catharsis that comes of feeling powerful emotions not normally encountered in daily life. Aristotle was talking about terror and pity,
and probably that serves perfectly well to encompass the world of a play
like *King Hedley II,* or Suzan-Lori Parks's *Topdog/Underdog,* or O'Neill's
Long Day's Journey into Night, or any number of the serious and unsettling
plays, whether originals or revivals, that have been mounted on Broadway

in recent years. These works of theater provide the moral and intellectual anchor of Times Square. The critics of the new Times Square complain that the "unsettling experiences"—experiences of the unpredictable, the incongruous, the unmannerly—central to urban life have been evacuated from this all-too-calculated global crossroads. They're right; and yet those disturbing experiences are still available inside the world of the theater. *King Hedley II* may not have constituted a cathartic experience for my father, but at the very least, it provoked a moment of troubled recognition— "They all seem very angry."

It is patent that theater doesn't "matter" in American culture; it's scarcely mattered in half a century. But it matters greatly in Times Square, and not only economically. The illusionistic worlds inside the theaters offer relief from, and an alternative to, the illusionistic world of Times Square itself. They are spaces carved out from Times Square's increasingly totalized environment. Some of them offer themselves as contrasts to, or subversions of, that environment. (One of the two main characters of *Topdog/Underdog* makes a living, when all else fails, playing three-card monte, presumably not far from the theater.) To emerge from these plays is to carry with you a memory, or perhaps just an image, of something that will not be assimilated into the glossy world of Broadway, just as King Hedley and his friends cannot be assimilated into Ronald Reagan's America.

Of course, most of these illusionistic worlds aren't meant to be disturbing in the least. They're meant to be—even if in fact they're often not—delightful, sentimental, splashy, and sparkling, just as they have always been on Broadway. Frothy escapism is the bread and butter of Broadway. Take a musical like *42nd Street,* for example. Just as the 1933 movie muted the bitter misanthropy of the 1932 novel, so the play—itself a revival of a David Merrick production from the sixties—gentles the Depression-era desperation of the movie. The kids who find a dime on the street and sing "We're in the Money" are urchins; but a moment later they're whisked away and the cast emerges in the gold spangles of the children's fantasy. Julian Marsh, the madly driven director, is here a lonely but lovable curmudgeon. Nick Murphy's gangsters may be naughty and gaudy, but they're hardly dangerous. And Peggy Sawyer tramples no toes on her way to the top. The show is about pluck—Peggy's, Julian's, the chorus's. And when, after two and a half hours of frantic hoofing, the cast capers its way madly, brilliantly, through a reprise, you think, "These kids are having the time of their life!" The life of a chorus girl was famously transitory and cruel; in the years before the First World War, George Bronson-Howard created an entire literature out of these beautiful, brittle, predatory creatures. But not here: the true subject of this *42nd Street* is the sheer wonderfulness of the theatrical well that is life on Broadway.

It is, of course, ever thus. There has always been an O'Neill, a Williams, a Miller; and a Ziegfeld, a Cohan, and, for that matter, a Minsky. Theater is the one aspect of Times Square that is immemorial: a play today looks like a play seventy years ago, and it is presented in the same space. You still need actors, musicians, writers, makeup artists, and ticket-takers, and you need producers willing to take a plunge on a risky project. Theater has remained the same, while everything around it, the context that is Times Square, and thus the context in which we experience it, has changed drastically.

This balance between the difficult and the accessible, the disorienting and the familiar, is an ancient pattern on Broadway. And yet the global firms that have come to dominate rental, food, television, and the like have now gained a foothold in theater as well. Two such firms, Disney and Clear Channel Communications, now constitute the largest forces on Broadway, the one as a producer, the other principally as a backer and a distributor, and both as theater owners. Their arrival in Times Square has been treated with a great deal of trepidation, though also some wary hope. Do they come as imperialists, or as rich uncles? The fear, generally unspoken, is that their advent will hasten the eclipse of the little voices of disturbance—the counterrealities of Broadway—and amplify yet more, as if it were needed, the bombast of the middlebrow musical. And then the Broadway theater, as it has been known for the last century, will linger only as Times Square's vestigial organ.

THOMAS SCHUMACHER, THE HEAD of what is known inside Disney as the Buena Vista Theatrical Group, does not produce an impression that corresponds in any way with that notorious term of abuse "Disneyfi-cation." Schumacher is a slight fellow, still almost puppyishly enthusiastic at forty-four, with thick, floppy hair parted down the middle and dark, squarish spectacles. He looks like a chic, media-savvy French intellectual. The medium, in this regard, is the message, for Schumacher is the living emblem of a very different kind of Disney. And he is at pains to distinguish his role on Broadway, and Disney's, from the epithet people so lightly toss around. "It's ironic," he said, when we first met, "that we use the term 'Disneyfication' when in fact the purest saving of what is the halcyon days of Times Square, the classic center of it, was actually the restoration of this theater." "This theater" is, of course, the New Amsterdam, on 42nd Street just west of Broadway. We were seated at a little table in an oval lounge ringed with murals depicting the history of New York City, from the first encounter with the Indians up through 1903, when the theater was built. The lounge had been submerged beneath a foot or so of water when Disney took title to the New Amsterdam in 1994; now, like the rest of the theater, it had been lovingly restored. "That's all we did," Schumacher went on, with a good deal of heat. "That's *all* we did."

"Disney" is, of course, a very sensitive subject for Disney. The word has become shorthand for the spurious and the engineered and the uniform-but-with-a-little-local-appliqué. "We didn't actually put up the McDonald's next door," Schumacher said, a bit wearily, "or the Chili's down the street, or Madame Tussaud's." He evidently knew the critique by heart. When I mentioned that restoring the New Amsterdam was not quite all Disney did, since the company owns ABC and ESPN, both of which have an extremely gaudy presence on Broadway, Schumacher raised his eyebrows. That's Disney-the-company; his Disney is the New Amsterdam Theatre and *The Lion King,* and *Beauty and the Beast,* and *Aida,* and the lineup of new shows he's got in the works.

Whatever "Disney" is, Schumacher himself is plainly not an alien life form on Broadway. He *is* Broadway. When we had lunch one day at a popular theater spot on 44th Street, Margot Lion, the producer of the hit musical *Hairspray,* waylaid him to say how much she had missed him while he was out of town. The restaurant's owner, another Broadway fixture, came by for a chat. Schumacher made a point of greeting a young woman at another table because she worked for him in some capacity, and he didn't want her to be embarrassed lest he overhear an unguarded comment. (Disney is probably the largest employer on Broadway.) It was like dining with David Merrick, or David Belasco. And Schumacher has the bona fides. When he challenged me to think of a musical that wasn't derived from an earlier work, I tried *Oklahoma!* "Completely adapted from *Green Grow the Lilacs*," he fired back. *Hello, Dolly!*? "Based on both *The Merchant of Yonkers* and *The Matchmaker*." When I complimented him on his erudition, he grinned and said, "Yes, the term 'show queen' does come up."

Schumacher is a San Franciscan who went to UCLA and then went into arts administration—first with a dance company, then with the 1984 Olympic Arts Festival in Los Angeles, then with the Mark Taper Forum. In 1987 he established the Los Angeles Festival of Arts, where he presented the English-language premiere of Peter Brook's *Mahabharata,* a production to which he often proudly refers. He then went to work in Disney's animation unit, which had just been revitalized by Michael Eisner. There he supervised the development and production of *Toy Story, Monsters, Inc., A Bug's Life,* and such more classically Disneyesque fare as *Tarzan* and *The Hunchback of Notre Dame.* Schumacher is proud of his work, and at times he skirts self-parody as he provides a gloss on the Disney output worthy of a man who produced the *Mahabharata.* When I asked him why one Disney heroine, or leading man, is indistinguishable from another, he said, "It's a retelling of the mono myth." The mono myth? "Who am I? What am I? What is my purpose?" In other words, as Joseph Campbell would put it, the hero with a thousand faces. Schumacher is a Disney true believer; of course, you wouldn't want to have a cynic turning out children's movies.

After the movie of *Beauty and the Beast* was greeted, at least by some critics, as a better musical than anything then running on Broadway, Michael Eisner, himself a native New Yorker and something of a theater nut, decided to produce a theatrical version of the show as an experiment in a new medium for Disney's animated characters. Disney executives came up with a noisy theme-park-style show that underwhelmed critics and delighted the plebes; *Beauty* has been running since 1994, making it, as of 2003, the seventh longest-running production in Broadway history. Schumacher makes a point of saying that he had nothing to do with the original production. I couldn't actually bring myself to buy a ticket, but Alex, who was forced to go by virtue of a class trip, found it so profoundly beneath his twelve-year-old contempt that he could barely bring himself to describe it. "Stupid," I think, was his chief impression.

Meanwhile, Disney was fixing up the New Amsterdam. Eisner now agreed to create a separate theatrical unit, and to run it he appointed Peter Schneider, the head of Disney Studios, and Schumacher. *The Lion King* had been released just as the theatrical production of *Beauty and the Beast* opened and was the logical choice for the next fable to grace the boards. There was no obvious reason why Disney wouldn't produce another connect-the-dots show like *Beauty and the Beast*. But Disney wasn't producing the new musical: Schneider and Schumacher were. And Schumacher, who was a man of taste but also a company man, found the place where personal taste and corporate strategy converged. He asked Julie Taymor, the sculptor and mask-maker—and then recent winner of a MacArthur Foundation "genius" grant—to direct the new play. Taymor was the least "corporate" of figures; she operated on the small, handmade scale of Very Off Broadway. And yet Schumacher recognized that her work, which revolved around myth and ritual, and nonverbal means of presentation—the whole Campbellian substratum—fit very well with the Disney oeuvre. He had, he says, tried to bring her play *Liberty's Taken* to the Los Angeles Arts Festival, and followed her work thereafter. And so he asked; and Taymor agreed.

When I asked Schumacher about the choice of Taymor, he said, "There is this impression that it runs counter to what we do. People don't realize that Salvador Dalí was in residence in the studio. People forget that Walt worked with Leopold Stokowski. People forget how arty *Fantasia* was. It has never seemed to me a choice outside of what we do as a company, but very much a choice outside of what people expected us to do." Of course, people forget these things because they took place half a century ago. Among the current generation of Disney movies, some are ingenious and charming—though I wouldn't have included *The Lion King* in that group—but most stay well within the Disney comfort zone, which often includes the downright cloying. (*Pocahontas,* anyone?)

There is, at any rate, no question that the choice of Taymor startled people who thought of Disney as the Standard Oil of children's entertainment. The news coverage in the run-up to the show's opening, in the fall of 1997, featured such arch conceits as Julie Taymor as Beauty, and

Disney, "the many-tentacled house of mainstream," as the Beast. Taymor conceded that many of her friends felt that she had, in fact, surrendered to the Beast. And of her new employer she said, "At first they worried that I was too far-out and I worried that they were Disney." And yet, she found that whenever an aesthetic choice had to be made, the suits from Disney, including Eisner, pushed her to take the bolder and more experimental route. Schumacher says that Disney and Taymor signed a contract permitting either to walk away in case of artistic differences. And then, he says, "we never looked at the deal again."

The Lion King offered irrefutable proof that "corporate theater" need not be a vaguely disreputable subspecies of the art form, like "dinner theater." The show bore the stamp of a single creator far more plainly than did the overproduced musicals pulled this way and that by a dozen different investors. It was a Julie Taymor show on a giant scale. And yet what was striking about it was how effectively Taymor had brought Disney's epic pretensions into human scale. "The grasslands" was indicated not by a great, billowing field of green but by two columns of stately figures rising from beneath the stage with square headdresses of green turf. A single tree with a great, spreading projection of lacy, irresolvable patterns stood for the bounty of nature. These allusive gestures, which Taymor described as "ideographic," summoned larger associations by virtue of being so sketchy and economical. And then of course there were the masks, also contrived as minimalist objects. A big bird was an actor carrying a rack of wings, a flock of little birds an actor wiggling a mobile hung with birdlike shapes. A leopard was an actor piloting a leopard figure like a wheelbarrow. Man and animal merge and mingle in an enchanted vision of unfallen nature—the Circle of Life, perhaps, without the movie's Mother Earth pieties. Apart from all the Disney-certified hokum about "Hakuna Matata"—which is to say, apart from much of the actual dialogue—it was an impressive production.

The Lion King won six Tonys, including one for best musical. Six years later, it was still playing to packed houses. On 42nd Street, and in ten other locations around the world, it had earned Disney over a billion dollars. What was perhaps even more important, it blotted out the image created by the schlocky Beauty and the Beast and materially altered Disney's status in the larger culture.

—

IF YOU'RE LOOKING FOR an example of an evil media conglomerate you couldn't do much better than Clear Channel Communications, an $8 billion company that enjoys a powerful, and in some cases near monopolistic, status in radio station ownership and program distribution; rock concert production; monster truck and motocross competitions; outdoor advertising; the management of sports stars; and, last and perhaps least, the nationwide distribution of theatrical productions. Clear Channel could have been described as one of the most powerful companies in the country that scarcely anyone had heard of until 2002, when suddenly it became the chief symbol of the evils of media concentration. Clear Channel owns 1,250 radio stations, making it by far the largest station owner in the country; and in the run-up to the war in Iraq, it was widely criticized for promoting pro-war rallies, pushing singers deemed patriotic and punishing those, like the Dixie Chicks, with the mettle to criticize the war effort. The company was said to engage in the illegal practice of "play for pay," forcing performers to ante up for airtime (a charge they have consistently denied). And Clear Channel's practice of using the exact same programming on many of its stations made it the single greatest cause of the numbing uniformity along the radio dial. Press reports described the company as "radio's big bully" and "the evil empire." And when the Federal Communications Commission deregulated media ownership in 2003, radio was conspicuously excluded from the fiesta—because of Clear Channel's naked abuses of its power, according to subsequent reports.

Clear Channel's role in the world of theater was practically an afterthought, and may be traced back to a company called Pace Theatrical. Pace had begun in the 1970s by booking tractor pulls and monster truck shows into arenas. In the early eighties, the company began to buy up theaters around the United States and in Great Britain; in many cities, it purchased the subscription series—in effect, the audience—rather than the theater itself. Pace then began to invest in Broadway shows, with a view to securing the right to distribute them in its network of theaters. Ever since the decline of the "road" back in the 1920s, theatergoers outside New York had largely had to content themselves with retread productions, of hardy perennials like *My Fair Lady* and *The Sound of Music*. In the late seventies and early eighties, the British producer Cameron Mackintosh began to mint Broadway-quality road companies for splashy shows like *The Phantom of the Opera, Cats,* and *Miss Saigon.* Mackintosh proved that you could charge more money for a better class of show and still turn a profit. Soon Pace was investing in practically every musical on Broadway and sending the most successful ones on the road in productions of its own. The company now owned the product, the audience, and the venue; it enjoyed the kind of monopoly over the road that Klaw and Erlanger, or Keith and Albee, had exercised ninety years earlier, though at that time the road was a good deal bigger, and more valuable, than it is now.

In 1999, a concert presenter called SFX purchased both Pace and Livent, the production company established by the Canadian entrepreneur Garth Drabinsky, which owned the Ford Center, across the street from the New Amsterdam, as well as several valuable properties, including *Ragtime* and *Fosse.* And then Clear Channel bought SFX, like the giant fish that swallows the big fish that swallowed the little fish. To give an idea of how very small that little fish was, the Theatrical and Family Division, the company's production wing, accounted for 12 percent of the revenues of Clear Channel Entertainment, which also included concerts, motor sports, and real estate (meaning the actual theaters)—and this entire branch of the company, in turn, accounted for only a quarter of its revenues. Nevertheless, that modest slice of the entertainment pie still made Clear Channel a giant force on Broadway—almost as significant a player in the world of musical theater as it was in, say, monster truck shows and billboards. In 2002, Clear Channel Entertainment moved into the Candler Building, a narrow, elegant limestone skyscraper built in 1913 on the southern side of 42nd Street. Clear Channel had now joined Disney, Viacom, and Toys "R" Us in the global entertainment axis of Times Square.

The offices of Clear Channel do not much resemble the raucous headquarters of Keith and Albee's United Booking Office on the second floor of the old Palace Theatre, though the function is not so very different. Lauren Reid, whose job is to supply a package of shows to Clear Channel's eighteen theaters, and its fifty-six subscription series, sits in a gray-carpeted office with a nice view east, toward the Condé Nast Building. Reid says that in most cities her big competition isn't the ballet or the opera, but sports teams. The average theater she's working with seats

2,800 people—immense, by Broadway standards—and this means that she has to find a crowd-pleasing product. "When we put together a package," she says, "we always try to round it out, so you have maybe one megashow, like *Lion King,* one new hot revival, like *42nd Street,* then you have a play slot and a slot for something different, like *Riverdance.*" She says that she would love to aim a little higher, but there are, she says, "a limited number of cities where you have an audience for a straight play." She would love to put together a circuit of smaller theaters for more modest and ambitious shows, but it hasn't happened yet. And so the folks out in Minneapolis or Portland get *David Copperfield* and *Seussical,* though also *Hairspray* and *The Producers*—not August Wilson or Suzan-Lori Parks, perhaps, but also not Top 40 radio.

Scott Zeiger, the president of Clear Channel Entertainment, compares the theatrical operation to a television network that has owned and operated stations—the theaters and subscription series—as well as affiliated stations, which in this case means the "strategic partnerships" Clear Channel forms with other presenters. The central imperative is to keep the network supplied with popular product. Clear Channel takes the role of "associate producer," "strategic partner," or "strategic limited partner" on various Broadway productions, but the ultimate goal is to field shows that will play well on the road. In the mid-nineties, the company also began producing kiddie shows in collaboration with Nickelodeon and others. Clear Channel may claim credit for such dramatic fare as *Rugrats—A Live Adventure, Scooby Doo Stagefright,* and *Blue's Clues Live.* Liz McDonald, who runs children's programming, says that some of these shows can sell out Radio City Musical Hall many times over. I attended one rehearsal of an upcoming show called *Dora the Explorer,* based on a popular cartoon of the same name. Dora is a feisty little girl with a pet monkey who engages in educational and prosocial activities in the course of solving knotty mysteries. At one point the director, a Broadway veteran accustomed to somewhat more ambitious productions, instructed the villain, Swiper, to "come downstage and take a feather from Red Chicken." Pausing to savor the sheer inanity of it all, he said, "I *know*: It's derivative of *Richard III.* I know that, but *the kids* don't know that."

In 2000, the principal officials of Clear Channel Entertainment decided that the time had come to commission adult works as well. Unlike

Disney, which has an archive of beloved material as well as a production line churning out mythopoetic cartoons on an annual basis, Clear Channel had to start from scratch. The company hired Beth Williams, a pianist who had conducted the pit orchestra in *Les Miz* and then worked as a line producer for shows Pace sent out on the road; she, in turn, hired six young producers to scour Broadway for talent and material. Clear Channel's culture would appear to be allergic to anything as unpredictable as actual creativity, but theater is too marginal an enterprise to be subjected to the same stultifying discipline as radio. Beth Williams describes herself as "a Mom-and-Pop producer," which is true in Clear Channel terms, if not in Broadway terms. Virtually everything has to be a musical, but Williams insists that it doesn't have to be an inane musical—Dora for grown-ups. She is very hopeful about *The Gospel According to Fishman,* a musical she has commissioned, set in 1963, in which a Jewish composer hooks up with a gospel group (a setting that sounds dangerously heart-warming).

It would not be the least bit surprising if Clear Channel's baby production unit unleashed on Broadway a cataract of gooey fudge, such as a Ben Vereen vanity piece now being developed. But you never know. Williams's executive producer, Jennifer Costello, spent her twenties running an "ensemble-based collective," Monsterless Actors, with her husband, who also now works for the company. She and Aaron Beall "flowed in the same circles," she says. Aaron flowed one way, and she flowed another, to *Rugrats—A Live Adventure.* But her aspirations lie elsewhere. Costello says, "I like theater that makes you feel uncomfortable," and she enjoys working with theater people who feel likewise. She has been trying to encourage a performance artist she admires to think Clear Channel thoughts. So far, she says, his ideas have been too avant-garde, but he's moving in the right direction. She's looking into a project about the drug-addled trumpeter Chet Baker. She would plainly love to produce something she doesn't find embarrassing. Of course, that may turn out to mean that she will be delighted with the untold story of Ben Vereen.

TOM SCHUMACHER PERMITTED me to see fifteen minutes' worth of a read-through for a musical of *Tarzan,* still in the very early stages.

Tarzan said things like, "Did you know there were others like me, Mother?" Jane said things like, "My interest in Tarzan is purely scientific," though also, "His eyes were intense and focused; I've never seen such eyes." Here was another romance in uncorrupted nature, like *Pocahontas* and *The Little Mermaid*. There may also have been elements of the mono myth in Tarzan's awakening. Afterward, Schumacher and I stood by the door, and he asked if I recognized any of the figures in the production. I drew a blank. "That's Phil Collins," he said, pointing to a balding figure sitting at a table. "He's written eight new songs. That's David Henry Hwang; he's writing the script. And the actor over there is Roger Rees, from *Nicholas Nickleby*." The director was Bob Crowley, perhaps the best-known lighting director on Broadway. All this for *Tarzan*.

Why do all these gifted people choose to work on a musical cartoon? The answer appears to be Tom Schumacher. Whatever horrors the word "Disney" may conjure up on Broadway, it is not Disney, but Tom Schumacher, who is buying lunch on 44th Street and choosing writers and directors. Schumacher says, "There's no Disney point of view, because Disney is not an idea. There's no gleaming granite board which says, 'We do this. We don't do that.' " Schumacher says that he always wants to be doing something new. That's why he has gone to Suzan-Lori Parks to write a script for *Hoopz*, a musical about the Harlem Globetrotters. It's why he asked Bob Crowley, who has never directed a play, to do *Tarzan*.

Rick Elice, a longtime Broadway publicist who now works as a consultant for Disney, argues that Schumacher should be understood as the David Belasco, or the David Merrick, of our day. Disney's wealth gives Schumacher the power, almost unheard of on Broadway, to make a project happen if he wants to do it; but he is not really free to exercise his own taste as a producer of old was, or even as many producers today are. Schumacher has put some of his own money into the kind of shows that Jennifer Costello might like, but he can no more make those shows for Disney than she can for Clear Channel. "Personally," Schumacher says, "as a guy who supports the arts, works in the arts, spent my life doing it, for me personally to produce a play is very interesting, but when I think of what I need to do for the company, it makes sense to do things with a great return." One can imagine Marc Barbanell saying much the same thing to Aaron Beall, though perhaps in slightly different words.

Disney may have a better record of creativity than Clear Channel, but the two companies operate under the same economic constraints. A big musical costs as much as $12 million to produce, and perhaps $400,000 to $500,000 a week to run. If the show is a flop, it's a catastrophe. But if it's a hit, it may gross $800,000 a week, which means that it will begin breaking a profit within a year and a half. A straight play would be much cheaper to produce, but the profit potential is far too modest for a company of Disney or Clear Channel's size. More important, success on Broadway means that the show is ready for the road; and it is the road that makes theater a business worth pursuing for Disney, as for Clear Channel. As Chris Boneau, a theatrical publicist, puts it, "Broadway is now a form of international branding." A hit musical is a global product.

Thus, by the fall of 2003, when productions opened in Sydney and Amsterdam, there were ten versions of *The Lion King* playing around the world. The initial cost of the play had already been absorbed; the road productions only had to earn more than they spent each week. This they did, with a vengeance. Although a ticket in New York generally costs more than a ticket elsewhere, the New Amsterdam has fewer seats than most of the other theaters where *The Lion King* will play. In 119 weeks, according to Schumacher, the show grossed $125 million in New York and $147 million in Los Angeles. *Beauty and the Beast* may be idiotic rather than ideographic, but the same economics apply. At its height, in fact, *Beauty* had eleven shows going at once.

Schumacher's ability to attract gifted writers and actors, and his own ambitions, make it unlikely that *Beauty and the Beast* will happen on his watch. But even *The Lion King* is not *Oklahoma!;* the language and characterization were stamped out in the Disney tool-and-die factory. Disney is itself the limiting factor in a Disney musical. What's more, the company's other current long-running Broadway hit, *Aida,* is considered neither as hackneyed as *Beauty* nor as inventive as *Lion King.* Perhaps that perfectly acceptable middle is where Disney will come to dwell. The projects closest to completion when I spoke to Schumacher were *Tarzan, The Little Mermaid, Mary Poppins* (a collaboration with Cameron Mackintosh), and a medley of songs from Disney films. Might they not turn out to be much of a muchness?

Calculations of profit do not determine everything on Broadway—not by a long shot. People have been pouring money into difficult and un-likely shows since O'Neill's first hit, *Beyond the Horizon,* in 1920. Broadway backers will continue to delude themselves about a show's merits, or its potential popularity, until the end of time. But giant corporations like Disney or Clear Channel face issues of scale that necessarily change their calculations; investments are not worth making if they can yield only a modest profit. And the imperative of mass appeal sharply limits one's op-tions, in theater as in every other art form. In fact, the dimensions of the theater audience mark out the borders both of corporate pandering and of corporate aspiration. Clear Channel will probably never dumb down theater as it has radio, because the theater audience is too small, too adult, and too variegated to make that strategy worthwhile. On the other hand, neither Clear Channel nor Disney is likely to nudge theatergoers very far from their comfort zone, because there's simply not enough money in discomfort. The one thing one can safely predict that both companies will do is to keep Broadway, and for that matter Cincinnati and Dallas, knee-deep in lavish musicals for many years to come. That is, in the world of global entertainment companies, a fairly benign outcome.

18

THE DURSTS HAVE
SOME VERY UNUSUAL
PROPERTIES

A N O R T H O D O X M A R X I S T H I S T O R I A N would say that the story
of Times Square is not the story of sex, or of theater, or of changing
mores, but of real estate. Times Square, that is, was forged by investors
making judgments about the profits to be realized from various potential
uses of real estate. Oscar Hammerstein built his Olympia Theatre on 45th
Street because land there was cheap. A few years later, the Shuberts began
amassing theaters in Times Square because the great mass of citizens arriving there through the new modes of transportation made entertainment the most valuable use to which local real estate could be put. The
theaters were converted to movie houses as movies became a more profitable use of space than plays. Those movie houses, in turn, became
"grinders," and then porn houses, and the trinket shops along 42nd Street
became massage parlors and peep shows, for the same reason. And
today's office tower, and retail-tainment complex, represents only the latest turn in the great evolutionary wheel of real estate usage. Who can
guess what tomorrow holds?

And yet, until the new age of massive redevelopment, Times Square
held very little appeal for the great clans that have dominated New York
real estate for close to a century. The buildings were too small, and thus
the stakes too low. What's more, the old clans tend to be extremely con-

ventional and painfully respectable, Donald Trump notwithstanding. The culture of Times Square was just too raffish for the Rudins and the Tishmans and the other titans of development. Times Square real estate has instead been controlled largely by theater families, including the Shuberts and the Nederlanders. The only real exception to that rule has been the one real estate family eccentric enough to feel at home in Times Square: the Dursts.

On one wall of the conference room in the Durst family headquarters, which is located in a nondescript office tower on Sixth Avenue and 44th Street, is a "Contract-Partnership" drawn up between Joseph Durst and one Hyman Rubin, and dated October 20, 1905. Like most of the other patriarchs of the real estate clans, Joseph Durst was a Jewish immigrant who began buying a building or two in the early years of the century. Joseph focused almost exclusively on commercial real estate in the booming neighborhoods of midtown Manhattan, abjuring his sons to stay away from rental properties. In the 1940s, Joseph anointed one of his sons, Seymour, as his successor.

Seymour Durst was probably the most far-seeing developer of his generation, and one of the wealthiest and most successful. He had two enormous gifts: he saw the potential of underdeveloped neighborhoods before others did, and he had the massive patience required to assemble plots one by one until he had a parcel large enough to build on. In the forties and fifties, Seymour built along Third Avenue, then a commercial wilderness but soon to be one of the city's great axes of commercial development. During the ensuing decade, he shifted to Sixth Avenue in the low Forties, another neglected area. And in the late sixties, he began buying the property between his Sixth Avenue holdings and Broadway. Seymour was a gentlemanly figure, soft-spoken and even withdrawn; but he was also a gambler. Not a single new building had been built in Times Square since the early thirties, and the area was beginning to take on its famously pathological character; but in the midst of the boom market of the sixties, Seymour was convinced that Times Square's moment had come.

Times Square was Seymour's greatest achievement in the field of assemblage. In a real-world version of Monopoly, he swapped his East Side properties for the West Side properties of Sol Goldman, a famous real estate troglodyte who still considered Times Square a wasteland. Seymour traded a Third Avenue building for fifteen or sixteen properties in the area owned by the real estate arm of Lazard Frères. It is hard to imagine, today, just how unprepossessing most of these parcels were; the Goldman property, especially, consisted mostly of empty storefronts, junk shops, rundown hotels, and the like. One of the properties, on 47th Street, was the Luxor Baths, a decrepit local landmark where Jack Dempsey and Walter Winchell used to soak their carcasses. By 1975, it was being used as a whorehouse. Seymour first tried to evict the operators, but then, when he failed, inexplicably decided to sell them the place instead. The new owners began chopping up the old baths into cubicles; the Luxor was well on its way to becoming the largest, and perhaps best-appointed, brothel in the city, if not the country. At the time, Seymour was serving, with no particular distinction, on a clean-up-Times-Square body called the Mayor's Office of Midtown Enforcement. Mayor Abraham Beame was so outraged at Seymour's laissez-faire attitude toward Times Square's image that he had him kicked off the committee.

And yet Seymour had a vision for Times Square—and not just a Third Avenue–type vision but a great and sweeping plan worthy of the great dreamers of the past. He planned to amass all the land from 42nd to 47th Streets, and from Sixth to Broadway, and then build a single complex, just as the Rockefellers had, half a century before, in the area between Fifth and Sixth Avenues a few blocks farther north. Seymour even called his proposal "Rockefeller Center South." But for once, he was too far ahead of his time: when the real estate market collapsed in the mid-1970s, Seymour lost several of his properties to the banks and was forced to abandon his plans. One of the parcels he had to surrender was the site of the decrepit New Criterion Theatre, which then made its way back to the Moss family. Seymour did, however, hold on to most of his properties, and the Durst organization later built a headquarters for U.S. Trust on West 47th Street, not far from the site of the Luxor Baths.

The model for Rockefeller Center South now sits on top of filing cabinets in an office in the Durst Organization: eight or nine black glass skyscrapers in two columns. Seymour never had much interest in fine architecture, and plainly he was thinking along the same lines that George Klein would pursue a few years later, though the Luxor Baths episode suggests that he lacked something of Klein's high seriousness. If he had had his way, Seymour would have turned Times Square into a western annex of the city's expanding corporate culture. "Maybe," says Douglas Durst, who has a parched version of his father's famously dry wit, "it's just as well it never happened."

Seymour was a character, a gaunt and gray-haired figure who walked everywhere, cut his own hair, wore his clothes until they were threadbare, and generally lived like an anchorite. He was a kind of homespun philosopher who kept his pockets stuffed with folded-up papers upon which he had scribbled his thoughts on the great issues of the day, and which he would withdraw with a flourish as the conversation turned to the relevant topic. He sent an endless stream of letters to *The New York Times,* often on the subject of rent control, which he considered the root of all housing evils. Seymour often purchased tiny advertisements at the bottom of the front page—"bottom lines," the family called them—in order to ensure that his views got the airing they deserved. Seymour could be extraordinarily creative in finding venues in which to ride his various hobbyhorses: in 1989 he mounted what he called the Debt Clock, on a building he owned just east of Times Square, in order to tick off the growing federal debt. He churned out immense "studies" and "reports" on housing problems that never saw the light of day, but toward the end of his life, in the mid-nineties, he found editorial fulfillment as the housing columnist of *Street News,* a newspaper distributed by the homeless.

Seymour knew the city, and perhaps even understood the city, as few men did. He had spent decades walking New York's streets and studying its buildings and its history; he was a beguiling and encyclopedic source of New York lore. He had begun to collect books about New York in the 1960s, and the collection had swiftly turned into an all-consuming mania. In 1985, he moved out of a brownstone whose supports were about to collapse from the weight of his books, and into a nineteen-room mansion on East 61st Street. One room after another was incorporated into this ever-expanding, Borgesian library. There were books in the fridge and books in the bathroom. There were filing cabinets bulging with articles about New York he had clipped from the papers. Each room of the library was devoted to a theme, with a décor arranged by Seymour to evoke the subject: the Infrastructure Room, the Biography Room, the Press Room, the Fiction Room (which also served as the Duplicate Books Room). Seymour kept the rare books in his own room, which was across from the Times Square Room—the collection of *Playbills* starting at the turn of the century, the books on theater, the nickelodeon with the nudie pictures, the posters for the live sex shows. Seymour devoted much of his life to amassing and cataloguing the collection; after his death, in 1995, it was moved to the Graduate Center of the City University of New York. It is now a matchless public resource, where the curious scholar may find *The Cries of New York,* a children's book from 1830 rendering the songs of street vendors as four-line poems, or Odell's epic fifteen-volume *Annals of the New York Stage,* detailing virtually every play mounted in New York up to 1894.

One of the curiosities of Seymour's career is that it seems never to have occurred to him that his development plans, especially in Times Square, might be laying waste to the culture whose artifacts he had spent his life lovingly preserving. One has to wonder about the nature of this remote, scholarly, quietly calculating, sharp-trading man. As his daughter, Wendy Krieger, observes, "He never said, 'I love New York.' He said, 'I have an interest in New York.'"

Seymour and his wife, Bernice, had four children. In 1950, when all of them were still quite young, Bernice jumped or fell to her death from the roof of the family house in Scarsdale, New York. Seymour never remarried, and he raised the children himself. He could be extremely charming, but in most settings he was cryptic and watchful, a sphinx in a world of backslapping bonhomie. His children absorbed a good deal of his social discomfort and his eccentricity. The oldest boy, Robert, grew up as a very confused rich kid in the sixties. He tried primal scream therapy; he studied with the Beatles' guru, Maharishi Mahesh Yogi. Robert went to work for Seymour, quit, opened a health food store in Vermont, married, and ultimately returned to New York and to the family business. Robert had the classic family makeup in a more extreme form; he would later be described as "sullen" and "reluctant to enter into conversation." In 1982, his wife, who allegedly had warned friends that he might do her harm, disappeared, and was never found. Robert remained with the family business until 1994, when Seymour, who had never chosen a successor as his father had with him, finally put Douglas, a younger brother, unequivocally in charge.

Robert then began to drift away into a life of wandering. He moved to Galveston, Texas, where his behavior became increasingly strange and perhaps psychotic. He posed as a mute woman whose name he lifted from a high school classmate. One journalistic account later described him as wearing "large-frame glasses that were completely covered with tape except for a small triangular opening over one lens." In late September 2001, several bags containing a human torso and a set of limbs, very professionally severed, washed up in Galveston Bay. The body belonged to Morris Black, a drifter who had lived next door to Durst. Evidence pointed to Durst, who had disappeared. After a nationwide manhunt, he was picked up when he stole a chicken salad sandwich from a supermarket in Bethlehem, Pennsylvania. Amid intense publicity, excruciatingly painful for this retiring family, Robert Durst was indicted for murder. In the trial, held in the fall of 2003, Durst admitted the killing but pled self-defense. To the amazement of many court experts and observers, he was acquitted. However, the investigation into his wife's disappearance twenty years earlier was reopened, and Durst remained under a very dark cloud.

Douglas, by contrast, is entirely sane, and yet one can see in him something of the same hesitancy, the same self-discomfort, that pathologically afflicted his older brother. He is a famously taciturn and private figure, uncomfortable in conversation, much given to pauses, which seem to begin in reflection and end in melancholy silence. Though unfailingly polite, like his father, he is prone to answer lengthy questions with a single word, often yes or no. He seems not to enjoy the company of his peers. He does not socialize, attend galas or, with a few exceptions, join the boards to which his money would give him access.

As a young man, Douglas had no intention of following his father into the family business. "I was in trouble in school, and I had problems dealing with authority," he says. Douglas enrolled at Berkeley in 1962, at the very moment when the cultural revolution of the sixties was getting under way. By the time he graduated, he looked like Jerry Garcia, with a great curly beard; he planned to work as a developmental economist in the Third World. It is hard to imagine any profession that would have been further from his aspirations than real estate. Then Douglas got married and had children, and suddenly he found his horizons closing in. He agreed to work for his father, and made an utter hash of the building he was given to manage. And so he lit out for the territory: with his wife and baby daughter, Anita, he moved up to Newfoundland, where he hoped to make a new life in a setting where he felt more comfortable. But this second attempt to escape the family orbit ended as suddenly and ineffectually as the first. Douglas had a serious accident when a wood-fired water heater blew up; he was dramatically rescued by Seymour and flown back to a hospital in New York. "I decided that New York was the safest place for me to be," Douglas says ruefully. And so he rejoined the family business, this time for good. It was, all in all, a rather sad story—a story of poor decisions, thwarted hopes, and a reluctant acceptance of an unavoidable destiny. It was Robert's story, without the catastrophic trajectory.

Douglas ultimately carved out a life for himself, satisfying his countercultural impulses by buying a farm in upstate New York that ultimately became the largest organic farm in the state. By the eighties, he was very much Seymour's partner. The Dursts had never built on their Times Square properties, and when the 42nd Street Development Project came along, they did everything they could to stifle it. Seymour had a long-standing philosophical objection to publicly subsidized and guided projects, and to the politicking that goes with them, though he and Douglas also had every reason to fear that the four heavily subsidized office towers George Klein proposed to build would swamp the market and thus depress the value of their own property in the neighborhood. And so, starting in 1988, when Klein looked as if he might be ready to build, Seymour, who was then head of something called the Real Estate Board of New York, regularly blistered the project in public as a shameless boondoggle, while the family mounted lawsuits against it and quietly funded a "grassroots" campaign. In 1989, the Dursts even purchased long-term leases to the derelict theaters on 42nd Street and commissioned a plan designed to prove that the private marketplace could bring them back to life more effectively and cheaply than the city could. It was widely believed that their actual motive was to sell the properties back to the city in the condemnation proceedings, and thus to net a huge profit.

The Dursts embarked on a conscious policy of delaying the project to death. In a furious 1990 op-ed article in *The New York Times,* Carl Weisbrod, the public official in charge of the project, alleged that the Dursts, acting in concert with the owners of the block's porno theaters, had forged "a litigation conspiracy trap aimed at preventing the reclamation of what was—and should be again—New York's most glorious street." Of course, the trap worked. But while the small fry who owned the theaters disappeared from Times Square, Douglas Durst returned in glory: when Prudential, George Klein's financial backer, forced him to sell in 1995, it was Durst, acting with the family gift for adroit timing and the well-calculated gamble, who bought the choicest of all the office parcels, at the southeast corner of Broadway and 42nd Street.

If there was any single moment that marked the emergence of the shining new Times Square of global media and entertainment firms, it was Durst's announcement that he had secured Condé Nast as the anchor tenant of 4 Times Square. And he had been able to do so by exploiting the enormous subsidies that the family professed to despise. Whether this constituted gross hypocrisy, or merely a very high order of gamesmanship, was perhaps simply a matter of perspective. Douglas, while protesting rather feebly that the family never really tried to impede the project, concedes, in his laconic way, that the outcome was "ironic." Lawrence Silverstein, a fellow mogul and old friend of the family, says, "Seymour, God bless him, as he looks down, what must he be thinking?" Of course, one should not entirely dismiss the possibility that Seymour is thinking, "Excellent deal."

Douglas had vindicated his father's faith in Times Square and paid for a twenty-five-year-old investment many times over. At the same time, he didn't seem to feel at home in the new Times Square he had wrought: he didn't eat in the fancy new restaurants or meet friends for a drink in the chic hotels. I persuaded Douglas, against the force of his habits, to have lunch with me one day by suggesting that we meet at the irredeemably unchic Howard Johnson's, where he could be certain of meeting no one who recognized him, much less knew him. As we sat in an orange booth on a blazingly hot day, Douglas pointed across the street and said, "I used to go to the Ripley's between Forty-fifth and Forty-sixth after school." He was, he said, a great aficionado of the arcades in the late fifties. When the kids were young, he would leave them to play pinball with Jimmy Glen, the owner of Jimmy's Corner, an old Times Square bar on 44th just east of Broadway, while he and his wife went out to dinner. That was the Times Square he cared about; and none of it, he said, was left (except Jimmy's). I asked Douglas how he felt about the new Times Square, which he had done so much to bring into being. There was a long, long pause. "I think," he finally said, "it could do without all the development—except, of course, Four Times Square." And he smiled ever so slightly at this shaft of Durstian wit.

AS I WALKED ALONG 42nd Street in the early months of 2002, I often looked at a shabby little structure huddled in the lee of the mighty Condé Nast building. On top of the storefront was a big billboard that featured a rendering of the American flag, an outline of a hand clutching a can of spray paint, and the slogan, "Declare Independence from Corporate Rule." Here, apparently, was a refreshing howl of protest at all that Times Square had become, and all that was embodied in that great glass tower occupied by the world's most glamorous media company. The storefront housed some kind of alternative arts complex called Chashama. It was Aaron Beall who told me that the founder and director of Chashama was Anita Durst—Douglas's older daughter. It seemed that the family predisposition to the peculiar had been passed on to yet another generation.

When I went to meet Anita, in a cubbyhole office on the second floor of Chashama, she was bouncing lightly on one of those big blue balls said to be therapeutic. She was, when she stood up, tall and slender, with a ferociously cropped skullcap of black hair and the almond eyes of a Modigliani—Douglas's eyes, actually—set in a narrow, triangular face. She was the kind of young woman (she was then thirty-two) who could war with her beauty and still look beautiful. We proceeded to have an oddly disjointed conversation; only later did I realize that Anita was so uncomfortable that she made me feel uncomfortable. She was terribly shy, as her father and grandfather were, but she also seemed to struggle in the medium of language; she would pull up short before fairly ordinary words. As a child, she had been severely dyslexic, and she still had trouble memorizing lines for a part; reading took real effort. Though trained as an actress, Anita was drawn to the kind of avant-garde work that often didn't require much in the way of speech. A few years before, she had played a mute and sullen secretary in Rainer Werner Fassbinder's *The Bitter Tears of Petra von Kant;* a critic in the *Times* had described her as "spectacularly creepy."

Anita was the oldest of Douglas's three children. She had been precociously ungovernable, appropriating a family car and driving it into trees at age thirteen—a story that Douglas told with some combination of awe and bewilderment, for she had set standards of willfulness that Douglas himself had never approached. School had been a nightmare: shipped off to prep school in ninth grade after proving a hopeless failure in public school, she was kicked out for smoking pot, took a one-year sabbatical to shack up with a biker, and was then enrolled by her obviously desperate parents in the kind of vocational school that was meant to be the last stop before the streets. "The classes were like ten minutes long," Anita said, "and then in the afternoon you worked." Anita earned her high school diploma by tending bar at a pizzeria. College was out of the question. She had no clear idea what to do with herself; her parents, having at least shepherded her through high school, asked her to move out. And then Seymour, of all people, invited her to move in.

Seymour was the kind of charming oddball who can seem highly appealing to a rebellious teenager. He passed no judgments, asked no probing questions, and wanted nothing more than a faithful listener, which Anita was formed by nature to be. She moved into the Fiction Room, way up on the fifth floor, and came and went as she pleased. After a few years, she was ready to leave, but Seymour couldn't bear to be parted from her. "He said, 'Bring all your friends here,' " Anita said. "At one point, I had four or five people living with me." And so Anita lived, very happily, in the midst of a commune. She browsed through the giant leather-bound two-volume set of *Mr. Vanderbilt's House and Collection,* and through the six volumes of I. N. Phelps Stokes's *Iconography of Manhattan Island.* She listened to Seymour's stories and crotchets, and she had breakfast with him every morning at the Burger Heaven down the street. Seymour recruited his librarians from among the waitresses there, since he claimed that professional librarians kept trying to improve on his "quintessimal" cataloguing system.

Like many shy people, Anita fell in love with acting. Unlike most of the others, she had a father who owned Broadway theaters. In 1990, Douglas agreed to let En Garde Arts, a "site-specific" theater company with which Anita was associated, put on a play in the wreckage of the majestic Victory Theatre. Douglas quickly became Anita's chief patron. He allowed her to use the semi-defunct Diplomat Hotel, on West 43rd Street, for a play called *The Law of Remains,* in which, Anita says, "Andy Warhol and Jeffrey Dahmer meet in Heaven." The play was apparently based on *The Egyptian Book of the Dead.* The hotel had a series of splendid, haunted-looking ballrooms. "The big ballroom was Heaven," Anita says, "and God was a Puerto Rican drag queen with an erection." Douglas says that Seymour would leave after the first few scenes of these shows and report, "I didn't understand it, but Anita was very good."

The Law of Remains had been mounted by Reza Abdoh, a celebrated Iranian multimedia artist who was Anita's mentor and collaborator. Later she played "a black wench slave" in an Abdoh production called *Tight, Right, White.* "It was very in-your-face," she recalls. Abdoh was an enfant terrible who infused Anita with a radical politics that goes rather oddly with her gentle nature and her very real fear of giving offense. Her actual politics seem to consist mostly of an abiding sympathy for all forms of disaffection or discomfort. Anita was proud to play host to the four-day Intergalactic Convention of Anarchists, though after the anarchists left she said that most of them had been peace-loving high school students who entertained themselves making puppets at another studio she ran. In Anita's utopia, everybody would make puppets and eat breakfast at Burger Heaven.

Reza Abdoh died of AIDS in 1995, and Anita then formed a company to carry on his work. After combing through books in her grandfather's library, she named the company "Chashama," a combination of the Persian words for "spring" and "eye," more or less. In 1997, as he had begun building 4 Times Square, Douglas gave Chashama the adjacent building, which had housed Herman's Sporting Goods. And as the leases of neighboring storefronts expired, he gave those to Chashama as well, though doing so cost him close to $2 million a year in forgone revenue. Chashama theaters and studios alternated with a Peep-O-Rama, Tad's Steaks, and a drugstore. The billboard had come courtesy of *Adbusters,* a radical antiglobalization magazine to which Anita's younger sister Helena was particularly devoted. Some members of the Chashama staff worried that Douglas might take the motto as a very public rebuke to himself and to all his building represented, as well he might have. But Douglas would not dishonor his inner Jerry Garcia. The billboard stayed, until Anita and her colleagues tired of it.

Anita was more or less the Mabel Dodge Luhan or Peggy Guggenheim of her particular early-millennial fringe artistic moment, though since even the most difficult artists can now gain the backing of powerful mainstream institutions, she was left with a fairly shaggy fringe. Anita faithfully maintained Abdoh's commitment to confrontational art, though it was often hard to say what end she had in view. She herself directed *The World of the P-Cult,* a production featuring a group of dominatrixes and neo-go-go girls she had rounded up from downtown as well as a young man with a terrible deformity that left his arms looking like flippers. The show had an atmosphere of portent, menace, and unleashed sexuality, with antlered S&M queens vaulting down from a catwalk to swagger through the audience. It was slightly reminiscent of the unfortunate climactic scene of *Eyes Wide Shut.* A pyromaniac named Flambeau kept columns of flame lit on the stage. And few who were fortunate enough to be there will soon forget the climactic scene, in which the naked flipper-boy, his genitals in a little bag, was borne onto the stage in preparation for ritual sacrifice, singing in his unearthly, androgynous voice a tune that mixed the first movement of Beethoven's Ninth Symphony with Madonna's "Material Girl."

Though Douglas was utterly baffled that his daughter, whom he considered an incorrigible space cadet, was able to run an organization of any kind, he backed her to the hilt in all things. If a movie production company wanted to shoot a scene in the Condé Nast Building, the answer was always the same: "Only if you give Anita a part." When Anita, in turn, had the ingenious idea of staging a series of tableaux vivants in the empty windows of 1 Times Square, the building at 42nd between Broadway and Seventh Avenue, she called her father, who in turn talked to the real estate broker. (No dice.) She once contemplated asking her father if she could broadcast a clandestine radio station from an antenna on top of the Condé Nast Building.

Anita, herself such a wounded creature, had no wish to wound anyone, least of all her own family. She was horrified at the suggestion that her plutocratic father might in any sense be the target of Chashama's radically anticorporate posture. "As a businessman," she said earnestly, "he's known for being very generous and very kind." In fact, Anita saw Chashama as a fulfillment of Seymour's crotchety worldview. "My grandfather hated Disney," she said. "He always said Times Square was meant to be built up by the community. That was one of his bottom lines." It would have been heartless to point out that Seymour had tried to create a Rockefeller Center Times Square, and that the Condé Nast Building played a starring role in the global entertainment-finance-media nexus of the new Times Square.

Like Aaron Beall, Anita wanted to offer something raw and unfiltered in a Times Square increasingly given over to "corporate rule." It was very important to her that Chashama have a presence on the street, so she had installed odd and often cryptic artworks in each of the storefront windows. These installations were often interactive, and thus offered a series of small-scale engagements between performer and spectator, animating Times Square's street life in a way quite different from, say, the transaction between spray painters and customers farther west on 42nd Street. There was the Deli Dance, which brought dancers out onto the sidewalk in front of a delicatessen. The Seder Installation, mounted during Passover, began as a window display of matzoh surrounding a chair, and then evolved into an actual seder on the crowded sidewalk.

I always made a point of walking by to see what was new. One afternoon, I noticed a young woman with a microphone sitting in the window, with a big bag of fortune cookies next to her. "Would you like to know your fortune?" she said into the microphone. I said that I would, and she broke open a cookie and read, "Kindness is the highest form of wisdom." When I asked whether it was a "real" fortune, she pointed a finger at me and said, "You mean if *I* wrote them, they're not real?" This was a pretty good point, and by the time I had formulated an answer I had a little audience of passersby, which made for a very odd and uncomfortable conversation. I realized that public engagement, and my discomfort with it, was part of the point; or perhaps it was an inadvertent by-product. Chashama productions often made me doubt whether having a point was the point.

What was plain, though, is that there was a wish, both in the window installations and in many of Anita's terribly of-the-moment productions, to bring back to life an old, knockabout, spontaneous Times Square, a Times Square devoted to the marginal and the odd—the Times Square of her grandfather's collection. Many of Chashama's productions dabbled in the forgotten forms of Times Square, like cabaret or vaudeville, and for all their rather mannered weirdness had something good-natured and fun-loving at heart. Chashama's hardiest production, which ran from July through December 2002, was a kind of neo-vaudeville production known as the Bindlestiff Family Cirkus. The circus consisted principally of two characters, neither of them actually named Bindlestiff, and was organized as a variety act, with old-fashioned rope tricks, sword swallowing, a bed of nails, and the like performed on a tiny stage before a tiny audience. Alex and I went one Saturday afternoon and found that most of the dozen or so people sitting with us were either wheelchair bound or mildly disturbed. The overall impression that we had wandered into the Twilight Zone was very much enhanced by the Museum of Times Square, located in the theater's lobby—a collection of old programs from Hubert's Museum, a carousel with odd little mechanical animals, and, in the back, behind a curtain, a collection of "frozen fetuses" in bell jars.

Anita had, perhaps unintentionally, created a kind of italicized, spoofy, self-conscious version of the Times Square that had been obliterated beneath the office towers. It wasn't "the real thing"; but, of course, if Chashama had been the real thing, it would have been a preposterous exercise in nostalgia. The old Times Square was not a thing you could bring back; but you could restore its spirit in an entirely new key. Chashama's marginalness, its pluckiness, even its amateurishness, was an antidote to the glittering Times Square of the office tower. It was a delicious, and very Times Square, irony that the man who made it possible owned the biggest office tower of them all.

19

A SIGN OF
THINGS TO COME

IN THE LATE SUMMER of 2001, a beautiful art object appeared in Times Square. This was, in itself, an almost unprecedented event. Works of art, in the form of plays, are regularly presented inside buildings in Times Square; but, considered as a physical entity, Times Square contains very little that is beautiful, or that even aspires to the status of art. And this new object was, in fact, a building, though it was, at the same time, a show. The building was a thirty-two-story office tower built for Morgan Stanley on the east side of Seventh Avenue between 49th and 50th Streets. It was an attractive enough building, though scarcely interesting as architecture. The art object wasn't the building, but its sign. Actually, it was hard to know how to characterize the relationship between the two— between the solid thing and the evanescent thing that played across its surface. In effect, the building *was* a sign, for imagery appeared, dissolved, and reassembled itself across the entire block-wide façade of the building and wrapped around either side, up to the twelfth-story setback.

The pictures had a wildly exaggerated pop vitality, as if Roy Lichtenstein had scripted the show. The best place to watch was from the street-side counter of the Starbucks across the way. There you could see immense red piggybanks performing a sort of piggybank shuffle; the dance gave way to a cascade of green apples bouncing down a chute. The piggybanks were of the reddest red, and the apples of the greenest green, you could imagine. The apples in turn gave way to a computer-animated image of a great suspension bridge soaring over a sparkling bay, and this in turn to an image of silhouettes walking down a long corridor, perhaps one inside the building itself. Words and numbers sometimes flashed on the screen—that is, on the building—but never the word "Morgan." This was a sign, but not a billboard or a television commercial. The images bore an intentionally tangential, sometimes almost a mocking, relationship to their sponsor. The piggybanks and the apples constituted a wry, children's-book version of the global marketplace in which Morgan operated.

Kevin Kennon, the architect chiefly responsible for the sign, was delighted to see that people would walk by the building, look up, startled, and then stand and stare, as they had half a century earlier, in the glory days of the spectacular. Kennon had hoped to design an idiom, or a medium, in which the new, corporate Times Square could express itself without blotting out the meanings that had made Times Square such an object of veneration. He had hoped to find a means by which an increasingly "virtual" Times Square could at the same time be thrillingly actual. And the reaction of those commuters and tourists told him that people wanted to be engaged, that they would stop and look if given something to stop and look at. But he also knew, like Aaron Beall, that he was pushing against the limits of his patron's patience, taste, and budget. He was trying to move Times Square in a direction it was reluctant to go; to put it more optimistically, he was trying to shape Times Square while its direction was still an open question.

TIMES SQUARE HAS NEVER, in all its long history, had so many signs as it has today. Forty-second Street is bedecked with signs as it never was in the heyday of Erlanger and Klaw, and even the upper reaches of Times Square are dense with billboards. The 1987 zoning regulations forced developers to put up brightly lit signs, while Times Square's rejuvenation filled it once again with the kind and number of people advertisers were eager to reach. The logic was no different than it had been in the twenties, when an adman had calculated that a spectacular could be erected for fourteen cents per thousand viewers; now, through some extremely creative math, Spectacolor, the largest sign company in Times Square, calculated that the cost-per-thousand of a Times Square sign was one-sixth to one-tenth that of a network television spot. For a brief period in the mid-nineties, Times Square signage had its own tulipmania. In 1995, a group of partners at Lehman Brothers stunned the real estate world by buying the Times Tower, essentially a nineteen-story signboard, from the Banque Nationale de Paris for $27 million. Within two years the building had been sold twice, each time for double the previous sum, so that the final price tag was an astounding $110 million.

But as signs increased in number and value, they became, inevitably, commodities—utilitarian articles designed to sell, not to dazzle. In an earlier day, the spectacular had been a medium of sheer virtuosity—the bigger, the brighter, the more wildly and improbably inventive, the better. O. J. Gude's dazzling Spearmen, or Douglas Leigh's Camel smoker, were something like the Super Bowl ads of their day—to be judged not by how much product they moved, but by how much glory they reflected on their sponsor. And in the days before television, how could any other advertising medium compete with a Times Square sign, either aesthetically or commercially? But that era was long gone by the 1990s. A few advertisers—Budweiser, Wrigley's Gum, Planter's Peanuts—returned to Times Square as a way of reminding viewers of past glories. But even Budweiser, according to Tama Starr, the third-generation chief executive of the venerable sign company Artkraft Strauss, couldn't be bothered to use most of the fancy graphics on its sign on the Times Tower, which Artkraft Strauss had designed. Most of the signs in Times Square could have been transplanted easily enough to, say, the Queens entrance to the Midtown Tunnel.

By the 1980s, sign-making had ceased to be a form of handicraft. The old sign companies were gobbled up by huge billboard firms that were in turn owned by multinationals like Viacom or Clear Channel. Artkraft Strauss, which has been building signs in Times Square for a century, is the last survivor, and today it owns only a dozen locations in Times Square. Tama Starr is afflicted with a rather extreme, if understandable, sense of declinism. Leaving aside her own signs, she says, Times Square has been overtaken by "video and vinyl": oversize screens showing commercials, and giant billboards of computer-printed vinyl, which can be discarded and replaced at a moment's notice. Even the executives of Spectacolor, a company founded in 1976, suffer pangs of nostalgia for a golden age they had no role in shaping. "You have an explosion of inventory," says Michael Forte, the company's president and CEO, "but you also have a lost art of spectacularity." Spectacolor's fourth-floor boardroom looks across Broadway to the spot where some of Times Square's most spectacular signs once stood—Wrigley's wiggling fish, the Bond waterfall, the giant Pepsi bottles. Today there is a forest of bodacious—but very vinyl—blondes strutting their stuff for Pony and Liz Claiborne. Forte gazes through the boardroom's picture window and says, with piercing regret, "To think that it went from that to this."

Signs have been banalized; at the same time, the rise of the office tower in Times Square has posed new questions about the relationship of signage to architecture. The 1987 zoning changes forced developers to think about signage in new ways. A few Times Square developers immediately embraced the new aesthetic. One, Jeffrey Katz, built a black glass hotel at 2 Times Square, between 47th and 48th Street, and used the entire south façade, which looks straight down at the Times Tower, as a rack for a column of giant signs, precisely what it had been throughout the century. The developer William Zeckendorf hired Alan Lapidus, an architect whose father, Morris, had designed many of the glitziest hotels in Miami Beach, to build a hotel on the west side of Broadway between 47th and 48th; Lapidus worked closely with the City Planning Commission to design a structure that would conform to the new rules.

But a hotel is, of course, the rare example of a tall building designed to evoke the idea of pleasure and excitement. An office tower, on the other hand, is traditionally meant to conjure up power, solidity, integrity. And the commercial developers who had fought the new regulations in the first place were loath to submit to them. David Solomon, who was putting up an enormous building, without a guaranteed tenant, at the corner of Broadway and 47th, was genuinely horrified at the prospect of signage. Tama Starr, whom Solomon and his wife, Jean, had retained to design signage if it proved unavoidable, says, "Their idea of a sign was very retro; it was a seventies consciousness of the tawdry 'HOTEL' with the 'E' flickering because the transformer was out. They did not see signs as having any class whatsoever." When the new rules were passed, the Solomons did their best to circumvent them. They worked with their architect, Charles Gwathmey, to create a system of lights and signs that would operate only at night; during the day, the building would look as solemn as a judge. Even at night the lights would be visible only from directly in front of the building. The City Planning Commission responded by amending the new zoning rules to specify that signs and lights must be visible during the day as well as at night. Times Square's new corporate tenants would have to find a way to adapt to the place's traditions, no matter how outlandish they seemed.

The Solomons ultimately lost the building, known as 1585 Broadway, to their lenders; in 1992, Morgan Stanley bought the property at a steep discount. The firm was profoundly skittish about Times Square; it was, in fact, so dubious about urban life generally that it was seriously thinking about moving its headquarters to Stamford, Connecticut, even though virtually the entire finance industry was concentrated in Manhattan. Now it had to find a way to live with Times Square, and with the Times Square zoning requirements. The bank had opposed the new zoning regulations as ardently as the Solomons had, if less publicly. As Susan Jarrett, now an executive director of Morgan Stanley, recalls, "The fact that there had to be any kind of sign—the fact that it had to be *kinetic*—the fact that it had to be *neon*—this was so anti-image for us." (Actually, it had to be bright, but not necessarily neon.) Tama Starr, who continued to work on the building, says, "Their first question was 'What's the cheapest thing we can do?' We said, 'We can give you some cutout plastic letters and stick them on.' And the answer was, 'How much will that cost?' "

Morgan plainly had to find a way to incorporate signage that enhanced, rather than damaged, its identity. Charles Gwathmey says that he always favored the idea of placing some kind of signage on the building's lower floors, among which would be trading floors that would not require windows. And Morgan officials, he says, put up very little resistance once they understood that the sign would serve not as an advertisement but as a new corporate emblem. Gwathmey's central innovation was, he says, "to integrate the sign into the façade rather than try to make it additive." He and the designer Massimo Vignelli came up with the idea of using financial information as a decorative motif—not, perhaps, the most far-reaching inspiration. The Morgan Stanley Building at 1585 Broadway has three bands of stock-ticker information, each ten to twelve feet high, running across the façade at different speeds. At either edge of the building are forty-four-foot-high cylindrical maps showing the time zones of Morgan Stanley's offices across the world. Decorative fins elegantly spell out the building's address. The bands themselves are sky-blue, and the data is the bright white of LEDs, or light-emitting diodes. The information comes from a real-time feed from the Reuters wire; the numbers appear to speed up as they round a curve leading from the façade of the building—an Artkraft Strauss optical illusion designed, says Tama Starr, "to give the feeling that the information was coming out of the building, crossing the front, and going back into the building to be reprocessed, as if it were a manufacturing process." This enormous sign, which Morgan Stanley executives once cringed at the thought of, makes a series of essential statements about the company: that it traffics in information and not just in money; that it is a central node and switching device in the global economy; that it is in the moment; and not least of all, that it is cool enough to claim a space for itself in the new Times Square. The sign was, in effect, a branding device both for Morgan Stanley and for Times Square.

By 1997, Morgan Stanley had so thoroughly accommodated itself to Times Square, and all it stood for, that it was looking to expand; it purchased a ground lease from the Rockefeller Group for the parcel on the east side of Seventh Avenue, between 49th and 50th Streets. The Rockefellers had long thought of the parcel as the western gateway to Rockefeller Center, and in 1989 had hired the firm of Kohn Pederson Fox to design a building that would essentially incorporate the property into Rockefeller Center. The architect, Greg Clement, had designed a building with Rockefeller Center limestone and a Rockefeller Center top that would line up horizontally with 30 Rockefeller Center, directly to the east. Here was yet another manifestation of the apparently irrepressible urge to subsume Times Square into Rockefeller Center—the urge that had guided Seymour Durst and George Klein and Philip Johnson. And then the market had collapsed, and Clement's building went into the deep freeze.

Now Clement and Kevin Kennon, who had since joined the firm, went back to work, this time for Morgan Stanley. Kennon says that he came to think of the new building, at 745 Seventh Avenue, as a "hinge" be-

tween two geographical axes, and a "hybrid" of the cultures of Rockefeller Center and Times Square. The new Times Square was, itself, a hybrid place—for, just as Toys "R" Us made Times Square into a more
"family-oriented" locale by placing its flagship store there, so Morgan
Stanley helped erase the distinction between the corporate world of midtown Manhattan and the old honky-tonk world of Times Square.

Kennon is a sandy-haired, soft-spoken man of an academic bent. His
father had been the head of the largest corporate architecture firm in the
United States and the dean of architecture at Rice University. While still
in college, Kennon had studied at the Institute for Architecture and Urban
Studies, a study group founded by a group of young architects and theo-
rists, including Peter Eisenman and Kenneth Frampton. One of Kennon's
fellow students was Rem Koolhaas, who was working on a project that ultimately became *Delirious New York*, a manifesto that celebrated Manhattan's raw power and indifference to traditional aesthetic standards,
somewhat as Robert Venturi, Denise Scott Brown, and Steven Izenour
had done with Las Vegas. Koolhaas wanted to celebrate Times Square,
and its frankly commercial and bluntly sexual traditions, rather than gentrify or erase them. In fact, *Delirious New York* includes a project Koolhaas
called the Sphinx, a giant complex facing the Times Tower that would
combine the functions of hotel, apartment house, sports complex, nightclub, auditorium, and sex parlor. Kennon was neither the theorist nor the
radical that Koolhaas was, but the Institute gave him a critical language
and approach that allowed him to operate beyond the conventions of corporate architecture.

At Kohn Pederson Fox, Kennon had designed the highly regarded new
Sotheby's headquarters on the East Side of Manhattan, as well as the
Rodin Museum in Seoul, a structure made almost entirely of glass and
thus open to passersby and to cars whizzing past. An architecture critic
wrote that the museum "inhabits both the site and Seoul in a way that
suggests a new dialogue between cities and buildings." Kennon was a
commercial architect with an intellectual program that involved forging
this new dialogue. "The big problem that architects have faced," he says,
"is how to energize public space. So much of what used to be public activity has now been superseded by television, the Internet, videoconfer-
encing. You're trying to say that a life exists in the public realm that's not

virtual; but because that virtual part of us is so ingrained in us, we have to work with it in order to reengage the real world." The task, in other words, was to revitalize that old sense of Times Square as an agora, a happy urban welter, even as entities like Morgan Stanley were turning Times Square into the central switchboard of the global information network—to harness the abstract, bit-stream world in the service of the face-to-face world that it seemed bent on eradicating. Kennon wanted to create a sign that had the evanescence, the ever-changingness, of information culture and that simultaneously worked as a transfixing object.

The obvious medium for the new sign was LED. Charles Gwathmey had already used LED technology on the first Morgan Stanley building, but he had been compelled to work with a more limited palette. LED uses tiny bulbs that have been placed in a chemical bath so that they emit light at different points of the spectrum, and thus in different colors. Only in the previous few years, however, had blue LED become commercially available, so that now it was possible to work in virtually any color. It had also become possible—though it was very expensive—to buy LED that would reproduce the visual quality of a movie, and thus create a stunningly vivid, color-drenched image. But Kennon didn't want to turn the new building into a giant TV set. "Normally you buy LED in eight-inch-by-eight-inch panels," he says. "But you can buy the panels like Lego blocks in whatever configuration you can think of. You can completely break the box." In other words, LED allowed you to project imagery in any size or shape you could think of; it was not only programmable, unlike neon or vinyl, but almost infinitely malleable. "There is," Kennon says, "a strong cultural tradition of receiving mediated information through a framing device"—a proscenium, a TV set. "Now you have something which has the possibility of being completely different. The frame can transform into a fragment, into pieces, into things that are not framed."

In the other post-1987 Times Square buildings, signs had been slapped onto buildings; even at 1585 Broadway, the sign was an afterthought. Kennon wanted to blur altogether the distinction between the permanent and massive material of the building's skeleton and the transitory and insubstantial material of its imagery—between architecture and media. He wanted to create panels of LED that would be fused into the façade of the building, so that the viewer would be reading not the sign, but the building itself. And Morgan Stanley had agreed that the sign would feature computer-generated programming, rather than the kind of electronic stock ticker used at 1585. That building was known around the company as "the head"; the new building was supposed to demonstrate the company's heart. "We wanted to portray Morgan Stanley as a service-oriented, family-oriented, global-oriented firm that cares not just about money," says Susan Jarrett.

In order to create the programming, Kennon and Clement hired a downtown design firm called Imaginary Forces, which specialized in using computer graphics to create whimsical and ingenious movie credits. But Imaginary Forces had also gained familiarity with LED when it was called on to design the giant screen at the Baltimore Ravens football stadium. Mikon van Gastel, the Dutch designer who headed the project, spent long hours with Kennon discussing the idea of a sign that not only was as big as a building but *was* a building. Van Gastel says that Kennon told him, "I want to question what a façade is. Is a façade a window into the building, is it a reflection of the environment, is it a reflection of the world? But the big word also was, 'I don't want it to be commercial. We want it to be soft branding.' It means you want to talk about the company without mentioning the company every three seconds, and it becoming much more of a reflection of its attitudes and values." Kennon was telling Van Gastel, a young and extremely hip figure whose hair stood straight up and was only rarely seen in its natural color, to do just what he would do if he weren't worried about the client's reactions. Kennon's aesthetic ambition appeared to coincide with Morgan's wish to speak from "the heart."

In January 1999, Kennon, Clement, and Van Gastel met at Kohn Pederson's offices with the clients—fifteen or so executives from Morgan Stanley, the Rockefeller Center Development Corporation, Tishman Realty, and Hines Development, the worldwide building firm based in Houston. After presentations by the two architects, Van Gastel showed the images he had worked up. "It was a disaster," recalls Kennon. "Lead balloon is kind of an understatement. After the presentation, there was dead silence. The comment from Morgan Stanley was 'All of our commercials are basically people in boats. What does this have to do with anything?' "

Kennon tried to explain that it was a sign, not a commercial; that he wanted to break the frame, and so on. But the executives liked the frame; they clung to the frame. To them, TV was not a "medium," but the natural means through which electronic information was consumed. And they didn't see much evidence of the service-oriented, family-oriented imagery they had in mind. One Morgan official who was at the meeting says that the pictures reminded him of "an MTV short"—abstract and ironic and full of ingenious one-liners. Kennon now concedes, in retrospect, that "It's very difficult to propose something this creative when you can't point to something [that already exists] and say, 'It looks like this.' "

And then there was the old-fashioned issue of money. Kennon and Clement wanted to use an immense amount of LED, and they wanted it to be the highest quality commercially available, which was sixteen-millimeter (the distance separating each cluster of bulbs). The complexity of the program would also require extremely sophisticated hardware. The sign they envisioned would cost in the neighborhood of $20 million to build, and perhaps another $1 million a year to operate. Morgan officials viewed the meeting as a useful starting point; now they began doing some thinking of their own. Could the sign be built more cheaply, using either less LED or a lower quality of image? Could the bank's own technology staff do the programming? The answer to all questions turned out to be no. After a year or so of research and planning, the bankers, to their credit, not only accepted the architects' proposal but increased the costs by adding a large vertical panel over the entrance to the building, to be used for showing more conventional, news-oriented imagery. Morgan re-hired Imaginary Forces; this time they had the designers work directly with marketing and communications officials from the bank.

The programming that the designers devised satisfied Morgan's concern about image without deviating very far from the original presentation. Van Gastel created six five-minute "themes," all of them meant to evoke the identity Jarrett and others described without turning the building into a commercial. Some of the imagery was nevertheless fairly direct and literal-minded. The "Aspiration" theme consisted of words and images demonstrating "how Morgan Stanley facilitates dreams," projected over pictures of people representing customers. There was an atmospheric theme, designed to use the building as a sort of giant mood ring:

in the morning, images of sunrise; in the evening, of the moon. But Van Gastel never lost sight of Kennon's directive to rethink the meaning of "façade." The "X-Ray" theme turned the building into a transparency: after a blueprint of one floor flashed on the sign, a schematic image of an elevator would rise to that floor, the doors would open to show the activities on the floor, ultimately leading to one particular employee at work; text superimposed on the picture might say, "Little League coach," or some other heartwarming—and fictitious—piece of identification. Instead of allowing the owner to project images onto the viewer, the sign was giving the viewer access, at least illusionistically, to the otherwise hidden core of the enterprise—to its "heart," as it were.

Kennon and Clement designed the building in such a way as to fully incorporate the sign. The LED panels, each forty feet wide and eight feet high, were placed inside pockets formed by structural elements of the façade. The three horizontal bands covered spandrels, dark areas that contain plumbing and wiring, and alternated with windows of equal height, so that when an image played over the building, a viewer would have to imaginatively fill in the blanks created by the intervening floors—another means of connecting the spectator in the street with the extravaganza in the sky.

No one had ever designed anything like this before, and the technical problems were staggering. Each horizontal panel contained 5,346 pixels; a standard movie screen, by contrast, has 2,048. So much imagery could run on the building at once that Van Gastel had to use three powerful computers to create separate images and superimpose them on one another in order to see what the façade would look like at any given moment. What's more, the LED panels were set inside the decorative mullions that ran up the façade; the software had to be programmed with five-pixel-wide blank spaces wherever a mullion would be located. The graphic information had to be programmed so that as it moved across the façade it would disappear or explode as it reached one of these vertical dividers—as if the building itself were a mediating device—and then reassemble on the other side. And the programming would grow more complex over time: Phase Two would add a layer of sound to the imagery, while Phase Three would incorporate sensors that would allow changes in weather or traffic to influence the imagery. After years of toil, the building would be everything the architects and designers had dreamed of—a sign that would be admired in Starbucks *and* anatomized in architectural journals and media studies departments.

By the summer of 2001, LED was beginning to emerge as the new medium of corporate spectacularity. NASDAQ had built a giant cylindrical sign jutting out over the street at the northeast corner of 42nd and Broadway, though all sign connoisseurs agreed that the quality of both the LED and the programming was poor. On the other side of Broadway, Reuters had commissioned the designer Edwin Schlossberg to create programming for a series of giant black panels that run down one vertex of the building and then continue just above the street level on two sides—and to use, as Morgan had, the highest quality of imagery.

Morgan planned to fully occupy its new building on November 15, 2001, so the programming was to be fully operational by then as well. Over the summer, Morgan installed the incredibly elaborate equipment required to operate the sign, and then began experimentally running the programming. It was during this period that passersby could see the piggybank gavotte, and the bouncing apples, and the pedestrians and the bridge. And then came the terrorist attacks of September 11. Suddenly, the idea of having your employees concentrated in the world's most famous urban space lost its appeal; within weeks, Morgan Stanley was scouting for new locations and for a buyer for its "heart." It quickly found the latter in Lehman Brothers, which had lost its headquarters, in the World Financial Center. In early October, Lehman bought the building, for $700 million. The sign, which had been four years in the making, was an afterthought. By the time Lehman formally took title, in early December, three of the six segments were up and running, but Lehman had suspended work on the rest.

In order to comply with the Times Square lighting regulations, Lehman continued to run the sign, but it kept only the most literal-minded images—the suspension bridge and the gallery of pedestrians—and ran them over and over until it was difficult to remember why the sign had been worth caring about in the first place. It was understandable that after the tremendous shock of 9/11, and the sheer logistical challenge of moving, reprogramming the sign was not exactly a top priority. Nevertheless, the bank hired Roger Dean, the Morgan executive who had been responsible for the engineering on both the sign at 1585 Broadway and the new one. When I went to see Dean in early 2002, he explained that Lehman had decided to at least temporarily strip away all the "foreground" images of data and graphics and to keep those few "background" images with which company officials felt comfortable. He had hired a new programmer, who had worked on the technical aspects of the new sign. He felt confident that Lehman would not reduce the sign to a commercial. "I don't get the feeling at the moment that we're likely to be blatant about it," he said. "There's enough blatancy in Times Square, and I personally would like to be removed from that."

The new programming went up in the summer of 2002; I stood in front of Starbucks to take a look. The words "Lehman Brothers" covered most of the building, save for two panels on which appeared the phrase "Where Vision Gets Built," apparently the company's rather awkward motto, since it was followed by a trademark sign. Then a background of blue mosaic tiles appeared, and once again the giant words "Lehman Brothers," this time sliding by as cutouts composed of the tiles. Then a mighty sea crashed against rocks; then "Lehman Brothers," and "Where Vision," etc., once again. Then came the bridge stretching over the sea, then rolling surf, then the company logo again, then the bridge, then a great mass of clouds, then the logo again, and then the blue tiles. I had had enough.

I called Roger Dean and asked how the corporate advertising squared with his antiblatancy pledge. "I don't know if I would consider it advertising," he said lamely. He was plainly uncomfortable. He added that his responsibility was "purely on the technical side." This was true, though it also seemed plain that he had lost some internal battle. "Our thinking has obviously developed," he said, and then asked, or rather pleaded, that I direct any further questions to Tony Zehnder, Lehman's head of corporate communications. Zehnder seemed utterly mystified by my sense of forfeited possibility. He said, "We took the content that Morgan Stanley had for the sign and we pared it down to what we thought were usable images, and we put our name on to identify the name of the building. That's what the sign is for the moment."

I called the new programmer, Steven Heimbold. Months earlier, he had been cautiously hopeful that Lehman would let him do something as inventive as Imaginary Forces had done. But they hadn't. "Lehman Brothers has not really embraced the sign in any way like Morgan Stanley," he admitted. "The imagery they want is more generic. They're not really looking for any higher meaning other than looking at the sign." Heimbold, like Dean, was having trouble being the good corporate soldier. "The public," he said, "really hasn't seen it in its full glory."

Might they someday? Zehnder had, after all, said "for the moment." A different moment could come, and all of the elaborate wiring and computer hardware would be there inside the building waiting to be used. One of the saving graces of Times Square is that nothing is forever.

20

À *LA RECHERCHE DES*
FRIED CLAMS *PERDUS*

UNLIKE THE STRIP in Las Vegas, or the E-Walk in Los Angeles, or the countless malls and festival markets and converted train stations all across this great nation, Times Square is full of old places—and, especially, of old places that do the same thing they did when they were new. Indeed, the building of all the new stuff, the office towers and the megastores, was justified in no small part as a way of preserving the old: that is, the Broadway theaters. The theaters evoke powerful feelings, and not only because of the shows mounted inside but because of the sense of antiquity, of unbroken tradition, provided by the buildings themselves. Disney bought itself immeasurable goodwill, perhaps especially among those otherwise inclined to deplore its presence in Times Square, by its meticulous and loving renovation of the New Amsterdam Theatre, even though the city footed the bill.

There are other places in Times Square famous for being old, beloved spots that bear the fossil traces of an all-but-vanished civilization. Most of these places are restaurants, like Sardi's, on 44th Street, where tourists have been coming for decades to ogle show folk, or what they suppose must be show folk. These sites have a special status as living proof that the indwelling spirit of the place hasn't died out. Perhaps the granddaddy of all such nostalgia magnets is the Edison Coffee Shop, universally known as the Polish Tea Room (a joke on the grandiose and self-important, and now late and lamented, Russian Tea Room). The playwright Neil Simon, a habitué, even wrote a play about the place, *Forty-five Seconds from Broadway* (the title a spoof of one of George M. Cohan's, *Forty-five Minutes from Broadway*). Located on 47th Street between Broadway and Eighth Avenue, the coffee shop was originally a salon of the posh Edison Hotel and is decorated like a giant Wedgwood tea set—blue for the ceilings, pink for the walls and columns that march incongruously down the middle of the coffee shop. The truncated remains of a grilled balcony look out over the luncheon counter, where a sign lists the featured specials of a bygone age of Jewish heartburn-producing cuisine—kasha varnishkes, blintzes, whitefish, gefilte fish, and so on. The cast of ancient regulars sipping tea at the counter looks like a lineup of George Segal sculptures. The actual Broadway folk sit in front, near the windows. You might be able to get a better pastrami on rye elsewhere, but the Edison is less an eatery than a tableau vivant, a show where lucky tourists are invited to mingle, as at audience-participation plays like *Tony n' Tina's Wedding*. Stubborn archaism and a kind of slapdash gemütlichkeit turn out to exert a tremendous atavistic appeal. The Edison is, in its way, a terribly fashionable place, and the tables are often filled with editors from *The New York Times* and masters of the universe from Morgan Stanley.

The Edison Coffee Shop teeters on some ontological knife-edge between the unself-conscious and the italicized, and thus between the lovable and the quaint. What is lovable—what you are willing to attach your emotions to—is not simply the old, but the unrenovated, the thoughtlessly preserved, the effortlessly itself. This, of course, is what no theme park can achieve. And the persistence of the unrenovated is the source of such charm as Times Square still has. This is especially true in what might be called Times Square's private spaces: the cross streets and the northern reaches, where the great crowds peter out. These are the places still patronized principally by actual New Yorkers. Irish bars still line both sides of Eighth Avenue. McHale's, a dark little pub on the northeast corner of 46th and Eighth, opened up in 1935 as the Gaiety Café, and in 1953 passed into the hands of the McHales, who ever since have been serving large hamburgers, modestly priced beer, and televised ball games. Upper Times Square still bears strong marks of the jazz and popular music culture that radiated from there half a century ago. Colony Music, at 49th and Broadway, opened up a few blocks to the north in 1948, at the site of the old

Alvin Hotel, where Billie Holiday used to perform. The owner, Richard Turk, grew up in the store, where his father worked as the accountant. Irving Berlin, aged ninety, once accosted him to ask, "How's 'White Christmas' doing?" To which Turk said, "It's doing fine, and 'Easter Parade' isn't doing so bad, either." Today the Colony offers an immense library of "music-minus-one" arrangements; what Turk calls the largest selection of karaoke machines in New York; and an odd assortment of rock-and-roll schlockabilia—e.g., Monkees lunchboxes—that appears to be only nominally for sale.

The Edison, McHale's, the Colony, and other such places, which together constitute the surviving vestiges of the indigenous, all occupy peripheral locations in the global crossroads that is Times Square. Within the four corners of the crossroads itself—which is to say, 42nd Street between Broadway and Seventh to the south, and 47th between Broadway and Seventh to the north—Times Square is almost as uniform, as gigantic, as "totalized," as Disneyland or the Strip: it is one pulsating global media–financial services–information–entertainment zone. All traces of an older, more localized, more organic life have been obliterated.

And yet not quite all. There is one holdout, one irrelevancy, one outpost not so much of nostalgia as of pathos: the Howard Johnson's on the northwest corner of Broadway and 46th Street. The Howard Johnson's is Times Square's very own "Night Café." When I sat down one day on one of the orange Naugahyde swivel chairs at the lunch counter, I had two other customers for company; another half dozen or so were scattered around the orange banquettes that ran back toward the bar—also empty. "Shake, Shake, Shake" was blaring out over the tables with their little hooked coat stands; over the silent, lingering waiters; and over the little wooden cubicle toward the front where the cashier sat, with the boxes of saltwater taffy displayed in the shelving above. I had never seen such a lifeless place in Times Square.

The counterman was a roly-poly man with a soft face and a black mustache. Irfan Anwar had been born in Kashmir, raised in Lahore, and then immigrated to this country; fourteen years earlier, he had landed a job at Howard Johnson's. Irfan moved with great deliberation, and not only because of his bulk: it had been many years since haste served any purpose. When he had first started working, Irfan said, "Every day we would be serving lunch to five hundred people, six hundred people. If you came here at lunchtime, you would see the people lined up four deep. And then came the war in the Middle East." Irfan maintained, not altogether logically, that the 1991 Gulf War had destroyed the restaurant's fortunes, and indeed had wreaked havoc on the block. "There was a Burger King just up the street. I think it was maybe a hundred years old," he explained. "And soon after that, it closed up." Irfan felt that everyone was hurting. I asked about the Edison Coffee Shop, just around the corner on 47th Street. The Edison, I pointed out, was usually jammed. "I do not know this place," Irfan said. This was after fourteen years.

There was something almost uncanny about the Howard Johnson's, so profoundly removed did it feel from the roaring world outside. Just up the block, at the 47th Street corner, fabulous-looking young people with money to burn were flocking to the Blue Fin, a glassed-in bar and restaurant affiliated with the new W hotel. Here was the new Times Square consuming class—the fashionistas from Condé Nast, the editors at Random House, the bankers from Morgan Stanley and Lehman Brothers. They might have enjoyed the retro warmth of the matzoh ball soup at the Polish Tea Room, but you wouldn't catch them at Howard Johnson's even on a lark. While the Blue Fin was hopping, a few old ladies sat at the Howard Johnson's counter delicately drinking ice cream sodas. Even the ice cream flavors bore the stamp of the retrograde: maple walnut, butter pecan, mocha chip. One day I ordered a turkey burger for lunch, and I received an article that bore no discernible relation to the austere, low-fat item that now graces coffee shop menus—a defrosted patty so thickly slicked with grease that even the pita bread in which it came was hard to hold on to.

The most exotic thing about Howard Johnson's was the waitstaff, which had been drawn from all corners of the globe. There was Ivan Pinto, a bald, coffee-colored, bespectacled gentleman in his mid-sixties whose name and accent were so unplaceable that he dared visitors to guess his origins. Trinidad? No. Guyana? No. "I come from Bombay," said Ivan, "but I am a Christian. We tend to live apart, and so do not pick up the Indian accent." There was a very black man with his hair shaved high above his temple on one side: Michel Valmont. "Like *Liaisons Dangereuses*?" "*C'est ça*," he said delightedly. Michel was a linguist. Born in

Martinique, he spoke French as a mother tongue, but he had also picked up some Danish and German. One afternoon I heard Michel saying something guttural to a Nordic-looking tourist he was escorting to the bar. "What was that?" I asked. Michel said that he had been speaking Dutch, and the young man confirmed that Michel had been speaking identifiable Dutch to him.

There was always time to talk to the waiters, who were pretty much the only denizens of Howard Johnson's in the long, lassitudinous period between lunch and dinner. By three-thirty, the place was virtually lifeless. Even happy hour, which started at four and lasted until seven, and featured mixed drinks for $3.25, only marginally enlarged the crowd. One afternoon, I sat at the U-shaped bar in the back talking with Victor, the bartender, who had spent the previous twenty-eight years working, first, at the Chock full o'Nuts on 50th and Eighth, and then here at the Howard Johnson's, which had opened up in 1959. I asked Victor why the bar didn't have a television set. "I been asking Mr. Rubinstein for years if we could put in cable," he said. Kenny Rubinstein owned both the franchise and the real estate it sat on. "He hasn't got to it yet." A few minutes later, two men in suits walked out of the kitchen, and Victor, pointing to one on the left, said, "That's Kenny."

Kenny Rubinstein was in his late forties, with curly brown hair and a solid build. I walked over, introduced myself, and congratulated him on having preserved this last little shard of old Times Square. It was the wrong thing to say: Rubinstein assumed that I was being sarcastic, for what real estate man would feel proud of having the last unimproved property in the core of Times Square? "I don't know how much you paid for that jacket you're wearing," Rubinstein said testily, "but I'm sure whoever sold it to you could make a pretty good profit if he sold one every week. But you can't sell one every week." I wasn't sure where Rubinstein was going with this conceit, but then he said, "People think that if you own a property here, it's easy to make a fortune, but they have no idea. They think IBM comes along every week; but I'm still waiting for IBM."

The Rubinsteins, it turned out, were another Times Square real estate family, like the Mosses, the Brandts, and the Dursts but not quite so successful. Kenny's father, Morris, had bought the parcel that included Howard Johnson's, as well as another right across the street, on the east side of Seventh, some time in the fifties or so—Kenny was hazy on the history, and Morris was dead. Morris had held the franchise for several of the Howard Johnson's in Times Square, as well as for the Chock full o'Nuts where Victor had worked, back when they were profitable entities. Now the land underneath the Howard Johnson's was worth immensely more than the restaurant, but Kenny's ship hadn't yet come in. He said, "I can count on one hand the number of serious discussions I've had." Kenny had fond memories of Times Square when he was a boy, but he would have unloaded the Howard Johnson's in a second; the only thing stopping him was that he was asking a very large number for a fairly shallow, and thus not altogether desirable, site.

Howard Johnson's was not, strictly speaking, an indigenous institution. Howard Johnson himself was a restaurateur from Quincy, Massachusetts, who made a better grade of ice cream and began building a local chain of restaurants in the late twenties. Johnson appears to have invented the idea of restaurant franchising, and in the thirties local entrepreneurs opened franchises up and down the East Coast and along the rapidly expanding network of thruways and turnpikes. Times Square, with its great mass of tourists, was a natural site for the new chain, famous not only for its ice cream but—a reminder of its eastern seaboard origins—for its fried clams. The first Howard Johnson's in Times Square opened on Broadway and 49th Street, across the street from Jack Dempsey's bar and just east of Madison Square Garden, in the late 1940s. It was a tiny place that sat no more than seventy-five people. Joseph Sherry, the manager of the current Howard Johnson's at 46th Street and the self-appointed custodian of the restaurant's Times Square history and cultural status, says that, as he understands it, the comic Lily Tomlin perfected her gum-popping wiseacre coffee-shop waitress routine behind the counter at 49th Street, while Gene Hackman, decked out in white gloves, worked as the doorman, for in those glorious days patrons of Howard Johnson's were greeted at the door.

Sherry himself began working straight out of high school, in 1966, at yet another Howard Johnson's, on the other side of Broadway at 46th Street. Sherry is a Jewish immigrant from a Middle Eastern nation where he was so ill-treated that he does not wish to dignify the country in question by allowing its name to be printed next to his. He is, by now, a worldly, well-traveled man, but he speaks with a more or less equal sense of pride of the United States, New York City, and Howard Johnson's, which took him to its great orange bosom and raised him over the years from waiter to manager. He avoided talking to me for weeks, possibly out of a sense that a person of his station need not stoop to press interviews, but once we sat down in a banquette, with the little placemats advertising A-1 Steak Sauce, he opened the spigot of reminiscence and a veritable geyser rushed forth.

"We opened at seven and we closed at three or four in the morning," Sherry said of the sixties. "And we were jam-packed. People *raved* about Howard Johnson's. They would come just for the fried clams. And the Howard Johnson's hot dog and hot dog bun was the talk of the town. Times Square was tremendously glamorous in those days. People were well dressed. They would come to eat at Howard Johnson's like they would come to eat at the Club 21. Remember, in those days the theater opened at nine, and people would come for dinner beforehand. Then the break was at eleven-thirty, and inevitably everybody would want to go to Howard Johnson's for a sundae or an ice cream soda. I would have two hosts that would only handle the overflow from the theater. The night manager would be back behind the counter helping the counterman make sundaes. Later on, the Latin Quarter down the street would close, and those people would come for ice cream." A waiter came over and whispered that a supplier had been waiting to talk to him for close to half an hour. "Make him wait," said Mr. Sherry imperiously, and he turned back to me. "This is to my knowledge the oldest restaurant left on Broadway," he went on. "There used to be an Automat right on this block, and a Schrafft's across the street, and the Nathan's where the Disney Studio is now. We had a stand across the street where we sold coconut champagne and nonalcoholic piña coladas. We used to sell hot dogs like hot potatoes."

Sherry dates the decline of Howard Johnson's, and of the neighborhood, not to the Gulf War but to the administration of Mayor David Dinkins, from 1989 to 1993, whom he blames for a crime wave which, to be fair to Dinkins, actually started three or four mayors earlier. In any case, Sherry understands that he is now the captain of a ghost ship. But he takes his job with the utmost seriousness, for he feels that Howard Johnson's offers the balm of the past to visitors dizzied by the spinning vortex of the present. "We've kept the décor of the eighties, we've kept the sense of nostalgia," he says—as if his boss, Mr. Rubinstein, had committed his fortune to keeping the restaurant just as it was. "You get tourists who come in—the older tourists, of course—and they're so excited to see a Howard Johnson's they can hardly believe it. They say, 'Is the ice cream the same? You still have the same clams?' We assure them it's the same. You have no idea how excited they become." It may be that you have to spend more time at Howard Johnson's than I have in order to witness such an episode.

IT IS FOR HIMSELF, I imagine, more than for those phantom tourists, that Joseph Sherry preserves Howard Johnson's in Naugahyde splendor. He's the nostalgic one—for those bygone days of Lily Tomlin and Jack Dempsey's and the Latin Quarter. For him, the old and the worn have special claims that the new can never challenge. But of course, that's his life. Why should we join him? Why celebrate a spot whose sole virtue is persistence in the face of change? Nostalgia is, of course, the easiest, and maybe the laziest, way of discrediting all that is new. Even the most ardent lovers of the Times Square *perdu* recognize the dangers of surrendering to this syndrome. Marshall Berman, the author of *All That Is Solid Melts into Air,* a fine history of modernism, and himself a famous celebrant of the literature and history of Times Square, once noted that "Times Square has the capacity to engender a 'discourse of nostalgia' that floats freely and unites people with radically different views of the Square and the world." Berman observed that even the *WPA Guide* of 1939 was nostalgic for the Times Square of 1920. One might add that the essayist Benjamin de Casseres was already shedding tears in 1925 over the collapse of the old booze forts of 1915.

In *Times Square Roulette,* the definitive account of the redevelopment of Times Square, Lynn Sagalyn, a professor of real estate at Columbia University, even provides a declension of the "varied voices of nostalgia," which include the "wistfuls," the "skeptics," the "retrogrades," the "reminders" (low-grade wistfuls), and the "resilients," who are actually a species of enthusiast about the new Times Square. It is, as Sagalyn writes, precisely because Times Square is a "touchstone" that choosing your orientation toward its redevelopment becomes a means of expressing an attitude toward mass culture, toward corporate monopolization of that culture, toward the role of the past and of memory in a world dominated by the idea of progress and constant change. Wistfulness about the oldest restaurant on Broadway is thus a means of expressing regret; and that regret, Sagalyn would say, is a kind of soft-core critique of the booming new Times Square which has obliterated the past—or rather, many pasts.

But wistfulness does not necessarily, or even usually, express a wish for things to be other than they are (as Sagalyn herself recognizes). It is more like an intuitive reaction to the inhospitality of a world that bears no traces of its own past, or of your own past in it. In its most blissed-out form, wistfulness is the delighted incredulity of those codgers who find that a Howard Johnson's chocolate sundae with coffee and butter pecan ice cream tastes exactly the way it did in 1962. Joseph Sherry says that Lily Tomlin came back for a plate of fried clams while she was starring on Broadway; it must have been, for her, a madeleine sort of moment (though others have, to tell the truth, found the fried clams distinctly vulcanized).

I am not, myself, a genuine specimen of a "wistful." I do not really wish that I lived in the era of Rector's, or of Hubert's Flea Circus, or that either of those places could somehow be teleported into our own time. Unlike Joseph Sherry, I do not have passionate memories of Times Square when it was swell, and though during my boyhood I must have eaten any number of grilled cheese sandwiches and even ice cream sundaes at various Howard Johnson's on various thruways, it would never have occurred to me to sentimentalize the place. (In fact, on the basis of a magazine article of mine, Sagalyn cites me as an instance of the optimistic variant of the "resilient.") And yet I will be very sorry when Kenny Rubinstein finally sells that plot of land to IBM. I will be sorry because the new Times Square is so smoothly engineered, and Howard Johnson's is so artless. I would go even further and say that Howard Johnson's appeal has to do with its haplessness: the appeal of Howard Johnson's is the appeal of genteel failure in the face of the brutally successful.

The truth is that the gentrification of Times Square over the last decade has done wonders for the food, and promises to do still more as the restaurant culture catches up with the new corporate presence. The cuisine at the Blue Fin is infinitely better than it was at Schrafft's or the Automat, if immensely more expensive as well. I like the Blue Fin, and I even like the almost comically chic bar in the W's eighth-floor lobby around the corner on 47th Street. I don't want everything to be Howard Johnson's, but I don't want everything to be the Blue Fin, either. I don't want Times Square to become a totalized, thematically unified place, like the Strip. It seems that I need some atavism; I'm inclined to think that we all do.

But the arrow of time is pointing unmistakably forward, and there can be no two ways about the destiny of that corner plot on Broadway and 46th Street. When I told Kenny Rubinstein that I planned to include the Howard Johnson's in my book on Times Square, he said, "I wouldn't wait too long if I were you."

21

ALL THAT IS SOLID

MELTS INTO AIR

Y OU CAN COUNT ON seeing the Naked Cowboy almost any afternoon on the little concrete island between Broadway and Seventh Avenue
at 45th Street. The Naked Cowboy is not, in fact, literally naked, like the
holy Jains of India. He wears a pair of undies that say "Naked Cowboy"
on the butt, and a cowboy hat and a pair of cowboy boots, and he carries
a guitar. As for the rest, he's all magnificent muscle and flowing blond
locks. The Naked Cowboy spends a lot of time in the gym; he is the
healthiest, handsomest, and possibly wholesomest street person in the
history of Times Square. He appears to have descended directly from
the Tommy Hilfiger billboard that looms far above his head, or perhaps
from the electronic sign on the World Wrestling Entertainment store
down the street—like a god come down to earth in human form. He is an
icon of cleaned-up sex for the sexy, cleaned-up Times Square—a daytime
cowboy rather than a midnight one. (He had never heard of *Midnight
Cowboy* until a reporter asked him about it.)

The Naked Cowboy is an actual, individual person; his name is Robert
Burck, and he hails from Cincinnati, Ohio. But he bears only a passing resemblance to the famous eccentrics who once haunted Times Square,
such as the religious crank Rose Harvel, who preached a garbled gospel
from the very same concrete island forty or fifty years ago. He has a persona, or a gimmick; and that gimmick, and the splendid expanse of gym-
hardened flesh the gimmick is designed to expose, has made him a media

figure. "I've been on *Howard Stern* thirteen times," he said when I first approached him, in the late fall of 2001. At the time, he had literally wrapped himself in the American flag, patriotism then being very much in vogue. "I've been on *Letterman,* I just finished doing German TV, I've been on *Good Morning America* three times. I'm on CNN all the time. When someone does Times Square, they pretty much always include me. I've got my own movie going to Sundance. It's a ninety-minute documentary about my life called *Legend of a Naked Cowboy.*"

The Naked Cowboy had done his routine—which basically consists of standing in his underwear and singing horribly—all over the country, but he had settled in Times Square because of the exposure it gave him. Like the hosts of *Good Morning America,* he was known to millions of people who had never seen him in person. When I told Alex that I had met a singing cowboy in underpants, he looked at me with the supreme condescension of the truly eleven, and said, "That's the Naked Cowboy. He's on *TRL*"—*Total Request Live,* MTV's most popular show—"*all the time.*" And so he was. But for the Naked Cowboy, as for the other products advertised in Times Square, media exposure is a means to an end. He operates a website, which sells the trademarked underpants for $15, as well as the Naked Cowboy guitar and boots and CDs and the Naked Cowboy autobiography.

The Naked Cowboy makes pretty good money as an actual person in an actual place: whenever anyone asks to take a picture, he says, "You gotta put a dollar in my boot." ("I'm only kidding," he would add, feebly.) His boottops are stuffed with bills even on an ordinary weekday. At the same time, he is a merchandising phenomenon, a brand name, a self-created cartoon character—an emanation of the new Times Square of global marketers and global media. The Naked Cowboy isn't a virtual street character, but he is the first street character of Times Square's virtual age.

TO SAY THAT TIMES SQUARE has a "virtual" dimension is to say nothing more than that it is known through representations of itself as well as through direct experience; and that, of course, has been true since people started sending postcards of the place or, for that matter, listening to songs about the place. Thanks to FPA and Irving Berlin and touring shows, millions of Americans have known all about Times Square without ever setting foot in it. Broadway's favorite subject has always been Broadway. But the production of images of itself is much more central to the new Times Square than it was to the old. When "the media" meant signs, songs, popular magazines and movies, one could say that the media played a central role in transmitting the life of Times Square to the world. But the media are now inextricable from that life. Disney or MTV, and even in their own way Reuters and Condé Nast, do not simply transmit popular culture; they *are* popular culture. These media institutions want to be in Times Square because Times Square is the center of popular culture; but the very fact of their choosing to be in Times Square is what makes it the center of popular culture, just as it is the Toys "R" Us flagship store that makes Times Square "the center of the toy universe."

But it is not enough to say that the great firms that traffic in imagery have a dominant presence in Times Square. The megastores and global retailers that have settled there are also, effectively, creatures of the media. They depend on Times Square to help shape their brand identity, as John Eyler of Toys "R" Us puts it. They want to be associated with the new Times Square brand—with that sense of unthreatening urbanness, contained exuberance, family fun. The power of the Times Square brand inheres in the fact that it is infinitely reproduced, and thus fixed in the minds of millions of potential consumers. This, of course, is precisely what Eyler understood when he booked Bill Gates for Toys "R" Us's opening night event, thus exploiting the media power of three global brands: Toys "R" Us, Microsoft, and Times Square. It is, in fact, only the media, with its blizzard of images, that makes it possible to instantaneously create or retool a brand.

What makes Times Square so powerful a place, at least in the calculations of global marketers, is that it is so intensely *there*—so dense with people, lights, buildings, history, emotion—while it is also one of the central nodes of the worldwide media network. It is Times Square's actuality that makes its virtuality possible, for McDonald's or Toys "R" Us as much as for the Naked Cowboy. When newscasters need an image that says "urban throngs" they often use a clip of Times Square. In the middle of the Oscars, ABC, which is owned by Disney, showed a clip of crowds watching the telecast on the big screen above the Disney studio in Times Square. ABC's *Good Morning America* broadcasts from the studio every day, sometimes showing images of the crowd from the ground floor, sometimes of the buildings from the second floor. NBC's *Today Show* broadcasts from Rockefeller Center; *Good Morning America* positions itself in a different way through its association with Times Square.

Total Request Live, MTV's version of *American Bandstand,* airs every afternoon at three-thirty from the MTV studio on the second floor of the Viacom Building, at Broadway and 45th Street, directly above the Naked Cowboy's patch of concrete. The outer wall of the studio is made of glass, so the studio audience and the performers, and the million or so kids watching at home, can see out to the street, and the people on the street can see in. When the Baha Men, or the Backstreet Boys, or Busta Rhymes, or No Doubt perform on the little bandstand, the camera shoots over their shoulders at the Pepsi billboard across the street featuring Britney Spears wearing a red garter saucily over her hip, or Pamela Anderson vamping for Pony, or Nelly at the Virgin Megastore. You could say that MTV is giving those brands—the human ones as well as the institutional ones—a free ride, or you could say that those brands are so central to MTV's identity that the show is exploiting its connection with them. The implicit message is that *TRL* is coming to you from the head office of the brands you love.

But the show has a much more complicated relationship to Times Square than that; or, rather, it offers a much more complex version of Times Square than is conveyed only by the billboard forest. Every weekday afternoon, usually starting around three, the show's adolescent fans, often with their parents, begin to gather on the sidewalk below the studio. On a low-profile day, just a hundred or so kids will stand under the studio; on a big day, the fans will fill the space inside the police barricades on the pavement, and then spill over to the sidewalk in front of Toys "R" Us, directly across the street and a good two hundred feet from the glass wall. When the Backstreet Boys came, in the fall of 2001, an estimated five thousand people choked the sidewalks, and the police were forced to close several lanes of traffic on Broadway. The crowd is real, their passions are real, and Times Square is reality itself; the relationship with the fans on the street gives *TRL* a special sense of authenticity.

But from the point of view of the crowd, it's the show that's real. The kids, and their parents, have parked themselves on the sidewalk in order to participate in a world they've only experienced indirectly, on TV. The show wants access to the crowd, but the crowd is only there because it wants access to the show—because it wants to be part of TV. The high point of the show comes when a star walks over to the window, strikes a pose or mimes a greeting or plays air guitar—and the crowd screams as one, and the kids frantically wave their hand-lettered signs: "I love you, Ashanti!" "I am your fatha', Ja-Rule." Sometimes a star even descends from the electronic realm to their own. Mariah Carey once waded out into the crowd and nearly caused a riot. And so there is a continual back-and-forth between the "inside" world of the show itself and the "outside" world of Times Square.

Total Request Live is staggeringly popular for a program that appears on cable television in the middle of the afternoon; and there is little question in the minds of the people responsible for the show that the feverish crowd on the street has a great deal to do with the program's cachet. And the fact that it was a happy accident adds to the program's air of uncalculated calculation. Bob Kusbit, the senior producer, says that when Viacom, the parent of MTV, first moved to Times Square, MTV executives thought the second-floor space overlooking the street would make a fine gym. Even when the studio was built, and *TRL* was launched as a live show featuring music videos (that was in September 1998), Times Square was expected to serve as a picturesque and demographically appropriate backdrop. "We never said, 'Come on down to Times Square,'" says Kusbit. "It just started to happen where you looked out the window the first week of the show and there were twenty people standing outside with a sign saying, 'Hey, Carson'"—for Carson Daly, the show's thoroughly adorable young host—"or 'Megan Says N Sync Is Number One.' So we invited somebody up. The next week there might have been fifty, then the next week it might have been a hundred, and pretty soon it started to become this sort of mecca for music fans to show up outside the studio." Kusbit and his colleagues knew they were onto something big when they conducted their "You Wanna Be a Deejay?" contest, and five thousand kids, accompanied by a battalion of TV cameras, showed up at the front door.

Kusbit talks about the way *TRL* benefits from its identification with Times Square in much the same way that John Eyler does about Toys "R" Us. "It is the center of pop culture," he says, "and *TRL* is so much about trying every day to be at the center of pop culture for its audience." The show has, in fact, been criticized for offering up a steady diet of teeny-bopper music to the exclusion of grittier, less mainstream performers; but in this regard *TRL* is no different from Toys "R" Us or the ESPN Zone or McDonald's or any of the other mass merchandisers of Times Square. It's a democratic show, in the lowest-common-denominator sense in which the developer Bruce Ratner describes 42nd Street as a democratic experience. *TRL* gives people what they want, rather than telling them what is worth wanting. As Kusbit says, "The beauty of it is that the show is about the people anyhow. They vote for the most popular videos, they pick the order of the videos, we talk to them out in the street."

Total Request Live is really about providing youth culture with an image of itself. It is, on the one hand, a sexually charged self-image. Both the lyrics and the videos themselves are overtly sexual in a way that would have left the kids on *American Bandstand* goggle-eyed. The same is true of those giant images of siliconized teen babes on the billboards out the window. And yet the atmosphere of *TRL* is friendly, wholesome, fun-loving, even innocent. The studio audience, which functions as a microcosm of that culture, consists of eighty or so teenagers, almost all of them nicely dressed and well groomed and wildly enthusiastic, sitting in bleachers around the stage. The girls are almost guaranteed to cry if they get a chance to meet J. Lo or a Backstreet Boy. Carson Daly himself has often been compared to Dick Clark, the host of *American Bandstand*. He asks innocuous, not to say vapid, questions, never pries, always finds nice things to say to the kids in the audience, and has pep to spare. And he makes a point of standing up for good values. At one show I attended, he introduced Joel, who appeared to be working at the show on some kind of internship. "Joel thought up 'The *TRL* Spelling Bee' and 'Spin the Bottle with Britney,' " Daly explained. "We made a deal with Joel—keep your grades up, we'll keep you in the show."

In other words, *TRL* has the same kind of reciprocal relationship with the Times Square brand that Toys "R" Us does: it offers an upbeat, consumer-friendly image of pop culture, and thus of Times Square, the world's capital of pop culture; and it uses Times Square's own image to help shape its own. It has, in effect, created a Times Square of its own—a sexy, friendly, brand-conscious, *rocking* Times Square, a Times Square of Naked Cowboys rather than Midnight ones—and made that place vividly real to millions of people who live far from New York. It is, in fact, something of a joke among hard-boiled New Yorkers that tourists will gaze rapturously at the Virgin Megastore on the other side of Broadway and say, "That's the place we saw on *TRL*." And of course they have seen it as well on *Good Morning America,* and on CNN, and in countless TV shows and movies. They have consumed the Times Square brand before ever actually coming to Times Square.

I SPENT AN AFTERNOON at Madame Tussaud's Wax Museum in the company of Mark C. Taylor, a philosopher at Williams College. Taylor is a deconstructionist, or perhaps a postdeconstructionist, who believes that the sharp distinction most of us insist on between "the real" and "the virtual," or "the not-real," is perfectly untenable and mostly reflects an atavistic wish for things to be just what they are, and no other. Taylor has written a book, *Hiding,* which advances the argument that the very idea of "depth," and thus of "deep meaning," is an illusion—that you can keep peeling away surfaces, and in the end you get . . . another surface. "This does not mean that everything is simply superficial," he writes; "to the contrary, in the absence of depth, everything becomes endlessly complex." Taylor loves the new Times Square of myriad reflective surfaces, of electronic apparitions fostered by global entertainment companies; it was his idea that we meet at Madame Tussaud's, the perfect place for a lesson in virtuality.

Madame Tussaud's is, of course, one of the chief "entertainment concepts" of Times Square, an international chain of "museums" which traffic in representations that confound the distinction between the real and the not-real. This particular Madame Tussaud's features a Broadway-inflected grouping of statues called "Opening Night," a party held in a kind of Roman courtyard featuring flawless effigies of Elton John, Elle MacPherson, Sarah Ferguson, Donald and Ivana Trump (separately, of course), Nicolas Cage, George Steinbrenner, network news anchors, and, rising majestically from the fountain in the center of the room, the famous cross-dresser RuPaul, naked under his sequins, à la Josephine Baker (whom we also see later). Elsewhere are world leaders, athletes, figures from the French Revolution; here, in the place of honor, are the heroes of the media culture. The room is itself a tribute to the endlessly repeated imagery that makes for modern celebrity.

As Taylor and I were standing at the edge of "Opening Night," I noticed an old woman with a handbag posed behind the newscaster Matt Lauer. Who in the world was she supposed to be? And then she moved: it was an old woman with a handbag. Taylor was delighted by this play of appearances. "Who's that?" he said to the friends of another woman standing next to Elle; and they all dissolved in a hail of giggles. "There are wax museums out west where they have Greek sculptures that have been colored," he said. But of course, many Greek sculptures *were* originally colored. The fake was truer than what we experience as the real. He had read, he said, that the criteria by which a forgery was detected were the same as those used to judge the original. "In other words, what constitutes the 'authenticity' of the authentic?"

Taylor showed almost no interest in the actual simulacra before us; what fascinated him was the idea of the simulacrum, and of Times Square as the center of a proliferating world of globalized images and messages and data. "Times Square," he said, "is now about globalization. Look at everything Virgin is into, and it just explodes." It was an airline that had ramified into a music store. "What they're trying to do is create the Virgin way of life. And who knows what Viacom owns, and how all these things connect? And then there's this whole question of inside and outside. You have these studios, ABC, MTV, or ESPN, which have shows where they will literally make the audience perform at certain moments—live TV." Taylor was, of course, thinking of *TRL*. He talked about Las Vegas, another node in the network of global imagery; the difference between the Vegas of Robert Venturi et al. and the Vegas of today, he said, was "the difference between automobile culture and driving down the road, on the one hand, and electronic culture and being inside a virtual reality terminal." The Times Square equivalent was the forest of electronic signs and studios, gesturing over our heads to one another. "There's a sense in which in Times Square you're inside an imagistic, virtual space,"

Taylor went on. "It's the image that is being continually replayed that is creating the space."

Taylor understood Times Square as the all-but-perfected form of a new world, a world whose essential commodity was information, and which was thus based on the insubstantial, the transitory, the instantly transmissible—information as a universal currency into which all the solid things of the world are translated. In the world of bits, distinctions between surface and depth, high and low, original and reproduction, fall away. This was the world described by the French sociologist Jean Baudrillard, who, in *Simulacra and Simulations,* declared the death of a stable world of correspondences, in which, say, the relationship of physical territory to map was understood as that of a real thing to its abstract representation. By contrast, in a world of simulations and infinite reproduction, Baudrillard writes, "The territory no longer precedes the map, nor survives it. Henceforth, it is the map which precedes the territory—*precession of simulacra*—it is the map that engenders the territory." The map engenders the territory: the TV show creates our sense of the reality of the place; the street figure as well as the toy store dissolves into "brand identity." And the territory—the original—does not survive the reproduction: "No more mirror of being and appearances," Baudrillard writes.

Like Taylor, Baudrillard is fascinated by the emerging world of global imagery; he has written an almost Tocquevillean account of America. And yet he describes the precession of simulacra as a species of death. "Something has disappeared," he writes: "the sovereign difference between [territory and map] that was the abstraction's charm. For it is the difference which forms the poetry of the map and the charm of the territory, the magic of the concept and the charm of the real." One might well say much the same thing about this new Vegas-ized Times Square whose advent Taylor was announcing. I asked Taylor how he *felt* about the place. Did it have any of the attributes of a "place"? Could you situate yourself in it, even find yourself at home in it, as people have found themselves at home in Times Square for a hundred years? Taylor considered this for a moment—he is a very fast thinker—and replied, "The question of home, and feeling at home, is a crucial one. In some sense, the real is always elsewhere. Part of the dilemma is to get over it and get on with it." Perhaps, Taylor said, the wish for familiarity, for charm, was itself an anachronism in the global city. "I don't think that kind of cozy gemütlichkeit is attainable, and I'm not sure it's desirable."

Isn't it, though? Are we really equipped to occupy a world of simulacra? Am I? I assume it's just that wish for "a cozy gemütlichkeit" that attracts me to the Howard Johnson's, and the Polish Tea Room, and McHale's. And surely what draws so many people to Broadway theater is the wish for a familiar, anachronistic kind of simulation, where the gulf between being and appearance is perfectly stable and legible, and where the very setting provides a powerful link to the past. (Mark Taylor himself lives in Williamstown, Massachusetts, a place redolent of its eighteenth-century origins.) We crave, still, not only the magic of the concept but the charm of the real, even if we no longer know exactly what we mean by the word "real." And that is why it is hard to share Rem Koolhaas's deadpan embrace of the rootless, postmodern "generic" city.

Standing at the corner of Broadway and 42nd Street, with Disney duking it out against Viacom, and Reuters against Condé Nast, we do, indeed, feel that we are occupying "an imagistic, virtual space." And it is a thrilling space, the crossroads of the colossal enterprise of pop culture—just as it was, mutatis mutandi, a hundred years ago. It is both a particular place and a virtualized, electronic no-place. The giant cylindrical NASDAQ sign reminds us of this new world, whose lifeblood is a bit-stream. There may be no other spot on earth where we feel so utterly a part of our new millennium. Baudrillard would, I'm sure, be mesmerized. And yet at the same time, we draw back—from the bit-stream, from the simulacrum, from the millennium itself. We stand in awe of this stupendous contrivance; but we are happy, in the end, to slip away to the quiet side streets toward Sixth Avenue, to the little bars and shops and restaurants that occupy an older, localized place where things are as they are, and not otherwise.

ACKNOWLEDGMENTS

OF THE TWO YEARS it took me to write this book, I spent about half in and around Times Square, and the other half in libraries. Virtually everyone I approached for an interview—real estate moguls, theater producers, street performers, former city officials, architects, sign makers, homeless people, corporate executives, waiters—gave me their time, whether they had a lot of it or very little of it. As for the indoor portion of my research, Madeline Kent, librarian of the Seymour Durst Old York Library at the Graduate Center of the City University of New York, was bottomlessly patient and endlessly helpful. I also could not have written this book without the intellectual guidance provided by two prior studies of Times Square: Lynn Sagalyn's *Times Square Roulette* and the collection of essays contained in *Inventing Times Square*.

I would not have written this book at all but for my agent, Andrew Wylie, who urged me to write a book about the city where I have lived for my entire adult life, and to which I have devoted much of my journalistic work. Nor would the book read quite the way it does without my editor, Jonathan Karp, who arrived in medias res and reminded me to tell stories about people, and to climb down off my high horse.

My friends David Scobey, Susan Margolis, and Giovanna Borradori read portions of the manuscript and made thoughtful comments. My wife, Elizabeth Easton, read the entire manuscript and asked the questions that I should have been asking myself.

CHAPTER ONE

Gouverneur Morris, Simeon DeWitt, and John Rutherford, "Commissioners' Remarks," in David T. Valentine, *A Compilation of the Laws of the State of New York Relating Particularly to the City of New York* (New York: E. Jones, 1862); Hendrik Hartog, *Public Property and Private Power: The Corporation of the City of New York in American Law, 1730–1870* (Raleigh: University of North Carolina Press, 1983); Rebecca Read Shanor, *The City That Never Was* (New York: Viking Press, 1988); David M. Scobey, *Empire City: The Making and Meaning of the New York Landscape* (Philadelphia: Temple University Press, 2002); Edwin G. Burrows and Mike Wallace, *Gotham: A History of New York City to 1898* (New York: Oxford University Press, 1999); Elizabeth Blackmar, *Manhattan for Rent, 1785–1850* (Ithaca: Cornell University Press, 1989); Miriam Berman, *Madison Square* (Salt Lake City: Gibbs-Smith, 2001); David C. Hammack, "Developing for Commercial Culture," in William R. Taylor, ed., *Inventing Times Square: Commerce and Culture at the Crossroads of the World* (Baltimore: Johns Hopkins University Press, 1991); William Dean Howells, *A Hazard of New Fortunes* (New York: Penguin, 2001); Mary C. Henderson, *The City and the Theatre* (Clifton, N.J.: James T. White and Co., 1973); Parson Zellers, *Tony Pastor: Dean of the Vaudeville Stage* (Ypsilanti, Mich.: University of Michigan Press, 1971); Tony Pastor Clip File, New York Public Library; *Harper's Magazine, Harper's Monthly, Electra Magazine, Frank Leslie's Illustrated;* Martha J. Lamb, *History of the City of New York: Its Origin, Rise and Progress,* vol. 2 (New York: A. S. Barnes, 1880); James Miller, *Miller's Stranger's Guide to New York City* (New York: James Miller, 1876); George C. D. Odell, *Annals of the New York Stage,* vol. XII (New York: Columbia University Press, 1940); Marvin Felheim, *The Theater of Augustin Daly: An Account of the Late Nineteenth Century American Stage* (Cambridge, Mass.: Harvard University Press, 1956); Stephen Burge Johnson, *The Roof Gardens of Broadway Theaters, 1883–1942* (Ann Arbor: University of Michigan Press, 1985); Rudolph

Aronson, *Theatrical and Musical Memoirs* (New York: McBride, Nast, 1913); Casino Clip File, New York Public Library; E. Ideall Zeisloft, ed., *The New Metropolis* (New York: D. Appleton, 1899); Theodore Dreiser, *Sister Carrie* (New York: Signet Classics, 2000); Lois W. Banner, *American Beauty* (Chicago: University of Chicago Press, 1983); Brander Matthews, *His Father's Son: A Novel of New York* (New York: Harper and Bros., 1896); Edgar Fawcett, *A Hopeless Case* (Boston: Houghton Mifflin, 1880); Arthur Bartlett Maurice, *New York in Fiction* (New York: Dodd, Mead, 1901).

CHAPTER TWO

W. G. Rogers and Mildred Weston, *Carnival Crossroads: The Story of Times Square* (Garden City, N.Y.: Doubleday, 1960); Mary C. Henderson, *The City and the Theatre* (Clifton, N.J.: James T. White, 1973); E. Ideall Zeisloft, ed., *The New Metropolis* (New York: Appleton, 1899); Edwin G. Burrows and Mike Wallace, *Gotham: A History of New York City to 1898* (New York: Oxford University Press, 1999); Clifton Hood, *722 Miles: The Building of the Subways and How They Transformed New York* (Baltimore: Johns Hopkins University Press, 1993); Gay Talese, *The Kingdom and the Power* (New York: World, 1969); Joe Laurie, Jr., *Vaudeville: From the Honky-tonks to the Palace* (New York: Henry Holt, 1953); Abel Green and Joe Laurie, *Show Biz: From Vaude to Video* (New York: Henry Holt, 1951); *Everybody Magazine,* October 1903; Mary C. Henderson, *The New Amsterdam: The Biography of a Broadway Theatre* (New York: Hyperion, 1997); Brooks Atkinson, *Broadway* (New York: Macmillan, 1974); *Theatre Magazine,* January 1909; Robert W. Snyder, *The Voice of the City: Vaudeville and Popular Culture in New York City* (New York: Oxford University Press, 1989); Peter A. Davis, "The Syndicate/Shubert War," in William R. Taylor, ed., *Inventing Times Square: Commerce and Culture at the Crossroads of the World* (Baltimore: Johns Hopkins University Press, 1991); George Rector, *The Girl from Rector's* (Garden City, N.Y.: Doubleday, Page, 1927); Parker Morrell, *Diamond Jim: The Life and Times of James Buchanan Brady* (New York: Simon & Schuster, 1934); *New York Plaisance: An Illustrated Series of New York Places of Amusement, No. 1* (Henry Erkins, 1909); Lewis A. Erenburg, *Steppin' Out: New York Nightlife and the Transformation of American Culture, 1890–1930* (Chicago: University of Chicago Press, 1981).

CHAPTER THREE

Timothy J. Gilfoyle, "Policing of Sexuality," in William R. Taylor, ed., *Inventing Times Square: Commerce and Culture at the Crossroads of the World* (Baltimore: Johns Hopkins University Press, 1991); Ethan Mordden, *The American Theatre* (New York: Oxford University Press, 1981); Charles Higham, *Ziegfeld* (Chicago: Henry

Regnery, 1972); Ziegfeld Clip File, New York Public Library; Robinson Locke Dramatic Collection, New York Public Library; P. G. Wodehouse and Guy Bolton, *Bring on the Girls: The Improbable Story of Our Life in Musical Comedy, with Pictures to Prove It* (New York: Simon & Schuster, 1953); Ethan Mordden, *Broadway Babies: The People Who Made the American Musical* (New York: Oxford University Press, 1983); *The Smart Set,* August 1926; *Playbill* Collection, Seymour Durst Old York Library; Gilbert Seldes, *The Seven Lively Arts* (New York: Sagamore Press, 1957); Marjorie Farnsworth, *The Ziegfeld Follies* (London: Davies, 1956); Julius Keller, *Inns and Outs* (New York: G. P. Putnam's Sons, 1939); Lewis A. Erenburg, *Steppin' Out: New York Nightlife and the Transformation of American Culture, 1890–1930* (Chicago: University of Chicago Press, 1981); Rupert Hughes, *What Will People Say?* (New York: Harper & Bros., 1914); Philip Furia, *Irving Berlin: A Life in Song* (New York: Schirmer Books, 1998); Julian Street, *Welcome to Our City* (New York: John Lane Company, 1912); George Bronson-Howard, *Birds of Prey: Being Pages from the Book of Broadway* (New York, W. J. Watt, 1918).

CHAPTER FOUR

Theodore Dreiser, *Sister Carrie* (New York: Signet Classics, 2000); David Nye, *Electrifying America: Social Meanings of a New Technology, 1880–1940* (Cambridge, Mass.: MIT Press, 1990); Tama Starr and Edward Hayman, *Signs and Wonders: The Spectacular Marketing of America* (New York: Currency Books, 1998); *Signs of the Times,* 1907–; O. J. Gude Clip File, in Artkraft Strauss archives; Rupert Hughes, *What Will People Say?* (New York: Harper & Bros., 1914); Bayrd Still, *Mirror for Gotham: New York as Seen by Contemporaries from Dutch Days to the Present* (New York: New York University Press, 1956); Gregory F. Gilmartin, *Shaping the City: New York and The Municipal Arts Society* (New York: Clarkson Potter, 1995).

CHAPTER FIVE

George S. Kaufman and Marc Connelly, *Dulcy,* in *The Drama Reader* (New York: Odyssey Press, 1962); Brooks Atkinson, *Broadway* (New York: Macmillan, 1974); Scott Meredith, *George S. Kaufman and His Friends* (Garden City, N.Y.: Doubleday, 1974); "My Lost City," in *Writing: A Literary Anthology of New York* (New York: Library of America, 1998); Ann Douglas, *Terrible Honesty: Mongrel Manhattan in the 1920s* (New York: Farrar, Straus & Giroux, 1995); F. Scott Fitzgerald, *This Side of Paradise* (New York: Scribners, 1995); Frederick Lewis Allen, *Only Yesterday* (New York: Harper & Bros., 1931); David Belasco, "A Flapper Set Me Right," in *Smart Set,* August 1927; Robert Baral, *The Revue* (New York: Fleet Publishing, 1962); Abel Green and Joe Laurie, *Show Biz: From Vaude to Video* (New York: Henry Holt, 1951); Edwin P. Hoyt, *Alexander Woollcott: The*

Man Who Came to Dinner (London: Abel and Shulman, 1968); Gilbert Seldes, *The Seven Lively Arts* (New York: Sagamore Press, 1957); S. N. Behrman, *People in a Diary* (Boston: Little, Brown, 1972); Phillip Dunning and George Abbott, *Broadway* (New York: George H. Doran, 1927); Eugene O'Neill, *Beyond the Horizon* (New York: Horace Liveright, 1920); Mary C. Henderson, *The City and the Theatre* (New York: James T. White, 1973); Moss Hart, *Act One* (New York: Random House, 1959); George S. Kaufman, *The Butter and Egg Man* (New York: Boni & Liveright, 1926); George S. Kaufman and Marc Connelly, *Beggar on Horseback* (New York: Horace Liveright, 1924); Philip Furia, *Irving Berlin: A Life in Song* (New York: Schirmer Books, 1998); George S. Kaufman and Ring Lardner, *June Moon* (New York: Sam French, 1929); Ethan Mordden, *Broadway Babies: The People Who Made the American Musical* (New York: Oxford University Press, 1983); George S. Kaufman and George S. Gershwin, *Strike Up the Band,* videotape in collection of New York Public Library.

CHAPTER SIX

Benjamin de Casseres, *Mirrors of New York* (New York: Joseph Lawrence, 1925); Stanley Walker, *The Nightclub Era* (New York: Frederick A. Stokes, 1933); Paul Morand, *New York* (New York: Henry Holt, 1930); Nils T. Granlund, *Blondes, Brunettes and Bullets* (New York: David McKay, 1957); Gilbert W. Gabriel, "Blind Pigs in Clover," in *Vanity Fair,* April 1927; Louise Berliner, *Texas Guinan, Queen of the Nightclubs* (Austin: University of Texas Press, 1993); Texas Guinan Clip File, New York Public Library; "Speakeasy Nights," in *The New Yorker,* July 2, 1927; Neal Gabler, *Winchell: Gossip, Power and the Culture of Celebrity* (New York: Knopf, 1994); John Mosedale, *The Men Who Invented Broadway: Damon Runyon, Walter Winchell and Their World* (New York: Richard Marek, 1981); "Texas Guinan Says" File, New York Public Library; Damon Runyon, *Broadway Stories* (New York: Penguin, 1993); Jimmy Breslin, *Damon Runyon* (New York: Ticknor & Fields, 1981); William R. Taylor, "Broadway: The Place That Words Built," in William R. Taylor, ed., *Inventing Times Square: Commerce and Culture at the Crossroads of the World* (Baltimore: Johns Hopkins University Press, 1991); F. Scott Fitzgerald, *The Great Gatsby* (Cambridge: Cambridge University Press, 1991); Gene Fowler, *Beau James: The Life and Times of Jimmy Walker* (New York: Viking Press, 1949).

CHAPTER SEVEN

J. Hoberman, *42nd Street* (London: British Film Institute, 1993); Abel Green and Joe Laurie, *Show Biz: From Vaude to Video* (New York: Henry Holt, 1951); Bradford Ropes, *42nd Street* (New York: Alfred H. King, 1932); *42nd Street* videorecording; Bill Ballantine, *Wild Tigers and Tame Fleas* (New York: Rinehart, 1958); Irving Zeidman, *The American Burlesque Show* (New York: Hawthorne, 1967); Stanley Walker, *The Nightclub Era* (New York: Frederick A. Stokes, 1933); *The WPA Guide to New York City* (New York: The New Press, 1992); Jack Lait and Lee Mortimer, *New York Confidential* (Chicago: Ziff-Davis, 1948); Felix Riesenberg and Alexander Alland, *Portrait of New York* (New York: Macmillan, 1939); Margaret M. Knapp, "A Historical Study of the Legitimate Playhouses on West Forty-second Street Between Seventh and Eighth Avenues in New York City," unpublished Ph.D. diss., City University of New York, 1982; Brooks Atkinson, *Broadway* (New York: Macmillan, 1974); Ethan Mordden, *The American Theatre* (New York: Oxford University Press, 1981); Clifford Odets, *Awake and Sing* (New York: working MS in New York Public Library); Thornton Wilder, *Our Town* (New York: Perennial Classics, 1998); Raymond Sokolov, *Wayward Reporter: The Life of A. J. Liebling* (New York: Harper & Row, 1980); Thomas Kunkel, *Genius in Disguise: Harold Ross of the New Yorker* (New York: Random House, 1995); A. J. Liebling, *Back Where I Came From* (San Francisco: North Point Press, 1990); A. J. Liebling, *The Telephone Booth Indian* (San Francisco: North Point Press, 1990); William R. Taylor, "Broadway: The Place That Words Built," in William R. Taylor, ed., *Inventing Times Square: Commerce and Culture at the Crossroads of the World* (Baltimore: Johns Hopkins University Press, 1991); Joseph Mitchell, *My Ears Are Bent* (New York: Pantheon, 2001); Joseph Mitchell, *Up in the Old Hotel* (New York: Pantheon, 1992).

CHAPTER EIGHT

The New York Times; Alfred Eisenstaedt, *Remembrances* (Boston: Bullfinch Press, 1990); Jan Morris, *Manhattan '45* (New York: Oxford University Press, 1987); Jack Kerouac, *The Town and the City* (New York: Harcourt, 1950); W. G. Rogers and Mildred Weston, *Carnival Crossroads: The Story of Times Square* (Garden City, N.Y.: Doubleday, 1960); Brooks Atkinson, *Broadway* (New York: Macmillan, 1974); Paramount Clip File, New York Public Library; Gary Giddins, *Bing Crosby: A Pocketful of Dreams. The Early Years, 1903–1940* (Boston: Little, Brown, 2001); Theatre History Society, Annual No. 6: Times Square Paramount Theatre; Arnold Shaw, "Sinatrauma: The Proclamation of a New Era," Bruce Bliven, "The Voice and the Kids," and E. J. Kahn, Jr., "The Fave, the Fans and the Fiends," in Steven Petkov and Leonard Mustazza, ed., *The Frank Sinatra Reader* (New York: Oxford University Press, 1995); James Gavin, *Intimate Nights: The Golden Age of New York Cabaret* (New York: Grove Weidenfeld, 1991); Helen Bloom, *Broadway: An Encyclopedia Guide to the History, People and Places of Times Square* (New York: Facts on File, 1991); Rivoli Theatre Clip File, New York Public Library; *Cleopatra* Clip File, New York Public Library; *Brigadoon* videorecording; *South Pacific* videorecording; *Kiss Me, Kate* videorecording; *Oklahoma!* videorecording; *Annie Get Your Gun* videorecording; Ethan Mordden, *Broadway Babies: The People Who Made the American Musical* (New York: Oxford University Press, 1983); Philip Furia, *Irving Berlin: A Life in Song* (New York: Schirmer Books, 1998); Douglas Leigh Clip File in holdings of Artkraft Strauss; Tama Starr and Edward Hayman, *Signs and Wonders: The Spectacular Marketing of America* (New York: Currency Books, 1998).

CHAPTER NINE

John Clellon Holmes, *Go* (New York: Scribners, 1952); Steven Watson, *The Birth of the Beat Generation: Visionaries, Rebels, and Hipsters, 1944–1960* (New York: Pantheon, 1995); Matt Theado, ed., *The Beats: A Literary Reference* (New York: Carroll & Graf, 2001); Barry Miles, *Ginsberg: A Biography* (London: Virgin Publishing, 2000); Jack Kerouac, *The Town and the City* (New York: Harcourt, 1950); William S. Burroughs, *Junky* (New York: Penguin, 1977); *The New York Times;* Timothy F. Gilfoyle, "Policing of Sexuality," in William R. Taylor, ed., *Inventing Times Square: Commerce and Culture at the Crossroads of the World* (Baltimore: Johns Hopkins University Press, 1991); John Rechy, *City of Night* (New York: Grove Press, 1963); James Leo Herlihy, *Midnight Cowboy* (New York: Simon & Schuster, 1965); Jay Gertzman, "Street-Level Smut," in *The Position* 5/26/2003; Josh Alan Friedman, *Tales of Times Square* (Portland, Ore.: Feral House, 1993); James Lardner and Thomas Reppetto, *NYPD: A City and Its Police* (New York: Henry Holt, 2000); Daniel Patrick Moynihan, *Family and Nation* (New York: Harcourt Brace Jovanovich, 1986); Fred Siegel, *The Future Once Happened Here* (New York: Free Press, 1997); *Taxi Driver,* videorecording; *The New York Times; West 42nd Street: The Bright Light Zone,* City University of New York study, 1978 (draft copy in Ford Foundation Library).

CHAPTER TEN

Documents, correspondence, clippings, etc., in City at 42nd Street File, archives of the Ford Foundation; Lynne B. Sagalyn, *Times Square Roulette: Remaking the City Icon* (Cambridge, Mass.: MIT Press, 2001); *42nd Street Development Project: General Project Plan,* 1981; *42nd Street Development Project: Draft Environmental Impact Statement,* 1984; and *42nd Street Development Project Design Guidelines,* 1981 (all in archives of 42nd Street Development Corp., O unit of the Empire State Development Corp.); *The New York Times; The New Yorker;* Hilary Lewis and John O'Connor, ed., *Philip Johnson: The Architect in His Own Words* (New York: Rizzoli, 1994); Franz Schulze, *Philip Johnson: Life and Work* (New York: Knopf, 1994); *Final Environmental Impact Statement* (1984, archive of the 42nd Street Development Corp., O unit of the Empire State Development Corp.).

CHAPTER ELEVEN

Robert Stern, *New York 1960* (New York: Monacelli Press, 1995); Robert Venturi, Denise Scott Brown, and Steven Izenour, *Learning from Las Vegas* (Cambridge, Mass.: MIT Press, 1972); Lynne B. Sagalyn, *Times Square Roulette: Remaking the City Icon* (Cambridge, Mass.: MIT Press, 2001); Marc Eliot, *Down 42nd Street: Sex, Money, Culture and Politics at the Crossroads of the World* (New York: Warner, 2001); *The New York Times; The New Yorker.*

CHAPTER TWELVE

The New York Times; Lynne B. Sagalyn, *Times Square Roulette: Remaking the City Icon* (Cambridge, Mass.: MIT Press, 2001); *42nd Street Now!* (1993); H. V. Savitch, *Post-Industrial Cities* (Princeton, N.J.: Princeton University Press, 1989).

CHAPTER THIRTEEN

Rem Koolhaas and Bruce Mau, *S, M, L, XL* (Rotterdam: 010 Publishers, 1995); Michael Sorkin, "Introduction: Variations on a Theme Park," in Michael Sorkin, ed., *Variations on a Theme Park* (New York: Farrar Straus Giroux, 1992); Alexander J. Reichl, *Reconstructing Times Square: Politics and Culture in Urban Development* (Lawrence, Kans.: University Press of Kansas, 1999).

CHAPTER FIFTEEN

Andrew Kirtzman, *Rudy Giuliani: Emperor of the City* (New York: William Morrow, 2000); Marshall Berman, *All That Is Solid Melts into Air: The Experience of Modernity* (New York: Penguin, 1988); Sharon Zukin, *The Culture of Cities* (Cambridge, Mass.: Blackwell, 1995); Robert Beauregard, *Voices of Decline* (Cambridge, Mass.: Blackwell, 1993); Herbert Gans, *The Urban Villagers* (New York: Free Press, 1962); Richard Sennett, *The Conscience of the Eye: The Design and Social Life of Cities* (New York: Knopf, 1990); *West 42nd Street: The Bright Light Zone,* City University of New York study, 1978 (draft copy in Ford Foundation Library); Laurence Senelick, "Private Parts in Public Places," in William R. Taylor, ed., *Inventing Times Square: Commerce and Culture at the Crossroads of the World* (Baltimore: Johns Hopkins University Press, 1991); Mary C. Henderson, *The City and the Theatre* (Clifton, N.J.: James T. White, 1973); Neil Smith, "New City, New Frontier: The Lower East Side as Wild, Wild West," in Michael Sorkin, ed., *Variations on a Theme Park* (New York: Farrar Straus Giroux, 1992); Albert LaFarge, ed., *The Essential William H. Whyte* (New York: Fordham University Press, 1990); William H. Whyte, *The Social Life of Small Urban Spaces* (Washington, D.C.: Conservation Foundation, 1980).

Lynne B. Sagalyn, *Times Square Roulette: Remaking the City Icon* (Cambridge, Mass.: MIT Press, 2001); Rem Koolhaas, *Delirious New York: A Retroactive Manifesto for New York* (New York: Oxford University Press, 1978).

Marshall Berman, "Signs of the Times," in *Dissent,* Fall 1997; Lynne B. Sagalyn, *Times Square Roulette: Remaking the City Icon* (Cambridge, Mass.: MIT Press, 2001).

Mark C. Taylor, *Hiding* (Chicago: University of Chicago Press, 1997); Jean Baudrillard, *Simulacra and Simulations* (Ann Arbor: University of Michigan Press, 1994).

ABOUT THE TYPE

This book was set in Monotype Dante, a typeface designed by Giovanni Mardersteig (1892–1977). Conceived as a private type for the Officina Bodoni in Verona, Italy, its first use was in an edition of Boccaccio's *Trattatello in laude di Dante* that appeared in 1954. The Monotype Corporation's version of Dante followed in 1957.